Observations on the Application of the West India Dock Company for a Renewal of Their Charter; With an Analysis of the Evidence Given Before the Committee of the House of Commons on Foreign Trade, to Which Their Petition Was Referred: and a Copy of the Report of the Said Committee

by Joseph Marryat

Address:
HardPress
8345 NW 66TH ST #2561
MIAMI FL 33166-2626
USA
Email: info@hardpress.net

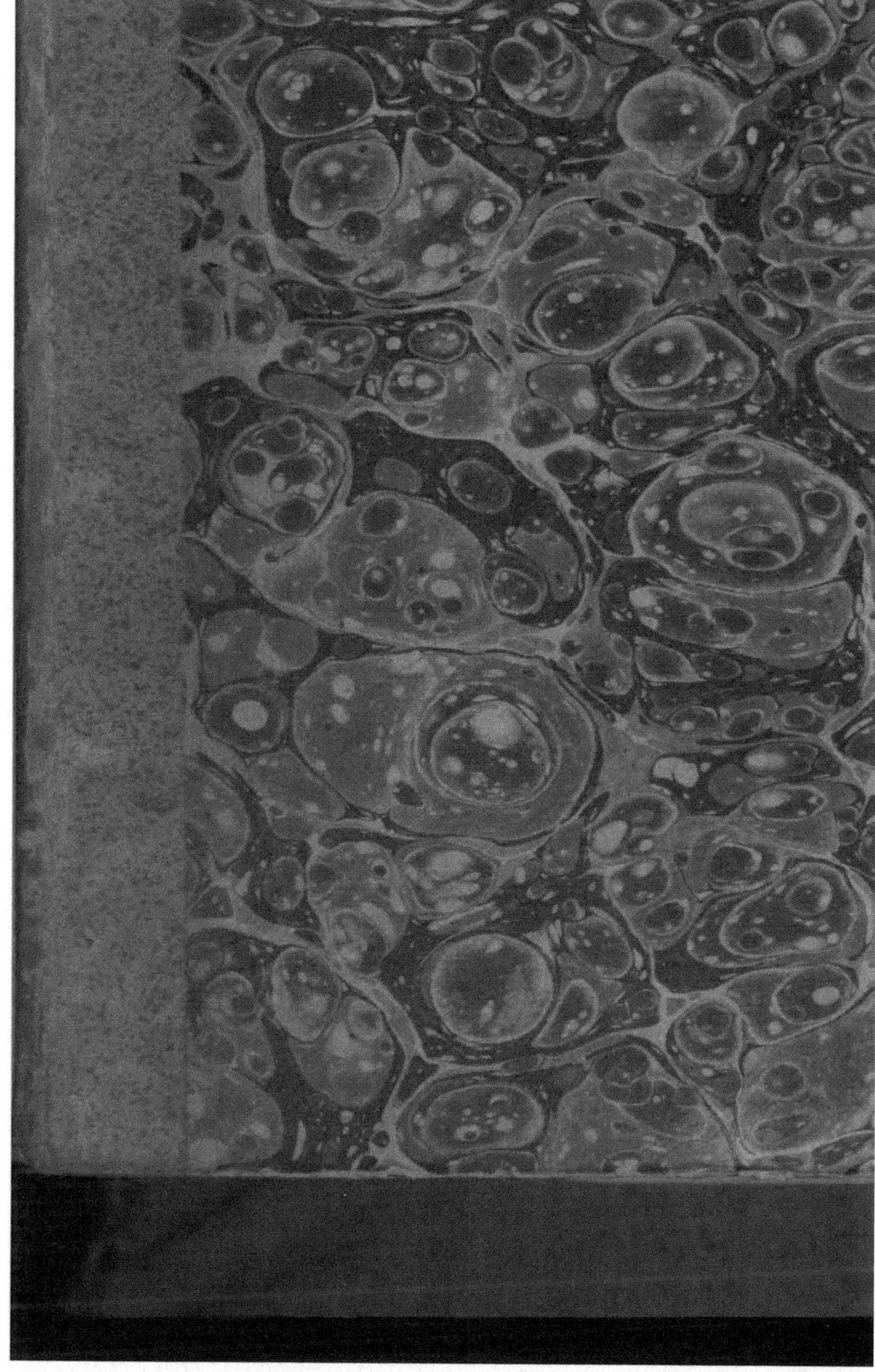

OBSERVATIONS,

&c. &c.

HUGHES, Printer,
Maiden Lane, Covent Garden.

OBSERVATIONS

ON

THE APPLICATION

OF THE

WEST INDIA DOCK COMPANY

FOR A

Renewal of their Charter;

WITH

AN ANALYSIS

OF THE EVIDENCE GIVEN BEFORE THE COMMITTEE OF THE HOUSE OF COMMONS ON FOREIGN TRADE, TO WHICH THEIR PETITION WAS REFERRED:

AND

A COPY OF THE REPORT

OF THE SAID COMMITTEE.

BY

JOSEPH MARRYAT, ESQ. M.P.

LONDON:

PRINTED FOR J. M. RICHARDSON, CORNHILL, AND RIDGWAYS, PICCADILLY.

1823.

INTRODUCTION.

Evidence given before a Committee of the House of Commons, from the nature and constitution of that tribunal, is extremely desultory and unconnected. Every Member of the Committee has a right to examine and cross-examine the witnesses; and consequently many questions are repeated, and followed up by a string of other questions, in the hope of obtaining answers more favourable to the views of the parties by whom they are put, than those which had been previously given. This mode of examination occasions much tautology and amplification: and where the subject of inquiry divides itself into many distinct branches, the information upon each being scattered throughout a voluminous mass of evidence, can scarcely be comprehended by the ordinary mode of perusal. In order, therefore, to bring it clearly and distinctly before the mind, it seems necessary to separate and arrange it under the different heads to which it relates; and if the summing up of a judge be necessary for the information of a jury, in cases where the evidence given occupies only a few hours, how much more necessary must some similar process be, with a large volume of evidence, that has occupied a Committee of the House of Commons several months to collect.

These observations occurred to the writer of these pages, after having attentively perused the Minutes of the Evidence given before the Committee on Foreign Trade, (which are printed at once for the use of the Members) respecting the application of the West India Dock Company for the renewal of their charter. Finding that the impression thus conveyed to his mind was very imperfect, and that he had by no means obtained a distinct or connected view of the leading points of the case, he sat down, during the interval between the last and the present Session of Parliament, to the task of analysing the evidence, for the better guidance of his own judgment; and found that by separating it into parts, he obtained a much clearer comprehension of the whole. It then occurred to him, that the fruits of his labours, on a subject of so much importance to the commercial interests of this great metropolis, and indeed of the whole British Empire, whenever they could be printed consistently with the orders of the House, might not be unacceptable to the public.

The analysis is divided into the following heads, which appear to comprise all the material points upon which evidence has been given.

		Observations.		Evidence.
No. I.	Advantages of the Dock System	- *page* 1	—	89
II.	Convenience of Situation - - - -	7	—	111
III.	Safety and facility of access . - -	10	—	122
IV.	Solidity of Buildings and Works -	13	—	153
V.	Means of Accommodation - - -	16	—	158
VI.	Machinery - - - - - - - - -	19	—	185
VII.	Security against Plunder - - - -	21	—	187
VIII.	Exclusion of Crews and Apprentices -	28	—	218
IX.	Classification of Commodities - - -	37	—	236
X.	Dispatch in landing Cargoes - - -	41	—	241
XI.	Mode of Housing and Sampling Sugars	44	—	249
XII.	Weighing Coffee after being Warehoused - - - - - - - - - -	51	—	276
XIII.	Making Cotton Merchantable - - -	54	—	284

		Observations.		Evidence
XIV.	Warehousing Rum - - - -	*page* 55	—	286
XV.	Moderation of Charges - - - - -	57	—	289
XVI.	Repairs and Improvements - - -	62	—	312
XVII.	Accumulated Fund - - - - - - -	*ib.*	—	*ib.*
XVIII.	Just Regard to Private Interests - -	66	—	337
XIX.	Discontinuance of Compulsory Clause	69	—	339
XX.	Competition of Dock Companies - -	73	—	357

Observations upon each of these points are prefixed to the analysis, so that the reader may compare the conclusions of the writer with the premises from whence they are drawn; and the Report of the Committee concludes and completes the information on this interesting subject.

OBSERVATIONS,

&c. &c.

No. I.

ADVANTAGES OF THE DOCK SYSTEM.

No conflicting evidence is found on this branch of the subject. All parties agree in the great security that has been given, both to the public revenue and the property of individuals, by the establishment of Wet Docks, for the reception of ships and cargoes, with warehouses contiguous to them, and surrounded with high walls. Under the old system, of ships discharging their cargoes in the river, and the commodities being conveyed in lighters to the legal quays, plunder took place to such an enormous extent, that it became a general subject of notoriety and complaint. In the year 1796, the merchants of London submitted various plans, for increasing the accommodation of the port of London, to the consideration of his Majesty's Ministers, which led to the formation of the existing establishments. The revenue officers, who were examined before the Committee on this point, prove in the most satisfactory manner, both the existence of the evil, and the efficacy of the remedy; and if any additional evidence were wanting, it is abundantly furnished in the testimony of Mr. Drinkald, who was himself both a warehouse keeper and lighterman, under the old system. He testifies, most unequivocally, to the malpractices that formerly existed; and admits that even at present, although better regulations have now taken place, goods would be much more liable to plunder in his lighters, than in the West India or the London Docks. From a statement given in by Mr. Hibbert, it appears that the plunder of West India produce alone, that took place in the port of London, in the years 1799, 1800, and 1801, exceeded £400,000 per annum.

In order to put a stop to this evil, it is true, as stated in the Memorial of the West India Dock Company to the Board of Trade, that the merchants readily consented to the compulsory clauses contained in the Charters of the different Dock Companies, and also to the payment of high rates both on goods and shipping for twenty-one years; but it is equally true, though not stated in that Memorial, that they did this, as the only means of inducing individuals to invest their capital in these great undertakings; and that they looked forward, at the expiration of that period, to the substitution of a system of open competition and moderate charges, for one of monopoly and high charges. In short, they submitted to temporary disadvantages, in order to secure the great and permanent benefits which were anticipated by Mr. Pitt, as the consequence of these establishments; "the perfect-"ing the warehousing system, lowering the "port charges, and making this metropolis the "emporium of the world."

The truth of these sentiments is fully established by the declarations of the most competent judges on this subject.

At a general meeting of the Merchants, Ship-Owners, and Traders of the Port of London, convened by public advertisement, and held at the City of London Tavern, on the 25th January, 1821, the following resolutions were passed unanimously:—

No. I.—Upon the motion of Thomas Wilson, Esq. M. P. seconded by J. W. Buckle, Esq.—That the system of establishing Wet Docks, for the reception of vessels laden with commodities subject to high duties on importation, or bonded for exportation, affords the greatest possible security to property, and therefore is alike beneficial to the merchant, the ship-owner, and the revenue.

No. II.—Upon the motion of John Forbes Mitchell, Esq. seconded by A. Rucker, Esq.—That the high rates granted to the different Wet Dock Companies in the port of London, with the monopoly of various branches of commerce for a limited period, were sanctioned by the legislature, with the view of inducing individuals to invest their capital in such establishments; and were comparatively of little importance, so long as the war gave to this country an unusual share of the commerce of the world, but have been heavily felt since the return of peace has placed us in a state of competition with the other commercial and maritime powers of Europe.

No. III.—On the motion of Robert Rickards, Esq. seconded by John Hall, Esq.—That the high rates, combined with other heavy charges to which commerce is exposed, tend to defeat the important object of making this metropolis the emporium of Europe; as merchants are thereby discouraged from consigning their goods, nor can ship-owners afford to bring cargoes on the same terms as to one of the free ports on the Continent; and that a great proportion of the benefits expected from the warehousing system have, in consequence, already been lost; and much of that commerce which would otherwise have centered in this country, has been driven into other channels.

No. IV.—On the motion of F. Kemble, Esq. seconded by W. Frampton, Esq.—That the monopolies of the different Dock Companies are not only injurious to the foreign commerce, but to the home trade of this metropolis, as they force consignments of merchandize to the outports, where the charges are more moderate, and by enabling the traders in those ports to deliver their goods upon lower terms, give them a decided advantage over those of the Port of London; and that as all charges fall ultimately upon the consumer, they operate as a partial and unfair tax upon the inhabitants of London and its vicinity, and the persons who are supplied from this market.

No. V.—On the motion of Sir Chas. Price, Bart. seconded by Geo. Lyall, Esq.—That in order to afford due relief to British navigation and commerce, and also in justice to the inhabitants of this metropolis, it is expedient, that whenever the Charters of the respective Dock Companies expire, their different monopolies should cease and determine; by which means the owners of ships and merchandize would be relieved from various inconveniences, delays, and expenses, to which they are now subjected; all charges would find their fair and proper level; and the commercial interests at large would derive those advantages from the said companies, in contemplation of which they were originally established.

No. VI.—On the motion of S. C. Holland, Esq. seconded by G. G. de H. Larpent, Esq.—That the advantage of a free and open competition is supported and confirmed by the fifth and seventh reports of the special commissioners, appointed by the Prince Regent to inquire into the customs and excise; by the evidence given to the Select Committee of the House of Commons, upon the petition of the merchants and others, for relief from the excessive charges of the East India Dock Company; and also by the evidence incidentally given to the Select Committee of the House of Commons, on the means of improving and extending the trade of the country; and that, in addition to this weight of testimony, every principle of political economy and the result of all mercantile experience, equally forbid the renewal of the exclusive privileges at present enjoyed by these several companies.

No. VII.—On the motion of Benj. Shaw, Esq. seconded by T. S. Benson, Esq.—That a copy of the foregoing resolutions be sent to the first Lord of the Treasury, the President of the Board of Trade, and the Chancellor of the Exchequer; and that a Petition to the House of Commons, framed in conformity with them, be left at the City of London Tavern for signature, and be presented by the chairman of this meeting.

These resolutions shew the real sentiments of the merchants and ship-owners of the port of London, on the dock system; and a petition founded upon them, after receiving more than 6,000 signatures, comprising names of the highest commercial respectability and eminence, was presented to the House of Commons.

No. II.

CONVENIENCE OF SITUATION.

In this and all the subsequent heads of examination the witnesses tread on debateable ground; for points of comparison perpetually arise between the different dock establishments, on which very different and indeed contradictory opinions are given. Most of the parties, as might naturally be expected, speak with partiality of the local advantages of those docks in which they are interested, or with which they are connected; and of that system of management which they had a share in framing, or under which they have been accustomed to act.

For the better understanding of this part of the subject, it may be necessary to state, that the London Docks have the advantage of the greatest proximity to the heart of the metropolis, their gates being only a quarter of a mile distant from Tower Hill. The West India Docks are between two and three miles lower down the river. The East India Docks are just below them, and the Commercial Docks nearly opposite to them, on the Surry side of the Thames: the London Docks therefore offer the greatest convenience to merchants, brokers, and others, whose business requires their personal attendance at the docks, more particularly with respect to commodities that must be tasted or examined, and cannot be sold by sample. A great saving in cartage is also made on all articles intended for home consumption, by their being deposited in the London Docks. On the other hand, all West India produce is sold by sample, and therefore no inconvenience in this respect is felt by the West India trade being confined to those Docks; but the staple commodity, sugar, is used almost exclusively for home consumption, and the cartage of it from the West India Docks is a considerable extra charge. The Commercial Docks are about the same distance from London Bridge as the West India Docks, and though somewhat more conveniently situated for Southwark, are less so for the great mart of consumption, the City. Both these Docks, and the East India Docks, possess the same advantage as to commodities intended for exportation, that the London Docks have as to those intended for home consumption. If the competition between them were thrown open, these advantages and disadvantages of situation would either lead to such a difference in rates, as would secure to each of them a participation in the general business of the Port; or would confine the business of each to these commodities, for the reception and delivery of which they are most conveniently placed.

Mr. Tilstone, in his second Report to the Commissioners of the Customs, argues upon two supposititious cases: one, that vessels were to discharge partly at one set of docks and partly at another, (which never was contemplated;) and the other, that they were to discharge in the river; when the only questions before him, as appears from the first paragraph of his Report, were "the "distribution and allotment of trade under the "*Dock System*, and the appropriation of the West "India trade to the West India Docks." The extraneous part of this Report has not therefore been copied from the Minutes of the Committee, but merely such extracts from it, as are relevant to the subjects of inquiry.

The result of the evidence given on this branch of the subject, without going into minute details, appears to be, that under the compulsory clauses in the Charters of the different Wet Dock Companies, various commodities are forced into situations very ill calculated for their reception, to the great expense and inconvenience of the proprietors, and to the consequent discouragement of the commerce of the Port of London; but that under a system of fair and open competition, these disadvantages would cease, all commodities would find their proper places, where they could be most conveniently and economically lodged, and the commerce of the Port of London, relieved from its present burthens and disadvantages, would revive and flourish.

No. III.

SAFETY AND FACILITY OF ACCESS.

On this point, the evidence is very contradictory; and the minds of some of the witnesses must either have laboured under very erroneous impressions, or a strong bias to favour particular interests.

Mr. Clippingdale, the pilot, after stating that "there is no danger at all in navigating "large vessels to the West India Docks, but "considerable danger in navigating them to the "London Docks;" on being asked, whether he ever heard of any risk or danger to ships going into the London Docks? says, "I do not "recollect any:" but on the same question being put to him, as to vessels entering the West India Docks, he answers, "Oh, yes." So that, according to his testimony, there is great danger where no losses have ever happened; but where they have repeatedly happened, there is no danger at all.

Mr. Drinkald, (who is a proprietor of West India Dock stock,) states, that "the advantages "of the West India vessels entering at once "from sea into those Docks, is very great in- "deed;" talks of its being "madness to drop a "large ship down, with a wind to the eastward, "after not being able to get her into the Lon- "don Docks:" and says, "there would be no "place for her to go to." It would seem, however, from another part of his examination, that he is apt to take rather an exaggerated view of cases in which he is an interested party; for being questioned whether he had a compensation paid to him as a lighterman, he answers, "I "never considered that I had. I had in my "house, for nearly six months, two accountants, "and they made out my loss of nearly £3,500 "a year; and I got £3,450." "You thought "you had not an adequate compensation?" "No: it was made out, not by me, but by offi- "cers employed." The Commissioners appear to have considered Mr. Drinkald's claim for a loss, which according to his estimate amounted to nearly £3,500 per annum, to have been sufficiently compensated by the sum of £3,450. If they were correct in this award, the extravagance of his estimate on that occasion, renders any extravagance in his estimate of the difficulty and danger of entering the London Docks the less surprising.

Mr. Inglis states, that in the year 1821, 1871 ships entered the London Docks; and that the average number that has entered them annually, since the opening, is about 1000. They have now been open nineteen years, and therefore, out of 19,000 vessels, not one has met with any accident whatever. The testimony of Mr. Inglis, in this respect, is confirmed by that of Mr. Chapman, and also by Messrs. Tooke and Wilson, both of whom state, that all their vessels have entered the London Docks with perfect safety. Mr. Eilbeck says, that he remembers the Union East Indiaman, of 650 tons, going into the London Docks, before the East India Docks were opened; and adds, "that ships now "go into those Docks with the same facility as "into the West India Docks;" the harbour master keeping better regulations than formerly, and the pool being less crowded. This latter circumstance, (as is stated in the evidence of Mr. Inglis,) is the necessary consequence of the pool being relieved from the 1000 sail of vessels that go annually into the London Docks; from all those employed in the East India and West India trade, which go into the Docks appropriated for their reception; and from those engaged in the timber trade, both from the Baltic and the British provinces in North America, most of which go into the Commercial and East Country Docks.

With regard to the Commercial Docks, Mr. Eilbeck, the superintendent, declares that they are capable of receiving a considerable part of the West India ships in their present state; and Mr. Walker, the engineer, speaks in the most positive terms as to the facility of making an entrance into them, of the same depth of water as that into the West India Docks.

Both Mr. Mitchell and Mr. Hibbert admit the loss of the ships Resolution, and General Miranda, in attempting to enter the West India Docks, probably owing to what Mr. Longlands, in speaking to another point, terms the "faulty position" of the Blackwall entrance, and explains, by saying, that "the set of the tide runs directly into it." No accident whatever has happened to ships entering any of the other docks; and therefore, if the judgment is to be governed by facts, the point of safety of access must be decided against the West India Docks.

No. IV.

SOLIDITY OF BUILDINGS AND WORKS.

In the memorial of the West India Dock Company to the Board of Trade, they mention "the extraordinary energy and rapidity display-" ed in the execution of this great work;" but from the evidence given upon this branch of the subject, they seem to have studied rapidity rather than durability; and to have verified the old proverb, "the more haste the worse speed."

Mr. Longlands states, that for a great many years the Blackwall entrance has been in a most alarming state; that it has now undergone repairs, and may last one year or several, the time is uncertain, and that its position is faulty. Mr. Rennie, the engineer, thinks both the Blackwall and Limehouse entrances are at present in a tolerable state of repair; but that it is extremely uncertain how long they may continue so; their lasting more than a few years is doubtful, from their not having been so well executed as they might have been. He states, that one of the mahogany sheds is tumbling down; that the extent of defective work is very considerable; that the works are defective in their execution with respect to the bricklayers' work, the foundations, and the work generally: that the works at the London Docks and the East India Docks are substantially executed, and free from defects; he cannot speak to the state of the Commercial Docks.

Mr. Mitchell says, that "undoubtedly some "of the works were not executed originally in "the substantial manner they might have been."

Mr. Walker, the engineer, thinks the wing-walls of the Blackwall entrance of the West India Docks in a bad state; and considers that a dock of that magnitude should not be confined to one entrance: that in case of any thing going wrong with one, there should be another; and adds, that according to his recollection, the Limehouse entrance is hardly wide enough to receive the largest loaded ships. Being asked, in cross-examination, whether the vessels which enter at the Blackwall entrance do not go out at the Limehouse entrance, he answers, "if they "do, they are then empty, and then their ex-"treme width is above the level of the walls. "He believes the one entrance to be forty feet "wide, and the other only thirty-two."

If the Blackwall entrance is in the alarming state described by Mr. Longlands; if it is subject to a great number of casualties, as stated by Mr. Rennie; if any casualty should actually befal it; and if, as Mr. Walker recollects, the Limehouse entry is hardly wide enough to receive the largest loaded ships, to what a situation is the West India trade exposed? Without, however, anticipating evils, which, although possible, are not certain, (but against which it is the duty of the West India Dock Company to provide,) the evidence of their own officers sufficiently proves, that in the execution of their works and buildings, they paid greater regard to rapidity, than to that solidity which they who deposit their property in them have a right to expect.

No. V.

MEANS OF ACCOMMODATION.

Mr. Mitchell states, that the West India import dock can contain 204 ships, the export dock 184, and the basins 48, making a total of 436 ships. That the import dock is capable of unloading at one time about 50 ships; and the export dock of loading with convenience 130 ships.

Mr. Inglis states, that the London Dock will contain somewhat more than 200 ships; and that they have the means of extending their water by making another dock; that their present warehouses would hold 200,000 hogsheads of sugar; and that many of them are only ground floors, which could be raised upon at any time.

Mr. Chapman says, that they can discharge 47 sail of ships at one time; and that the vaults at the London Docks will contain 57,000 pipes of wine.

Mr. Gibson states, that at the Pennington-street warehouses, carts might load on the outside, without coming into the dock gates, provided that mode of doing business was thought necessary.

Mr. Eilbeck states, that at the Commercial Docks there are six docks, covering 53 acres, and capable of accommodating 300 sail of vessels; that the present warehouses could accommodate 20,000 hogsheads of sugar, and that warehouses to any extent could be built, if necessary; that the Company have purchased land, in the view of making an additional entrance to the docks, nearer London-bridge.

Mr. Manning states, that the Commercial Docks are not, at present, equal to the West India Docks, in point of accommodation for West India produce; but that they are capable of every improvement.

Mr. Tooke sees no reason why the London Docks could not, in proportion to their extent, give the same accommodation as the West India Docks.

The means of accommodation for West India produce, in the West India Docks, are undoubtedly complete and perfect; but the question to be considered is, whether the same accommodation may not be obtained elsewhere. The evidence proves, that the London Docks in their present state are capable of accommodating a great proportion of that trade; and that the mode of loading carts from the back of the warehouses, without their entering the dock gates, (as practised in the West India Docks) might be adopted there, if thought expedient; but the want of a sufficient extent of water is a defect in that establishment which requires to be remedied by the formation of an export dock, upon the land which the Directors have reserved for that purpose.

The Commercial Docks rather possess great capabilities than present means of accommodation. Their number of separate docks is a great advantage; but before they can accommodate the West India trade, many of those docks require to be deepened, an additional entrance into the river must be made, additional warehouses and vaults must be built. If, however, the proprietors raise funds for these undertakings, (and capital may always be found in this metropolis, for any object in which it can be invested to advantage,) improvements upon their premises may be carried to almost any extent that the trade of the metropolis can be expected to require.

No evidence was offered to the Committee respecting the East India Docks, the East Country Dock, and the Surry Canal; but sufficient proof has been given, that ample means of accommodation, for every branch of commerce, are provided by the different dock establishments in the port of London.

No. VI.

MACHINERY.

The West India Dock Company, in their memorial to the Board of Trade, mention "the "costly machinery which the Company have "provided, and which was adapted to the dif-"ferent descriptions of goods, under the able "superintendence of the late Mr. Rennie."

Mr. Filstone confirms this idea, by answering in the affirmative to a question put to him, "whether those docks have not the advantage "of very valuable machinery, which does not "exist elsewhere?" although he admits, "that "any other Company might have the same "machinery, if they choose to go to the ex-"pense of it." This assumed superiority, however, is extremely weakened by the cross-examination of Mr. Mitchell, who allows "that "no extraordinary machinery is requisite for "warehousing sugar and coffee; and that the

" costly machinery of the West India Dock " Company is confined to the landing and stowing wood; some of the logs of which are of " immense weight." On the examination of Mr. Manning, this assumed superiority vanishes altogether; for he states, that " at the Commercial Docks they are in the habit of landing and housing cargoes of teak wood from " Sierra Leone, the logs of which weigh five " or six tons each; and that they have machinery for that purpose." In another part of Mr. Mitchell's evidence he observes, that " machinery produces a great saving of manual " labour;" and as it is obviously, therefore, the interest of every Dock Company to introduce machinery, no doubt can remain but that it will be introduced, wherever it can be advantageously substituted for manual labour. The mahogany to which this extraordinary machinery is applied in the West India Docks, is not in fact the produce of the West Indies, though included in the compulsory clause in the Company's charter; but of Honduras, a British settlement in Spanish South America. The produce of the West Indies, properly so called, is lodged, as Mr. Mitchell observes, " in warehouses provided " only with the common machinery of cranes, " jiggers, and trucks, which must be had, in " order to warehouse commodities of any and " every description." From this evidence it is clear that the West India Dock Company, although entitled to great credit for the masterly application of scientific principles to practical purposes, in many parts of their establishment, have no right to claim any extraordinary superiority on account of the costly machinery mentioned in their memorial.

No. VII.

SECURITY AGAINST PLUNDER.

This is a subject of very great importance, and necessarily involves various points of comparison, between the regulations of the West India Dock Company, and those of the other Dock Companies.

Mr. Tilstone "thinks it impossible that the "revenue can be effectually protected in a "dock of promiscuous trade, such as the London "Dock, where vessels are unloading inwards "and loading outwards, lying alongside each "other." Having never done duty at the London Docks, he cannot say what plunder, or that any plunder has taken place there; but because he knows there is none at the West India Docks, he supposes there must be more at the London Docks.

Mr. Burne states, that some frauds were

formerly practised upon the revenue, at the London Docks, which arose from the system being a bad one, with respect to the Crown; or as he afterwards explains, "to the remissness "or ignorance of the revenue officers stationed "there." He thinks there is no reason to expect pillage or depredation of sugar at the London Docks. He prefers the system of the West India Docks, which appears to him to approach as nearly to perfection as any imperfect system can do. He considers that an Import and Export Dock, the turning out the crews, and the not permitting carts upon the quays, render the security at the West India Docks, preferable to all others.

Both Mr. Mitchell and Mr. Hibbert lay great stress on the system established at the West India Docks. Mr. Hibbert thinks that the same security cannot be afforded, by any establishment having but one large dock; and states, that the system of the West India Docks could not be applied to a dock where different trades were admitted.

Mr. Turner believes that great plunder formerly took place in the delivery of the ships in the river, and afterwards in the warehouses; that the same danger of plunder must attend the transit from Gravesend to the West India

Docks, as to the London Docks, which is only a difference of a few miles.

Mr. Colville thinks, that the same security could not be obtained by the merchants and planters at the London Docks, as is at present obtained in the West India Docks, and for nearly the same reasons as those given by Mr. Hibbert and Mr. Mitchell.

Mr. Drinkald does not think the system adopted at the London Docks fit for the West India trade; says, that the West India ships would be exposed to plunder, in the night, by the crews of the foreign ships; and that they have not another dock to put the empty ships into.

Mr. Stuart is of opinion, that the same security could not be afforded at the West India Docks, if other trades were admitted; but thinks the system of the London Docks preferable for the wine trade, and never knew any inconvenience arise to the revenue or the merchant from that system.

Mr. Inglis states the London Docks to consist of two basins and a dock, all used for export or import, according to circumstances; and that being surrounded by walls, and checks being established at the gates, they give as great security as can be given: that a regular watch is kept night and day; that no article of merchandize, nor any individual is suffered to pass the dock gates, without being examined: that the crews of many of the ships remain on board, and that in his opinion, this circumstance does not expose the property to plunder; but the contrary, because the masters, officers, and crews, being liable for the plunder, have an interest in protecting the property: that he has heard of no instances of plunder on board any of the ships; and that they must have come to his knowledge, especially for the first fourteen or fifteen years of the establishment, because he went weekly to the docks, and attended the committees during that time: that the carmen who enter the dock gates, are subject to a penalty if they leave their carts and horses, and if they were to range about, the constables would prevent it.

Mr. Chapman does not consider there is any thing in the London Docks worthy of the name of plunder; perhaps, once in two or three weeks, the gate-keepers discover a man with some trifling things, but nothing beyond that has ever come to his knowledge: that vessels cannot go in or out before or after day-light; the hours are fixed by Act of Parliament.

Mr. Gibson states, that there is only one public entrance to the London Docks, for goods to be carted in or out, at which five revenue gate-keepers and police-officers appointed by the Dock Company, are constantly stationed; the other entrance is only used by special leave, which is very seldom granted; and a third entrance, to the tobacco warehouse, is used by the revenue officers alone: that all persons going out are searched, both sailors and day-labourers; that they frequently make them take off their shoes: that watchmen attend upon the quays by night and day; and the Company's officers, as well as the revenue officers, in the warehouses, in the day-time; that under these circumstances, he considers it impossible that goods in the warehouses, or lying on the quays, can be plundered: he thinks the system established at the London Docks, is perfectly sufficient for the security of the revenue. If he had his choice, he would prefer the system of the West India Docks, because, where there are no persons there can be no plunder; but without that degree of perfection, he thinks the system of the London Docks sufficient, and has no doubt that the revenue upon the West India trade would be sufficiently secure there. He should require no greater security for his own property than is afforded by the regulations of those docks.

Mr. Eilbeck says, that in his judgment, a wooden fence, twelve feet high, with the watchmen they have in the Commercial Docks, is a sufficient protection to West India produce; because if a man is resolved to take down a fence, he can take down a wall.

Mr. Marten depends upon such regulations as should render plunder impossible: does not think there is great security in walls, when whole bales of muslin have been got over the high East India Dock wall. Regulations and good attention, in his opinion, give the best security: they have, at present, in the Commercial Docks sufficient security for the trade that comes there; and if they had more trade, they should provide accordingly.

Mr. Glennie has been perfectly satisfied with the protection afforded to his property at the London Docks.

Mr. Lampson does not know that there is more liability to plunder, from crews being permitted to remain on board, unless they can remove articles out of the ships; and he does not know where they could take them to. He imagines they could not be carried out of the Docks. He never was there at night; but he supposes the dock gates are shut, and they are guarded during the day-time, and persons searched on going out.

Mr. Manning considers the property of the merchants as safe from plunder in the Commercial Docks as any where else; and that the system of the London Docks affords perfect security to the revenue.

Mr. Tooke had frequent occasion to complain of deficiencies, which he could only ascribe to plunder, previous to the erection of the London Docks; but has had no complaint to make in respect to articles imported into those docks.

Mr. Wilson imports a great deal of silk into the London Docks, which is a very valuable article, and extremely liable to plunder; and knows of no merchandize of any description or quality having suffered from plunder in the London Docks: considers both that establishment, and the West India Docks, to be well regulated, and thinks there is adequate protection in both.

That effectual protection is given to property in the West India Docks is admitted on all hands: but the point at issue is, whether the very rigid system adopted in that establishment is essential to that protection; and whether greater accommodation may not be perfectly consistent with the security both of the public revenue and the property of individuals. It is very natural, that they who have framed a system should extol it as a model of perfection. We have the same partiality for our intellectual as for our natural offspring; and as Gay asks,

"Wherever yet was found the Mother
"Would give her booby for another?"

It appears, however, from the evidence, that in the estimation of all the witnesses, those connected with the West India Docks excepted, full security is given to property, by the regulations adopted in the other Wet Dock establishments.

No. VIII.

EXCLUSION OF CREWS AND APPRENTICES.

This is a point of considerable interest, not only as it affects the security of property, but as it relates to the owners, officers, crews, and apprentices of the shipping employed in the West India trade.

Mr. Tilstone says, that in his judgment, there

being no concourse of persons in the West India Docks, except those in the immediate employment of the Company, tends materially to protect the property from plunder; but admits, that such a rigid system of management would not be practicable, consistently with the fair convenience of the public in general, where trade is admitted promiscuously. He farther admits, that the crews of ships might be employed to discharge the cargoes, as well as the common labourers hired by the West India Dock Company: does not know that there is any advantage in employing labourers instead of the crews; and is aware that the crews must be exposed to idle habits, during the time they are out of employ.

Mr. Burne thinks the labourers discharge the cargoes in less time than the crews, but that there would be no difference as to plunder: that there may be honest sailors, as well as honest labourers.

Mr. Groves thinks that turning the crews out of the ships in the West India Docks is no inconvenience to the owners: that this system saves the necessity of having revenue officers on board the ships at night, and diminishes the risk of plunder.

Mr. Longlands considers the exclusion of

the crews as a material security to the revenue and the merchant: that the pay of the seaman being responsible for his plunder, would not operate as any restraint upon him, especially in the plunder of spirits; says, that the Company give regular employment to a certain number of labourers, some of whom have worked with them fifteen, sixteen, and seventeen years, persons whose characters are well known in every respect; that they also hire occasional labourers, and though they are not able to ascertain the good character of them all, at least two hundred of them are known to their officers, both as to honesty and industry. He will not assert that those men whose characters they are unacquainted with, are more to be depended upon for integrity than the seamen and apprentices of vessels, under the superintendence and controul of their proper officers; but thinks they are more competent under the superintendence of the officers of the Company, to do the duty required in those docks.

Mr. Mitchell considers the excluding the crews of vessels from the docks, as one of the restraints upon which the security of the planter is founded. Judging from what he has heard, with respect to the seamen on board West Indiamen, and also from what is the practice, he should certainly say that this description of seaman, is not the person he would rely upon in preference; and that if the owners of West Indiamen were allowed to lump out their own ships, they would not do so with their own crews. That vessels are unloaded in the West India Docks by persons who have had experience in unloading vessels for a number of years; and therefore that it must be done better by such labourers, than by the seamen of the vessels.

Mr. Hibbert, having been owner and part owner of eight ships in the West India trade, never discharged a ship by means of the crew. In war, it was out of the question; and, in peace, it was the practice for the crew to leave the ship, on her coming to her moorings. He adds, that the risk of plunderage would be increased, by suffering the crews to remain on board.

Mr. Drinkald considers the discharge of the crew is a measure of importance, but that it would be impossible to adopt it in the general trade of the port; says, that the officers of the London Dock have no controul over the crews, nor the officers of the ship over the labourers.

Mr. Inglis says, that at the London Docks, they have no naval school; that the apprentices are kept on board the ships, and sent by their masters to schools in the neighbourhood, in the day-time; that he considers the crews being kept on board the vessels, to be of great importance to the protection of the seamen and the apprentices, and to the nursery of seamen for the navy: that the West India ships are compelled, by Act of Parliament, to carry an apprentice for every 100 tons, and if 500 ships enter the West India Docks in a year, supposing them to average 300 tons, there must be 1500 apprentices attached to that tonnage; that the school can give accommodation to only 350; that the remainder are turned loose upon the public, during the time they are at home, and exposed to every sort of mischief that can happen to young men in such circumstances. He declares that he never heard of any instance of plunder taking place by the crews, or persons connected with the ships, in consequence of their being permitted to remain on board; and that if seamen were to plunder, they could not carry it out of the docks, for every man that goes out of the gates is searched; that officers of the customs have been let in at night to examine all the empty ships, on a suspicion that plunder might exist, but none was discovered; that before the establishment of the docks the officers and apprentices always remained on board, the crews were generally discharged.

Mr. Chapman states, that at the London Docks, it is optional to discharge the crews, or to continue them on board; that he does not recollect any cargo being plundered by the seamen; that he certainly should consider the crews as honest as the labourers.

Mr. Gibson gives it as his opinion, that a system where the crews, together with the revenue officers, remain on board, not being allowed to leave their ships at night, and watchmen being employed on the quays, fully protects the property: and that this opinion is derived from his experience in the London Docks, where he has been employed from the beginning of the establishment.

Mr. Sawtell, (having been employed at both the West India and London Docks,) cannot give a preference to either system; does not think the discharging the crews gives greater security to the property.

Mr. Eilbeck, (who formerly commanded a West Indiaman,) being asked, if all the docks were opened, by what he should be led to prefer one dock to another, answers, "I do not know "that it would make any difference with me, as "master of a ship, except at the West India "Docks, the turning the boys on shore, which "I consider hurts their morals a good deal: no "master of a ship likes that. In the London "Docks I could keep them on board. The "being obliged to send all the apprentices to

" lodgings, would induce me to prefer the Lon-
" don Docks to them, for there I could keep
" them on board."

Mr. Lampson does not consider that the keeping the crews on board is a security for the preservation of the cargo; says, that if they were allowed to pass in and out of the docks, after a certain hour, they might carry away small quantities, which might in the whole be considerable. He does not know the night regulations of the London Docks, not being on duty after four o'clock; but has no reason to think that the security to the revenue is not as great in the London Docks, as in the West India Docks.

That docks cannot be plundered when no persons are in them, is an incontrovertible position; but whether this object is best secured by the West India Dock system, of turning every body out at night and locking the gates, is a very different question; for when premises are abandoned within, they may the more easily be plundered from without. This was the case with the East India Docks, from whence bales of goods to the amount of £8,000 were taken in one night, by scaling a wall twenty-five feet high. No wall is insurmountable; and when that is once got over, the very circumstance of there being no person within the premises, gives the depredators full security against interruption or detection. It would seem, therefore, that a system of good internal protection, is most efficacious for the security of property; and to this the officers and crews of vessels, when suffered to remain on board, in a certain degree contribute, as they at least prevent the plunder of the cargoes confided to their care.

With regard to the interest of the ship-owners and the parties in their employ, the evidence given by no means justifies the expediency of excluding the crews and apprentices, and employing day-labourers. Many of the witnesses, practical men, who speak from long experience, state that the one class is as likely to be honest as the other; and if no strong case of necessity is made out for this very rigid system, and cogent objections may be urged against it, it surely ought to be abolished. Every ship-owner wishes to encourage his officers and crews, as much as possible. A West India voyage does not occupy them, in general, more than seven or eight months, and the remainder of the year they are without employment. The wages they earn on the voyage will not furnish them with means of subsistence while their ships remain at home, and thus most of the seamen are obliged to change their ship every voyage. Instances however occur, of their making shift, by occasional employment, to continue with the same master for many years together: but how much would their so doing be facilitated, and the interval they are out of work be shortened, by their being employed to discharge their own vessels, instead of being turned out of them the moment they arrive at the dock gates? By continuing in regular employ, men acquire regular habits, contract an attachment to their officers and owners, and are ambitious of gaining their good opinion; but all these ties are broken and destroyed, by the roving and unsettled mode of life forced upon them by the West India Dock system. The grievance is particularly great as to the apprentices, a great number of whom, instead of living on board their own ships, under the care of their officers, are lodged in the different public-houses at Wapping. Surely, some regard is due to the interests, the comforts and the morals of British seamen and apprentices, on whose character, in a national point of view, so much depends. Be it farther recollected, that if any thing can promote a disposition to plunder, it is the loose and vagrant habits of life now forced upon those valuable classes of individuals. In whatever point of view it is considered, this system cannot be too strongly deprecated, nor too soon abolished.

No. IX.

CLASSIFICATION OF COMMODITIES.

The Directors of the West India Dock Company, in their memorial to the Board of Trade, assert, "that the advantages anticipated from "the arrangement and classification of goods, "were among the principal motives for the "establishment of Docks;" and they invite inquiry into "the very beneficial effects of this "classification," which they assert, "tends more "than any other circumstance possibly can, to "the security of the revenue, and the facility "and consequent economy with which it is col-"lected." They also assert, that "it has ano-"ther important tendency, that of rendering the "law more clear and certain in its application; "all that relates to our West India trade, thus "becoming insulated in its details." The meaning of this last passage lies rather too deep for comprehension, but it is sometimes useful to puzzle, where we cannot convince; and therefore, perhaps, it was thought that these dark sayings might assist in bringing their Lordships to the desired conclusion, that "when "your Lordships enter into the examination, "you will without doubt perceive the harmo-"nious system which has arisen from this classi-"fication, and feel the danger of destroying it."

In support of their arguments, the directors offer the evidence of Mr. Irving, inspector-general of imports and exports; who, being asked, "would "not that system of warehousing be best, which "keeps most separate and distinct, merchandize "of the greatest value and subject to the high-"est duties?" answers, "I am of opinion that "merchandize of a similar nature, and imported "from particular countries, would be best se-"cured in separate docks, or different apart-"ments in those docks." This answer contains the whole merits of the case: the plan of having a separate dock for merchandize of a similar nature, and imported from each particular country, is too impracticable to be entertained for a moment; but all that is necessary, as Mr. Irving says, is the securing them in separate apartments; and his evidence is confirmed by that of all the witnesses examined before the Committee.

Mr. Tilstone says, that it is necessary a certain decree of classification should take place in every dock; that goods of different descriptions should be distributed in different warehouses, or in different floors, parts of the same warehouses; and that the same security to the revenue, as is afforded in the West India Docks, would be afforded in any other docks, under similar regulations.

Mr. Burne says, the same security might be obtained by classification in different warehouses, as in different docks, if the regulations were good.

Mr. Mitchell admits that East India sugars are landed in the East India Docks, and Brazil sugars in the London Docks; East India coffee in the East India Docks, and Brazil coffee in the London Docks; that cotton also is landed in both those docks, as well as in the West India Docks; and that none of these staple commodities of the West Indies are landed in the West India Docks exclusively; that the classification of none of them, as being in one particular dock, is complete; only the classification from particular countries: that articles not the produce of the British Plantations, are kept in the West India Docks in distinct warehouses, and that he has heard no complaint of that system not answering every purpose of classification.

Mr. Stuart says, that the practicability of keeping commodities separate, depends upon the number of warehouses any set of docks may have on their premises; and that if a greater variety of commodities comes to any dock, it only requires a greater number of warehouses to give the requisite accommodation; that if the present number of warehouses at the London Docks is not sufficient, more might be built.

Mr. Inglis says, that the articles received into the London Docks are classified in the warehouses; that they could classify sugar and other articles; that they do classify the Brazil trade, and that he never heard any complaint of their mode of classification.

Mr. Gibson states, that the articles imported into the London Docks are so miscellaneous, that it is impossible to separate them entirely; but that they are classified sufficiently for all the purposes of the revenue; and that if the goods at present imported into the West India Docks were brought there, they also could be sufficiently classified.

The foregoing evidence proves, that the classification in the West India Docks is so far imperfect, that all the great staple West India commodities, sugar, coffee, and cotton, are landed in other docks: and it also proves, that the same practical purposes of classification are answered by keeping commodities separate in different warehouses, or in different apartments of the same warehouse, as by keeping them in different docks.

No. X.

DISPATCH IN LANDING CARGOES.

Mr. Tilstone, in giving evidence on this subject, states, that ships are discharged in the West India Docks, on an average, in five days; that for several years they have regularly been discharged without waiting for their turn; but that during the war, when they arrived in fleets, they were obliged to wait. He cannot say the accommodations now provided, would have been sufficient for the immediate discharge of the ships, without detention, during the war; that fifty ships can be discharged at one time, but he has known from 150 to 200 daily coming in. He can make no comparison between the dispatch given at the West India Docks and any other dock, because the cargoes are of so very different a nature.

Mr. Drinkald says, that he can get as much work done in one hour at the West India Docks as in three at the London Docks; that he certainly should give the West India Docks the preference for expedition; that their system cannot be surpassed!

Mr. Domett says, that he had a brig that delivered in the London Docks ten or twelve years ago; that he did not command her at the time; that he has been as an idler there for an hour or two, and he sees that they do not discharge the ships so quickly as in the West India Docks; that in 1820, a brig of his was discharged in the West India Docks in nine hours and a quarter.

Mr. Inglis states, that from the variety of articles that are landed in the London Docks, and from the attendance that is required of revenue officers, no fair comparison can be made between the dispatch given there, and in landing West India produce in the West India Docks.

Mr. Chapman, speaking of the London Docks, says, that if a ship comes from America with rice and cotton, which are articles of the same kind as those which are discharged at the West India Docks, they can discharge them fully as quick; but that if the cargo consists of a great variety of articles, requiring more strict examination, it requires a longer time. He conceives that among other causes for the Brazil ships giving a preference to the London Docks, is their finding more dispatch there than they would at the West India Docks; otherwise, they would give the West India Docks the preference. He states, that the average time of discharging a Brazil ship of

300 tons, in the London Docks, is about five days; that the King's duties are not ascertained in the same manner as in the West India Docks; that the lowest weight used in the West India Docks, for sugar, is a 4lbs. weight; in the London Docks, they weigh with a 1lb. weight; they try it two or three times, first with a 2lbs. weight and then a 1lb., and probably will take four or five minutes in weighing a cask; that they could dispatch as quickly as at the West India Docks, if the revenue was ascertained in the same manner. He says, that greater dispatch in landing cargoes is given by labourers than by crews, because a greater number of labourers are employed than the crews consist of.

From this evidence it appears, that the greater dispatch given in landing cargoes at the West India Docks is owing to two causes,—one, that the same mode of ascertaining the revenue, by very exact weighing, is not adopted with respect to sugar, as to commodities paying very high duties; and the other, that in the mode of landing cargoes by labourers, a much greater number of persons are employed than the crews consist of. But no claim to superior dispatch, under equal circumstances, is made out by the West India Dock Company; nor any proof offered, that West India commodities would not be landed with the same dispatch in any other dock. Another important consideration is, that it appears in evidence, however satisfactory the dispatch given may be in time of peace, should war return, and ships arrive in fleets, the accommodations provided in the West India Docks will be inadequate; and the same inconveniences that were formerly felt will recur, unless the compulsory clause in the charter of that Company be repealed, and other docks be opened for the reception of ships in the West India Trade.

No. XI.

MODE OF HOUSING AND SAMPLING SUGARS.

The ancient and established mode of housing and sampling sugars in the Port of London, has been altered by the West India Dock Company; and the buyers complain, that the interests of all parties have suffered by the innovation.

Mr. Hibbert does not deny that the present mode, of sampling sugars when first landed, is attended with less trouble and expense to the Company, than the former mode of drawing them only when intended for sale; but is confident that was not the consideration which led to the law. As to housing the casks on the bilge instead of the head, he thinks that though the sugars might be the better for losing 7lbs. of molasses, their being subjected to a regulation which prevents their losing 7lbs. is still a better thing. He admits, that samples of sugar, if kept for a considerable time, may vary by the change of weather; and that many houses have their sugar redrawn occasionally, but he does not think the practice frequent.

Mr. Bowman believes the regulations of the West India Dock Company met with the approbation of the sugar refiners in general; but says, that the regulations are not always implicitly followed by the Dock Company's servants; and that the sugar refiners are dissatisfied with the manner in which the samples are kept after they are taken, which does not rest with the Company.

Mr. Glennie says, that for a considerable time after the West India Dock Company was in existence, they were seldom able to sell a board of sugar, without being obliged to make an allowance for the false drawing of the samples: that the sugar bakers and grocers complain, that placing the cask on the bilge, throws the syrup into the sugar more than when it is pitched on the end; that they can separate it more easily from the sugar when the hogshead is pitched on the end, and the rolling of the cask does not mix it so much as when it is on the bilge; that common sense will tell us this.

Mr. Kemble states, that they hardly knew what it was to have a complaint of sugars, in the old mode of warehousing them on the head; that the new mode of warehousing them is on the bilge, and that this new practice is disadvantageous to him, as a wholesale dealer in sugar, to a most enormous extent. That when the sugars were pitched upon the bottom head, the foot (which is the technical phrase for that sugar which has become saturated by molasses, and which is wet and moist,) was found at the bottom; it was in smaller quantities, and could be easily removed without having injured the rest of the sugar. That now, by the present mode, the foot remains on one side of the cask; and it increases in quantity, because the stratum immediately over the saturated stratum becomes also impregnated, and rises in the hogshead; that if the cask of sugar is not quite full, in the operation of rolling it over, which never takes place till after the sample is drawn, the deteriorated sugar becomes mixed with the good, and frequently so entirely alters the quality, that a common observer would not suppose the sample came out of the hogshead at all. That this injures the trade of London; that they used to have a decided preference over the out-ports as grocers, and now the preference is against them; that he would pay a higher price for sugars, if drawn and warehoused in the mode formerly used; that it would save him some thousands per annum in the charges of trade, the whole expense of sending the sugars from the docks to his own warehouses, to make them equal to sample, and then sending them to the wharfs: that he offers his customers 1*s.* 6*d.* per cwt. to receive them from the docks, and take the chance of their turning out well or ill; that the effect of the present system is, to give a better price to the merchant; but that it is ultimately counteracted by the loss of trade; for it has occasioned such a disinclination to buying before hand, or any thing like speculation, that sugar is frequently left on the hands of the importers, which, but for this distrust of the samples, would be scattered among the buyers: that he has heard many West India merchants and planters express their disapprobation of the mode adopted, and their wish that it might be altered.

Mr. Frampton states, that within the last three months, he has lost £300 by sugars not answering the sample: that he now holds 100 hogsheads, of which he should not have had one, if they had answered the description for which he bought them, which he attributes entirely to the mode in which they are warehoused, and the samples being drawn at the time of landing: that if one set of merchants adopted one mode of drawing, and another another, he and the trade generally would give more for the samples taken in the old way than the new; that a very small quantity of molasses being left in a hogshead, and that hogshead being warehoused on the bilge, mixing with the good sugar afterwards, when the cask is rolled over, very much deteriorates the quality of the sugar in that cask; that the present system occasions a considerable quantity of trade, which would otherwise be brought to London, to be transferred to the out-ports, and has a tendency to lower the price of sugar in London; that the West India merchants have an apparent interest in continuing the present system, as the effect of it is to give a better appearance to the article than properly belongs to it.

Before casks are filled with sugar in the West Indies, they are set upon stancheons or joists in the curing-house, on the bottom head, in which holes are bored, but partly filled with pieces of sugar-cane, so as to leave room for the molasses to drain through. The sugar is then poured in, and when the molasses has exuded, it is considered as sufficiently cured for shipping. In the hold of the vessel, the casks are placed upon the bilge for the convenience of stowage; and while in that position, during the voyage, a fresh fermentation takes place, and consequently a fresh deposit of molasses, which has no opportunity of escaping at the bilge, the staves in that part of the cask being perfectly tight. Formerly, when landed here, the hogsheads were placed in the warehouses, on the same end as they stood upon when on the stancheons in the West Indies, by which means the molasses discharged itself through the holes originally made for that purpose. At present, when landed in the West India Docks, the casks are moved on a truck, and warehoused without any change of position, so that the molasses is kept in; but when delivered to the buyers they are necessarily rolled over, and then the molasses mixes with and deteriorates the whole body of the sugar, in the manner explained in the evidence. Under the old system, samples of sugars were never drawn till the importer wished to bring them to market. Under the system of the West India Dock Company, they are all drawn when first landed, whether the importer intends to sell them or not; and if the samples are kept for a considerable time, they bleach in fine weather, or become damp in wet weather, so that the same justice is not done, both to buyer and seller, as formerly. In the year 1808, a memorial upon these subjects was presented to the

West India Dock Directors by the wholesale grocers and other buyers of sugar. The answer to it is given in evidence by Mr. Hibbert; and a summary of it is, that the mode of taking samples of sugar for sale, after previous consideration by the West India Merchants, was submitted to and sanctioned by the legislature; and that the Dock Company have no power to alter it. That the mode of stowing sugars in the warehouses, is that which is used at the principal out-ports; and that in a great and extensive establishment, formed for general purposes, it is not practicable to vary and model their business, so as to meet the wishes of individuals, and even of particular branches of the trade with which they may be connected: and that an important body of importers, have refused their assent to any variation in the mode of stowing complained of. The grocers having failed in obtaining redress on that occasion, when the renewal of the charter of the West India Dock Company came under consideration, presented a petition against it to the House of Commons, repeating their complaints, and requesting to be heard in support of them. This petition was referred to the Committee, and the evidence given by Mr. Kemble and Mr. Frampton, which is unopposed by any counter-evidence, leads to the conclusion, that the old mode of housing and sampling sugars is preferable to that adopted by the West India Dock Company.

No. XII.

WEIGHING COFFEE AFTER BEING WAREHOUSED.

Mr. Tilstone has always been of opinion, that weighing articles on landing before they are deposited in warehouses, enables the consignee to detect any plunder that may happen between the shipment and the landing; and states, that this was the practice when coffee was landed at the legal quays, before the West India Dock Company were established.

Mr. Burne says, that the distance of the warehouses from the dock, in the London Dock, is about 25 yards, which is double that at the West India Docks.

Mr. Groves states, that coffee landed in the West India Docks is not weighed before it is warehoused; but that was the usage prior to the establishment of those docks. He states, that that usage created great confusion in the books and accounts of the revenue, and therefore that the present system was adopted. That in the West Indies they can pack coffee in less space than it can be done here; that when the coffee is poured upon the floor, in order to tare the cask, the same quantity cannot be got into it again; that the duty attaches upon the quantity landed, and is charged upon the quantity re-packed; and that till this practice was adopted, there was nothing but confusion. That the plan occurred to himself, in the time of the late Mr. Milligan; and was at first very much opposed, but has been tried and found to answer. He is aware the Act of Parliament directs that all goods should be weighed on landing; but that this could not be done at the West India Docks.

Mr. Tanner says, that the Act of Parliament is disregarded in that respect, and that the enactment was intended as a security to the revenue, and probably to the merchant also. That the coffee could not be weighed on the quay at the West India Docks; there is not room for it. It would impede other business. It could not well be done. He sees no objection to the cask being weighed in the open air, and the tare being taken afterwards in the warehouse; but then there must be another weight ascertained, inasmuch as the same coffee could not be returned into it.

Mr. Mitchell states, that as a West India merchant, he has frequently found so great a variance between the invoice weight and the actual weight, that he can place no reliance upon the invoice; but that it would be convenient in many respects that coffee should be weighed upon the quay at landing. That the importers of coffee have complained of being deprived of that remedy which other importers have; and that the Secretary of the Company was directed to make application to the Commissioners of Excise, to allow them to alter the present system, but that they have not been able to obtain permission, and that the complaints of the parties remain unredressed; that there are sufficient means for weighing the coffee on the quay, if it should be thought expedient.

It appears, that by this new practice of not weighing the casks of coffee before they are warehoused, an Act of Parliament is violated, and the proprietors are deprived of that remedy against plunder which the legislature thought necessary for their protection. It also appears that this innovation occurred to Mr. Groves, in the time of the late Mr. Milligan, and was recommended by him in order to prevent the confusion that existed in the accounts of the excise, under the old system. As the same difficulty still exists, that the whole of the coffee emptied from the casks cannot be got into them again, it does not appear how the confusion arising from this cause can be remedied by the new system; but it does appear that the old system would be attended with great inconvenience to the West India Dock Company, from the contracted space of their quay; and that, as Mr. Groves says, "*another weight must* "*be ascertained;*" which would of course occasion additional expense to the Dock Company, and additional trouble to the excise officers. Whether these objections justify a departure from the old system, is the real question at issue.

No. XIII.

MAKING COTTON MERCHANTABLE.

Mr. Hibbert admits that a complaint was made on this subject, by the importers of cotton-wool, in the year 1805; and a promise given by the Directors of the West India Dock Company, that as soon as the surplus funds of the Company enabled them to take into consideration the reduction of rates, the rates on cotton should be one of the first objects of their consideration: but he doubts whether that assurance was accurately fulfilled. He states, that there was no reduction of the rate on cotton previous to the year 1817, and admits that the circumstance of excluding the buyers of cotton from the West India Docks, may have been inconvenient to the importers of that commodity.

Mr. Glennie says, that the monopoly of the West India Dock Company was particularly felt in the cotton trade; and that his house were under the necessity, for a very considerable time, so long indeed as they had any consignments of cotton, of taking it away from their warehouses, and carrying it up to other warehouses in London, where it could be made merchantable. None of the buyers would purchase it, until it was made merchantable in other warehouses. They felt this inconvenience most severely, and most extensively.

This evidence scarcely requires any comment, except to observe, that the system of the West India Dock Company, by subjecting this commodity to very high charges, and the buyers of it to very great inconvenience, has contributed to drive the consignments of West India cotton so completely to the out-ports, that very few are now made to the port of London.

No. XIV.

WAREHOUSING RUM.

Mr. Mitchell, having given in an account of the difference between the landing gauges and the delivery gauges of rum, in the year 1821, was asked for a corresponding account of the year previous to the building of the present rum-vaults, but said that he had none; and being asked whether the deficiency was not much more considerable, and a subject of great complaint among the merchants, admits that he has seen a statement, whereby it appears that the loss was considerably greater before the vaults were made. He also admits, that more evaporation must take place, when rums are kept in cellars having wooden floors over them, than when they are in vaulted cellars. Being reminded that Mr. Longlands had stated the new rum-vaults to have been built between 1817 and 1819, and asked why that evil which had existed from the year 1802 had not been sooner remedied, he answers, that long before that time he believes there were vaults belonging to the Company, but not sufficient for the quantity of rum which afterwards came to the Port of London; and therefore the Company, when they found they had the money to devote to that particular object, executed the work, and provided greater accommodation for that article.

Mr. Stuart stays, that the wastage or evaporation on spirits deposited in vaults, is half per cent., but would be nearly double that, in warehouses above the vaults. That in the deposit of wines or spirits in the London Docks, no part of them is deposited in warehouses, but the whole of them in vaults.

The directors of the West India Dock Company cannot be supposed to have been ignorant of the loss to which rum deposited with them was exposed, by being kept in warehouses instead of vaults; and though they admit it to be their duty to provide proper accommodation for the West India trade, they suffered this evil to go on for fifteen years, rather than provide a remedy for it at their own expense, but waited till they could do so, out of the surplus funds which they had accumulated, from the high rates granted them by their monopoly.

No. XV.

MODERATION OF CHARGES.

The principal circumstances adverted to in the evidence on this subject, are, a provision in the West India Dock Act, that the directors were not bound to lower the rates granted them by the Act, till all the money they had borrowed was repaid; their having borrowed £30,000 from the consolidated fund in 1807, and not having repaid it till 1817, although they had ample means of so doing long before that period; their paying the proprietors the property-tax on their dividends, in addition to their dividend of ten per cent., contrary to the Act of Parliament; their expending more than £750,000 out of the rates, in repairing and improving their works; and their refusing to reduce the maximum of their dividend below the present amount.

Mr. Longlands states, that the Act provides that the dock-rate should not be lowered till all the money borrowed was paid off: that the £30,000 borrowed from the consolidated fund in 1807, was not paid off till the year 1817; that the Company certainly had the means of paying it off previously; that their balance in hand was then £482,980; that from the first half-year after the docks opened in Sept. 1802, they divided seven and a half per cent. and ten per cent. ever since; that to the year 1810, when it was objected to in a Committee of the House of Commons, they paid that dividend clear of the property-tax, which they also paid out of the funds of the Company; that taking the substitution of new works for old, and every thing that has been expended on the establishment, he has no question that it may be nearly two millions; that every original proprietor has received his capital back with interest, and that the selling price of the stock is now 185 per cent.; so that if it were 200, he would have his capital three times told; that from the year

1802 to the year 1817, the whole of the rates were charged on the trade.

Mr. Mitchell states, that in the year 1817, after the termination of the war, and as soon as the directors could judge what their situation was likely to be during a period of peace, they came to the determination of lowering the rates; that on viewing the present income and expenditure of the Company, taken on an average of the three last years, which are the three years during which the reduction of the rates in 1817 has had its proper effect, the last reduction of rates proves to be considerably more than will allow of giving ten per cent. dividend to the proprietors of stock; that any expense saved by an alteration in the West India Dock system, would not prove a beneficial economy.

Mr. Turner thinks most decidedly, that the planters and merchants have a strong equitable claim to the benefit of the £700,000 which the Company have expended out of the rates in new works, and to the £500,000 more they have in hand; that a great number of persons would be willing to come forward for the establishment of new docks, provided they could obtain a monopoly for twenty-one years, at a much lower rate than that charged by the West India Dock

Company; thinks they would come forward at a maximum of seven per cent., now that the interest of money is considerably lower than it has been; and that the Company ought to reduce their surplus by a farther reduction of their rates, though they have already lowered them to a considerable degree: that in dividing ten per cent. interest on their capital for twenty years, they have received back considerably more than their capital, with five per cent. interest; that they had received that in fourteen years and a quarter.

Mr. Stuart says, that the charges at the West India Docks are fair and reasonable; that the rent upon a puncheon of rum is only threepence per week, but admits, that till very lately it was sixpence.

Mr. Pallmer thinks the dock charges unquestionably too high; and that the West India trade, from the present value of produce, is not so well able to bear those heavy charges as it has been hitherto. This gentleman also gave in to the Committee a copy of the terms offered to the West India Dock Company by the West India Committee, which were rejected, the Directors refusing even to propose to the Dock Proprietors, any reduction in the present maximum of their dividend of 10 per cent.

Mr. Martin says, that he has referred to the West India Dock rates, and is satisfied the Commercial Dock Company could do the business under, and be glad of it too.

Mr. Glennie repeats that assertion, with the exception of rum.

Mr. Tooke, in stating that the expenses of the Port of London were high, meant to exclude the charges at the London and the Commercial Docks; and meant to include the charges on a quantity of pepper in the East India Docks, which were very extravagant; says, that the present charges in the Port of London are apparently high enough to drive away a considerable portion of the trade.

Mr. Wilson is of opinion, that under the reduction that has lately taken place, the charges upon rum at the West India Docks are lower than those at the London Docks. He believes the West India Dock Company have reduced the rent on rum from *7d.* to *3d.* per week; that at the London Docks, the charge on brandy is, for the first twelve months *6d.* and afterwards *7d.*

Mr. Frampton states, that at the period of

the establishment of the West India Docks, assurances were held out to the wholesale grocers, that they should be indemnified for the extra cartage from the Isle of Dogs; that was one of the things that prevented the trade from making any opposition: but immediately on the bill being passed, they were told they must consider it in their sales.

The evidence given on this point is certainly not very favourable to the moderation of the West India Dock Directors, who might have averted the opposition of the West India body to the renewal of their charter, by acquiescing in that reduction in the maximum of their dividend, which is consistent with the general reduction in the rate of interest that has taken place since the peace; but the Directors refused even to submit such a proposal to the consideration of the Proprietors of West India Dock stock.

No. XVI.

REPAIRS AND IMPROVEMENTS.

No. XVII.

ACCUMULATED FUND.

These subjects are so connected with each other, in the evidence given before the Committee, (provision for both having been made out of the surplus rates,) that it is impossible to treat them separately. They involve, however, many points much more fit for the discussion of gentlemen of the long robe than of any unlearned individual.

In framing the Act of Parliament for the incorporation of the West India Dock Company, a clause was introduced, which gave them the power of applying the rates to the extension and improvement, as well as to the repairs of their works; but it is alleged, that a construction has been given to this clause, which never could have been contemplated by Parliament. The Directors of the West India Dock Company appear to have been extremely anxious to come into possession of the high rates granted to them as soon as possible: and this they accomplished, (to use the words of their own Memorial,) by "the energy and rapidity which they displayed "in the execution of this great work." In short, they ran up their buildings in so hasty and imperfect a manner, that as Mr. Rennie, their own engineer, says, "they are defective "with respect to the bricklayers' work, and "the foundations, and the work generally." His testimony is corroborated by the statement of Mr. Mitchell, that no less a sum than £754,186 has been expended from February 1st, 1810, to

February 1st, 1822, in works and repairs; a sum which never could have been necessary, had the works been originally built in a substantial manner. Exclusively of this money actually expended, a sum of £400,000 more has been accumulated out of the rates; and, according to the statement of the West India Dock Directors, will be required for the same purposes.

Whether it was not the intention of the legislature, that the West India Dock Company should make their works and buildings complete, at their own expense, or whether they meant to give them the power they have exercised, of making them so out of the rates, is a subject of much controversy. The plea set up by the Dock Directors is, that if these expenses had not been defrayed out of the rates, they must have been provided for by an increased capital of the Company, on which they would have been entitled to receive a dividend of 10 per cent.; and therefore, that the mode they have adopted is the most advantageous to the West India body. To this the West India body reply, that unless the charter of the Company is renewed, the money so expended on their works, is for the benefit of the Dock Company, and not for that of the West India trade; and that, according to the Act of Parliament, the whole of their accumulated fund ought to have been applied to the reduction of rates, which now cannot possibly be done before their exclusive privilege will expire. The Dock Directors farther contend, that their accumulated fund was derived, in a great degree, from the rates paid on the produce of the foreign colonies, and not from those paid on the produce of the British West India colonies: but the answer to this is, that all their rates, from whatever source derived, are appropriated by an Act of Parliament, to which they are bound to conform.

Under these circumstances the Dock Directors consider these funds as the property of the Company, while the West India body contend that they have an equitable interest in them. It can scarcely be thought, that while Parliament restricted the profits of the West India Dock Company to ten per cent. on their capital, they meant to render that limitation nugatory, in the manner contended for by the Dock Directors; and give them, in addition to that dividend, these sums of £750,000 expended on their works, and £400,000 of accumulated fund. Gentlemen learned in the law, who have been consulted on this subject, agree that the latitude of discretionary power vested in the West India Dock Directors by the Acts of Parliament is so great, that no redress can be obtained from any court of justice, nor in any other mode, than by applying to Parliament to explain its own intentions. The Acts direct the surplus funds, after paying the necessary expenses of the Docks, and the dividend of ten per cent., to be appropriated to the reduction of rates; and appoint the West India Dock Directors trustees for that purpose. Independently of the injustice of their retaining, for the benefit of the Dock Company, what ought not to have been accumulated, it is obvious that this fund may be so applied as to operate very unfairly against the other Dock Companies, in the competition which it is intended to establish. It seems therefore expedient, either that this fund should be taken out of their hands at once; or some arrangement be made, by which it shall be exhausted during the period when the West India Dock Company will labour under the peculiar disadvantage, of their exclusive privileges having expired, while those of the other Dock Companies remain in force.

No. XVIII.

JUST REGARD TO PRIVATE INTERESTS.

This is one of the objects stated by the West India Dock Directors, in their Memorial to the Board of Trade, to have been in the contemplation of the Legislature in establishing the West India Docks; and as it may be presumed that the same considerations which influenced them when the charter was originally granted, will not be lost sight of now the continuance of it is requested, a few observations upon this point appear necessary.

Mr. Inglis states, that the capital invested in the London Docks is £3,250,000, and was subscribed with a view to a participation in the general trade of the port of London, when the period for which the exclusive privileges were granted should have expired. That the effect of the exclusive privilege of the West India Dock Company is, to make their capital of £1,200,000 equal in value to the £3,250,000 of the London Dock Company. He cannot very well judge whether the continuance of this exclusive privilege would be such an interference with private property, as would entitle the London Dock Proprietors to an indemnity.

Mr. Marten states, that the Commercial Dock Company had the promise of a monopoly in the outset, which promise was not made good; and that they have looked forward to the opening of the other Docks from monopoly, as the only means of remuneration.

When the wet dock system was first established, indemnities to the amount of more than one million of money were paid out of the public purse, to wharfingers, warehouse-keepers, lightermen, and various other classes of persons, whose occupations and emoluments were interfered with by this new mode of conducting the business of the port of London; and this is probably the just regard to private interests, which is alluded to in the Memorial of the West India Dock Company. But if this exclusive privilege operates with such serious effect as is stated by Mr. Inglis, how can it possibly be continued with any just regard to private interests? The London Dock Company, in order to obtain the advantage of local situation, paid as much money in many instances for a square yard of land in Wapping, as the West India Dock Company paid for an acre in the Isle of Dogs. The former establishment required a capital of £3,250,000; and the latter, though upon a larger scale in point of extent, only £1,200,000; and yet, under the exclusive privilege now in force, the emoluments of the latter Company are greater than those of the former, and the former are deprived of all those advantages of situation for which they have actually paid so valuable a consideration. This is an interference with private property, as inconsistent with justice as with the spirit of a free Government; and the

London Dock Company, the Commercial Dock Company, and all the other Dock Companies, who have invested their capital in the expectation of sharing in the general trade of the port of London, when the present monopolies expire, appear to have as just a claim to indemnity, if those monopolies are continued, as the wharfingers, warehouse-keepers, lightermen, and others had, when they were originally established.

No. XIX.

DISCONTINUANCE OF COMPULSORY CLAUSE.

The evidence given on this point relates rather to the effect of continuing than discontinuing the compulsory clause; but the one may be judged of by the other.

Mr. Mitchell states, that the West India Docks are very short of being full during a considerable part of the year; that at the time he was giving his evidence, there were only 6,400 casks of sugar in the warehouses, and that they will contain 120,000 to 140,000 casks; that raw sugars are generally used for home consumption, or refined for exportation; that the average general import of sugar into the docks is 180,000 to 190,000 hogsheads; that the West India Docks are at a greater distance than the London Docks from the principal establishments of the sugar refiners; that the produce of the Brazils is uniformly landed in the London Docks, and (cotton excepted) must be exported again.

Mr. Hibbert thinks that if the compulsory clause were not continued, it is very likely that the West India Dock Company might continue to divide 10 per cent. He considers a monopoly of the trade essential to the system that at present protects both the planter and the revenue, but does not consider it essential to the prosperity of the dock proprietors.

Mr. Colville states, that without the continuance of the compulsory clause, supposing the general trade of the port of London should not decrease, and taking it for granted that Parliament will take no measure in contravention of those Acts, upon the faith of which the docks have been established, and the money for their erection subscribed, he has a very confident opinion that the business of the Dock Company could easily be so managed as to give the proprietors 10 per cent. dividend, and that rather than accept of 7 in the place of 10 per cent. he should feel it his duty to state his candid opinion, that the Company should stand upon their Act, rather than accept of any renewal of the compulsory clause upon a less dividend than is at present allowed them by Act of Parliament: that he does not contemplate any improper combination, and should in all instances advise the proprietors against it.

Mr. Drinkald should not be afraid (if he had them as a legal wharfinger) of doing much better with the West India Dock warehouses, under the present system, than by having a monopoly of the West India trade, and being excluded from all other trades, as they now are; says, that the West India trade might go elsewhere in the first instance, till experience taught them better; but afterwards he has no doubt the whole trade would come back again, from their superior management and system: that in his opinion their establishment is more than sufficient, if they are confined to the West India trade.

Mr. Pallmer gives in the conditions upon which the West India body wished the restrictive clause to be continued; but if it should not be continued, sees no reason to fear that a competition among the Wet Dock Companies should not produce the usual and natural effect of competition, in a reduction of charges.

Mr. Inglis says, that if the renewal of the exclusive privilege of the West India Dock Company should not be granted, though he cannot answer for what a general court of proprietors would do, as an individual he should feel no hesitation in proposing to the proprietors of the London Docks to resign their exclusive privileges also; and he believes that sentiment to prevail with the Directors.

Mr. Glennie thinks that it would be advantageous to the commerce of the City of London, that the monopoly should no longer continue, and that it is believed to have had the effect of driving away part of the commerce of the metropolis.

Mr. Manning speaks to the extra charge incurred upon wood shipped to the West Indies, by the compulsory clause, under which it is necessary to send it in lighters from the Commercial Docks, to the exporting vessel which lies in the West India Docks, instead of shipping it direct from the Commercial Docks.

It appears from the evidence given on this subject, that the compulsory clause forces commodities intended for home consumption, to be landed in docks low down the river, from whence they must be brought up to the City at an extra expense of cartage; and that commodities intended for exportation, are landed in the London Docks, close to the City, from whence they have to be carried down the river again; but that if the compulsory clause were discontinued, all commodities would find their proper places, where they could be deposited and delivered, with the least expense, and the greatest convenience to the proprietors. This evidence also relieves the mind from the apprehension of any injury being sustained by the proprietors of the West India Docks, from the discontinuance of the compulsory clause; for it proves, on the authority of the Directors, that this clause is not essential to the prosperity of the Company; that they would in all probability still continue to divide 10 per cent. on their capital, and therefore one of the Directors declares, that he should advise the proprietors to stand upon their Act, rather than accept any renewal of the compulsory clause upon a less dividend than 10 per cent. The most important effect of discontinuing the compulsory clause, will be the substitution of a system of competition for one of monopoly; but this will be best considered under the next head, of competition of dock companies.

No. XX.

COMPETITION OF DOCK COMPANIES.

Mr. Mitchell, on being asked whether the opening of the trade of the port of London would not lead to competition between the different dock companies, and induce them to vie with each other in establishing such a system as would give the most effectual security to property, and the greatest accommodation to trade, at the most reasonable rate, says, he should rather fear it would be the reverse, as it relates to the West India trade.

Mr. Hibbert admits that the original intention of the subscribers to the Wet Docks in Wapping, was to leave their plan to its own merits for public encouragement, wishing for no monopoly, compulsion, or restriction; but says, that they soon departed from those principles, and took a monopoly. He believes that the first monopoly was given to the West India Dock Company, and that another monopoly was given to the London Docks. He knows the fact, but does not know the reason to be, to encourage them to proceed with their undertaking. He is satisfied the monopoly with which he is most conversant, was granted upon the most solid grounds.

Mr. Colville thinks, that if the effect of competition was to reduce the rates too low to give an adequate profit on the business, the evil would be corrected by a combination on the part of the dock companies; that what occurred in the violent competition among the water companies, led him in part to give that answer; but he thinks it is the necessary consequence of competition being carried too far, and there would be much facility in such a combination, because there are fewer docks than water companies. He conceives that the West India trade could not be carried on separately, by different docks in competition with each other, with equal advantage to the planter or the merchant; because it would be impossible to adopt the same restrictions that are now adopted in the West India Docks, and which he considers as essential to the security, both of the revenue and the merchant.

Mr. Turner is of opinion, that by competition, as between dock and dock, the business might be done at a cheaper rate in the first instance; but he looks upon a monopoly to be almost essential to the system. He is quite satisfied that any competition between the docks, would be something like the competition between water companies; that though for a short time it might induce persons to do the business at a cheaper rate, still it being concentrated in one spot, would enable the parties to do it really at a cheaper rate, than it could be done if it were more dispersed; that whether it would do so, is a different question. He adds, that in consequence of the clear statement that has been made, that the rates which have been levied (by the West India Dock Company) during the last 21 years, have been equal to pay a dividend of 10 per cent. during that time, and also to raise very nearly, if not more than a million of money besides; he does not think it too much to say, that men of sense and capital would undertake a new dock, secure of the same business as the West India Dock Company are to receive, supposing they get a renewal of their charter, who would be content with 7 per cent. in the present times. He believes that the London Dock Company makes a dividend of only 4 per cent.

Mr. Inglis states, that the London Docks have a monopoly of wines, spirits, tobacco and rice; that it was not solicited by them, but offered by the Lords of the Treasury for the protection of the revenue; that the London Dock was established on the principle of freedom of trade, which in his opinion is the proper principle for docks to be established upon: that, as a merchant, he would prefer a system of open competition, to one of monopoly: that if the trade of the port of London were opened, and more came to the London Docks, they could give it every accommodation: that competition would lower the charges: that the dividends which have been paid, and the sum that remains in the hands of the West India Dock Company, prove that the business can be done for less.

Mr. Chapman says, that if the monopoly of

the West India Dock Company should expire, a considerable portion of the West India trade could be well accommodated at the London Docks, as cheaply, as safely, and more conveniently, because the cartage to the sugar bakers and grocers would be cheaper. He considers competition best for the merchants and the docks also.

Mr. Marten is satisfied that fair and open competition is the best means of obtaining accommodation at the cheapest possible rate; and that unless something of that kind is thought of, the port of London will lose its trade. In his opinion, it would be for the benefit of trade, that the exclusive privileges of the different dock companies should be done away. He thinks they could give greater accommodation at the Commercial Docks, than is now given at the West India Docks, from competition rousing up all their powers. They would not seek a preference, by giving indulgence to any body who might be disposed to plunder; but should be disposed to enter into a competition of lawful and proper indulgences: that if the West India business was open, which gives another Company 10 per cent., they would make a race of that business, by doing it on lower terms, but without any indulgence whatever to smuggling: that they would not pay court to the captains and crews of ships, and relax the regulations against plunder, because, according to the old proverb, honesty is the best policy, and so is morality too: he should look upon it as their first interest to secure the revenue and the merchant, and let all other things take their course. He has referred to the West India Dock rates, and is satisfied that they could do the business cheaper.

Mr. Glennie is confident that the Commercial Dock Company could and would do the business cheaper than it is done at the West India Docks. In his judgment, it would be highly advantageous to the general commerce of the river, that there should be an open trade, and competition among all the dock proprietors: that the Commercial Dock Company would be satisfied with the trade at 10 per cent. reduction from the present rates, excepting rum; and thinks they might improve upon the present system of the West India Dock Company. He knows some of the trade has been driven to the Continent, by the high charges in the port of London: at one time he had a considerable share of the Havannah trade, but found the charges in this port so high, that he was obliged to give it up.

Mr. Tooke has no hesitation in giving the preference to an open trade over a monopoly, on all occasions; thinks that the commerce of the port of London would be better accommodated, and at less expense: considers that the commerce of the port would be very much benefited, by the cessation of the monopoly of the West India Docks: that the charges in the port of London are higher, taking all the trade collectively, than those of any other port, probably in Europe, certainly higher than those of any other with which he is acquainted: says that to reduce the port charges would tend mainly to promote the prosperity of the port of London.

Mr. Kemble is of opinion, that if the West India trade were extended to the different docks in the river Thames, there would be a greater disposition to give accommodation to the trade, than has been shewn under the monopoly of the West India Dock Company. He states that many merchants have expressed a wish to store and sample their sugars, in a way that would be satisfactory to the buyers; and that if a fairer mode were adopted at any one dock, he presumes ultimately it would be adopted at all, not excepting the West India Docks.

Mr. Frampton thinks, that if the West India trade were open to competition among all the different dock companies, that mode of housing and sampling sugars would be adopted, which was considered most advantageous by the importers and the buyers.

The result of this evidence is conclusive, as to the advantages of competition; and the same sentiment is most forcibly expressed by the Commissioners of Inquiry into the Customs and Excise, who conclude their seventh report with the following luminous observations on the Wet Dock Companies.

" We are fully satisfied, that they afford the " means of protecting the revenue, not only more " effectually, but more economically than it could, " under any regulations, be secured, if the vast " transactions now conducted within the docks, " were carried on, as formerly, upon the open quays: " and we find it generally admitted on the other " hand, that they have been highly useful to the mer- " chant, by the safeguard he has found in them, " against the frauds and pillage to which his goods " were formerly exposed. These are advantages of " great value, and more especially under a general " warehousing system. It is therefore, in our view " of the subject, most desirable, that the dock estab- " lishments should be maintained upon the pre- " sent respectable footing: but we are at the same " time far from being prepared to state, that for " that purpose the continuance of the whole of " their exclusive privileges would be necessary or " expedient. We are sensible, on the contrary, " that the interest of the mercantile community is " deeply concerned, in being enabled to obtain the

" accommodation which these docks afford (and to " which, for the advantage of the revenue, they are " compelled to resort,) at the cheapest rate at which " it can be yielded; and after all the consideration " that we have hitherto been able to bestow upon " the subject, we are not aware of any other mode " of securing that object, than by opening a com- " petition between the several dock establishments, " and other warehouses and quays, such as cannot " exist consistently with the exclusive rights by " which the former are now protected: and which " rights have been granted for certain periods, as " a fair remuneration to the proprietors for the " expense of the undertaking. By what modifi- " cations of their several privileges, at the expira- " tion of those periods, *this competition, which in " our judgment can alone protect the merchant " against arbitrary charges,* may be effected, we " propose to consider, and submit to your Lord- " ships in a future Report."

Apprehensions are expressed by some of the witnesses before the Committee, that competition between the dock companies might lead to combination between them, something like that which took place a few years ago between the water companies; and the Memorial of the Directors of the West India Dock Company to the Board of Trade, countenances this idea, in the following passages. " An open competition between dock and dock,

"your Memorialists submit, would create a com-
"petition of indulgences to the captains of ships, "and the persons employed by them to discharge "their cargoes; and that the business would soon "revert to the state in which it was before the estab-"lishment of any of the docks, when it was not "uncommon for men to offer to lump out, or "discharge ships for nothing, on an understanding "that no notice should be taken of the breakage "or plunder of the cargo." On what principles the West India Dock Company may have determined to conduct that establishment, when this competition is opened, they know best; but it may safely be affirmed, that whenever that event takes place, the dock company which gives the greatest accommodation, on the most reasonable terms, will have the preference, and that any company that permitted the practice of such abuses, would soon lose all its business. Substitute competition for monopoly, and a new spirit will be given to emulation and invention; the different dock companies will vie with each other, in making improvements upon their present systems; and competition, so far from being injurious, will be found as beneficial in this, as in every other respect. The Directors of the West India Dock Company assert, in their Memorial to the Board of Trade, that they give superior security to property, have a better system of management, and at as low a rate of charge as any existing establishment. If so, they have no-

thing to fear from competition; but if these assertions are not borne out by proof, (and the directors of other docks pledge themselves to do the business on lower terms), then indeed their dread of competition may easily be accounted for.

Several of the witnesses state their conviction, that the charges at the port of London are higher than at any other port in Europe; that they have the effect of driving away trade to foreign countries; that open competition will reduce these charges, and promote the prosperity of British commerce. These considerations have acquired additional weight from the bills passed last session of Parliament, which open the ports of all Europe to the produce of our West India colonies, and thus bring our charges in direct competition with theirs. The difference in the charges on sugar is not in evidence; but it was proved before the Committee, by Mr. John Hall, in the year 1820, that the warehouse rent on coffee, in various ports on the Continent, was only one-fourth of that then charged by the West India Dock Company; that the rent of one hundred tons of coffee, at Antwerp and other adjacent places, for twelve months, was £60, and at the West India Docks £240; being charged in the former at the rate of one shilling per ton per month, and in the latter at one shilling per ton per week. It may not perhaps be reasonable to expect, that the charges in London should be altogether so low as on the Continent; but unless they approximate much more nearly than they now do, the British planters will have a great inducement to send their produce direct to the Continent, instead of continuing to ship it to the mother country; and the same observation applies to every article of foreign produce. All the advantages we enjoy; our free government, which gives the best security to property; our central position, so favourable to intercourse with every part of Europe; the mildness of our climate, which renders our ports accessible at seasons when those on the opposite coast of Europe are frozen up; the capital and integrity of British merchants, which tend to make this country the emporium of the world; will be counteracted and overborne by the continuance of our present enormous port charges. If the exclusive privilege of the West India Dock Company be renewed, those of the other dock companies must be renewed also, and the whole of our commerce be bound up in monopolies, which will fetter and cramp the enterprise of British merchants. The public have performed their part of the contract with the West India Dock Company; they have amply remunerated them for investing their capital in that establishment; and therefore have a right to enter into possession of those advantages, which they were taught to expect at the expiration of the charter. They rely, with confidence, on the assurance given them by the Committee on Foreign Trade, in their first Report, that "the time when monopolies could "be successfully supported, or would be patiently "endured, seems now to have almost passed away," and they call upon them to fulfil that prediction, by refusing the petition of the West India Dock Company for a renewal of their charter.

WITNESSES *called by the West India Dock Company.*

1. John Tilstone, Esq. Principal Surveyor of the Customs at the West India Docks.
2. Thomas Burne, Esq. Comptrolling Surveyor of the Customs at the West India Docks.
3. Thos. Groves, Esq. Inspector General of the Imports at the Port of London.
4. Thos. Tanner, Esq. Comptrolling Officer of the Excise.
5. Henry Longlands, Esq. Secretary to the West India Dock Company.
6. John Rennie, Esq. Engineer to the West India Dock Company.
7. W. Mitchell, Esq. Chairman of the West India Dock Company.
8. Geo. Hibbert, Esq. Director of the West India Dock Company.
9. Saml. Turner, Esq. West India Merchant.
10. And. Colville, Esq. Director of the West India Dock Company.
11. Fred. Bowman, Esq. Sugar Refiner.
12. Mr. John Clippingdale, River Pilot.
13. Mr. John Drinkald, Ship Owner and Lighterman.
14. Mr. Chas. Stuart, Wine and Spirit Broker.
15. Nath. Domett, Esq. Ship Owner.

Witnesses called by the Committee of West India Planters and Merchants.

1. C. N. Pallmer, Esq. West India Planter.
2. John Inglis, Esq. Chairman of the London Dock Company.

3. Mr. Dennis Chapman, Comptroller of Charges and Deputy Superintendant of the London Docks.
4. Fred. Gibson, Esq. Principal Surveyor of the Customs at the London Docks.
5. W. Sawtell, Esq. Comptrolling Surveyor of the Customs at the London Docks.
6. Mr. Beeby Eilbeck, Superintendant of the Commercial Docks.
7. Jas. Walker, Esq. Engineer to the Commercial Dock Company.
8. R. H. Marten, Esq. Director of the Commercial Dock Company.
9. Alex. Glennie, Esq. Director of the Commercial Dock Company.
10. John Lampson, Esq. Landing Surveyor of the Customs at the Legal Quays.
11. John Manning, Esq. Landing Surveyor of the Customs at the Commercial and other Wood Docks.
12. Thos. Tooke, Esq. Merchant.
13. Fletcher Wilson, Esq. Merchant.

Witnesses called by the Grocers.

1. Francis Kemble, Esq. Wholesale Grocer.
2. W. Frampton, Esq. Wholesale Grocer.

MINUTES OF EVIDENCE.

No. I.

ADVANTAGES OF DOCK SYSTEM.

Mr. Tilstone's First Report to Commissioners of Customs.

"The insulated state of the docks and warehouses, the military guard, and the vigilant and well-regulated police of the Company, give safety to the premises, the revenue, and the merchant's property, from fire, plunder, and every species of depredation.

"The property of the ship-owner is also completely protected, during the time the vessels are in the docks; and the expedition with which the ships are unladen, is highly advantageous to the owners, for, upon an average, ships are now discharged in these docks in five days. When in the river, the delivery often exceeded five weeks, and the average time could not have been less than a month; in fact, the article of rum was seldom unshipped under thirty days, the time allowed by the excise laws, before it became liable to seizure.

"Thus, the former protracted discharge of the cargo, with its attendant expense of demurrage, and loss of time to all parties, are by this establishment wholly averted; and the ship, in the course of a few days after her arrival, is cleared inwards, and ready to proceed on another voyage.

H

"With respect to the convenience of trade, no doubt can be entertained but that it is greatly promoted by the West India Dock system: the landing, housing, sampling, and certifying to damage and deficiencies (arising from bad stowage or otherwise) to enable the importer to make proper deductions from the freight and the delivery of all goods for home consumption or exportation, being performed by the Dock Company, greatly facilitates the operations of commerce; subjecting the merchant to an inconsiderable expense to what was formerly incurred at the legal quays, where he was obliged to employ clerks and others, personally to superintend and to adjust matters relative to freight, &c.

"The dock rates on goods landed, unshipped or discharged, were established by the 39th Geo. 3d, cap. 68, section 85, founded on the legal quay charges. They were afterwards raised, by Act of 42d Geo. 3d, cap. 113, section 21; and in March 1817, lowered again by the Court of Directors, to the original standard; with this material difference, that the warehouse-rent at the legal quays commenced on the ship's report, whereas the West India Dock rates include warehouse-rent for three months from the commencement of the ship's discharge. . . . . .

"An expense has been imposed on the trade, (compared with what it might have been under the former system,) in consequence of the distance of the West India Docks from London, the cartage of goods being more than it was from the legal quays; but this, we conceive, is counterbalanced by the excellent condition in which the goods are now delivered to the purchasers; formerly they were exposed to the weather, from the time they were unshipped to the landing at the quays, and consequently delivered to the buyer in a deteriorated state. . . . . .

"The dock system, as it concerns the Planter, has

been truly beneficial; for when the ships discharged in the river, his property was exposed to plunder, from the unshipping to the landing; and even after it was deposited in the warehouses, the loss on sugar (which article *now* undergoes no diminution, except from drainage, and the usual samples drawn for the purposes of sale) was calculated at 44 lbs. per hogshead.

"The advantage to the Revenue is obviously great, when we consider the opportunities that presented themselves for smuggling in the unshipping, during the transit of the goods to the quays, and whilst lying there, for days and weeks before they could be landed, and brought to the King's beam.

"Indeed the average plunder of sugar, before it was weighed for the duty, was ascertained, (in the year 1810,) from very good data, to be 27 lbs. per hogshead; rum, $2\frac{18}{25}$ gallons per puncheon; coffee, $\frac{1}{40}$ part; and the plunder on other goods was estimated at one per cent. on the value.

"This establishment, therefore, which connects the docks, wharfs and warehouses, with the immediate arrival of the ships from sea, has entirely put a stop to the enormous plunderage which took place in the river."

Mr. Tilstone's Second Report to Commissioners of Customs.

"Further, if ships were to discharge West India produce in the River, and send it to various places, all the precautions that could be adopted would (judging from former experience) prove insufficient for the protection of the revenue, and the merchant's property; and a revival of the old system (the detrimental effects of which led to the establishment of docks at the Isle of Dogs) would soon follow.

Examination of John Tilstone, Esq.

Does not the security given to the revenue, and the property of individuals, depend upon the system itself, of landing cargoes immediately on the arrival of the vessels in wet docks, containing warehouses surrounded by high walls?—I do not think that does give security.

Explain why?—Because the ship is resorted to so frequently, and not brought alongside the quay to discharge. At the West India Docks, the entries are all passed before a ship can break bulk; then she is brought alongside to discharge, and the landing goes on until the whole of the cargo is landed.

Do you mean to state, that at other docks, for instance at the London Docks, or the East India Docks, the ships are not brought alongside the wharf, to discharge their cargoes?—No, I do not mean to say that; but I believe in the London Docks they frequently take goods out of the ship before she is alongside, or when the ship is lying in a tier, at a distance from the quay.

Even in that case, is not the security of the revenue, and of the property of individuals, vastly improved beyond the old system, of ships being discharged in the river Thames?—Oh, certainly; I think there is a material difference between ships discharging in the river Thames and discharging in the docks, though not with the perfect security of the West India Docks.

In your first report delivered in, the comparisons are drawn, not between dock and dock, but between the dock system and the system which previously existed?—Yes, certainly, the comparisons in my report are drawn between the West India Dock system and the system which previously existed.

Many of the statements which you make there, are not

peculiarly applicable to the West India Dock, but to the dock system generally, as compared with the system which previously existed?—I conceive they apply particularly to the West India Dock system, compared with the system previously existing.

The West India Docks were the first that were opened? —They were.

Therefore you had no other comparison to make?—No.

Mr. Thomas Burne.

Have you a recollection of the inconveniences which prevailed in the River, before the dock system?—Perfectly well.

In the event of the Dock Charter expiring, and that a combination between the docks should render it necessary to permit vessels to discharge in the River; are you aware of any circumstances which could prevent the recurrence of the same mischiefs?—I have no doubt the same mischiefs would arise immediately.

If ships that now discharge their cargoes in the West India Dock, were permitted to discharge their cargoes in any other dock, but not permitted to unload them in the River, as was formerly the case; would the revenue be any more exposed to fraud than it now is, or to a recurrence of the plunder that formerly took place in lumping out cargoes?—It would depend on circumstances; if the crew were allowed to remain on board, probably plunder would arise in consequence; if the crew were suffered to work out the ship, I think they would probably be half as long again; it would be longer exposed in consequence.

Supposing the crew were not suffered to remain on board, but the ships were worked out by persons in the employ of the Dock Company, would not the same security from plunder be given in one set of docks, as in the other?—No doubt of it.

Thomas Groves, Esq.

Have you been called upon to make any report upon the subject?—I have.

Officially?—Yes.

By whom were you directed to make that report?—By the Commissioners of Excise, in consequence of directions they received from the Lords of the Treasury.

Have you that report here?—I have a copy of it; the original report went to the Commissioners.

You know it to be a correct copy of the report which went to the Commissioners?—Certainly it is.

[*The Witness delivered in the same, which was read, as follows:*]

"Honourable Sirs—The present Dock system at the port of London, originated in the increase of commerce and trade.

"In the years 1793, 1794, and 1795, such was the crowded state of the river Thames, the legal quays, and warehouses for the reception of merchandize, that goods remained at times for some months, before they could be warehoused or put in a place of safety; and therefore the harbour itself, although perhaps one of the best and largest in Europe, being too small for the current trade, it became indispensably necessary to enlarge or extend it; for this purpose, recourse was had to docks.

"But in order to show how very little the utility of the Dock System pursued, was known, I beg to remark, that in a Report of the Commissioners of Customs, of the 16th May, 1796, to the Lords of the Treasury, upon several plans that were presented to their Lordships, for improving the port accommodations, it was stated, that the Commissioners viewed docks, merely as places of reception of ships, in easement of the river, to unship their cargoes on board lighters, but not as places for the due examination and final delivery of their cargoes; and then they went on to state their objections, and to show, that the legal quays were preferable to any other place, for the landing and examination of merchandize.

"Subsequent experience, however, has abundantly proved, that a dock properly constructed and regulated with quays and inclosed warehouses, affords that protection to the revenue as well as to the merchant's cargoes, that cannot be had by any other means whatever; indeed, unless a dock is so constructed, it is the worst of all port accommodations.

"*The West India Docks*, consisting of an Import and Export dock, were erected and regulated by the Acts of 39 Geo. 3, chap. 69, and 42 Geo. 3, chap. 113. Under these Acts, the hatches of each laden ship are put under the locks of the officers of revenue, from the time of entering the dock to the final discharge of the cargo.

"Bulk is not allowed to be broken, until entry is made or bond given for the duties on all the goods on board the ship.

"The shutting the gates and entrances, and obliging every person to quit the dock after the hours of business, being an experiment never made before, it has been found necessary strictly to prohibit either lighter or craft of any kind, capable of removing goods, to remain in the dock in the night-time. And during the day, no labourer leaves the dock without being previously searched at the dock-gates; nor are any goods allowed to be removed from the warehouses, which are strong, substantial, and secure, until proper documents are produced for that purpose; so that it becomes impracticable to smuggle, or even to plunder to any extent.

"A military guard sent by Government, is also placed on the outside of the dock in the night-time, to give an alarm in case of fire, and also to be an additional safeguard to the merchant's goods.

"The ship-owner's property is well protected during the time the ship remains in the dock, and the expedition with which the cargoes are landed, must be advantageous to them. In the year 1801, which was the last year in which the whole of the West India ships discharged their cargoes in the river, it appears that they were, upon an average, twenty-eight days from the date of report to the clearing of the Excise tidesmen; and those tidesmen having frequently been cleared before the cargoes were delivered, the detention of the ships must have exceeded this calculation.

"The average time for clearing the West India ships in the dock, in the year 1818, is no more than fifteen days, when the ships were liberated and allowed to proceed on another voyage, or to remain in the Export dock free of expense, for six months.

"I have heard objections to the West India Docks, on account of the distance at which they are situated from the seat of business; but when it is considered, that almost every article of West India produce is sold by sample, which sample is sent to the dock house, a central situation in the City, and there delivered to the proprietor or importer; that the charges are less than under the old system, or even than the London Dock system; that the state and condition of all goods are examined, on landing, by competent persons, and the damages, if any, assessed between the ship-owner and the merchant; that plunder and depredation, which formerly were carried on to a great extent, may be said to be entirely prevented; that all goods, whether for home consumption or for exportation, are delivered with dispatch and expedition; and that for the export trade, the situation is a good one; it does appear to me, that these advantages do more than counterbalance any objection that is made to this public concern.

"In a Revenue point of view it is impossible to calculate the benefit derived. The saving of expenses must be obvious to every one; and it is well known, that in all detached warehouses, more especially in such as are situated at remote distances from the quay or landing place, it is impracticable to prevent the mixing and shipping for exportation British spirits for Foreign spirits, and thereby effecting frauds to a serious amount. Several instances might be adduced in support of this position; but two, which lately occurred, the one at Leith and the other at Liverpool, and which will be in your Honours' recollection, may be sufficient.

"At the West India Docks it is impossible to carry on any fraud of this kind.

"I have gone at greater length in my remarks concerning this than the other docks, because it seems to be required by Mr. Harrison's letter.

"*The London Dock*, which consists of one dock only, appears to have been erected for the purpose of improving and extending our commerce; as well as for affording relief to the merchant from paying down on the nail very high duties, to which some of the articles warehoused on bond are now subject.

"The exciseable articles, which it may be said to be almost imperative on the importer to land, and which, with a few exceptions of small quantities, are invariably landed at this dock, are tobacco, wine, brandy and geneva.

"There are also large quantities of other valuable goods landed and warehoused, as rice, silk, cotton wool, sheep's wool, coffee and cocoa, not the produce of the West Indies; hemp, flax, tallow, barilla, brimstone, dye woods, drugs, &c.

I believe, myself, that the duties on the exciseable articles, were tolerably well secured under the old system, except as to some evasions in the export of tobacco; though certainly they must all be still better secured when the goods are lodged in strong and secure warehouses, inclosed by high surrounding walls, which, whilst they afford complete protection to the revenue, have been productive of laws and regulations tending materially to improve our commerce, by the export of articles for which the Legislature had hitherto thought it dangerous to make any provision. And indeed I know of no other practical method than this, of effectually guarding the revenue on some of the high-dutied articles, lodged here for commercial purposes.

"In point of situation this dock is undeniable.

"*The East India Dock*, consisting of an Import and Export dock, may be considered as a place for the discharge of ships cargoes, rather than for the reception or stowing of them. The warehouses, on and near the spot, being of comparatively small extent, except those for the reception of saltpetre, pepper and drugs, the great bulk of the goods and merchandize landed are removed to the East India Company's warehouses in London, by caravans under the revenue locks.

"It is situated near four miles from the Custom-house, and being obscure and lonely, the walls of the Import dock, though of the same height as those at the West

India Docks, have been scaled, and depredations practised; and on account of such depredations, (as the Dock Company have refused to heighten the walls, or to make them more secure by other means), a watch or patrol is kept within the dock, in the night-time, by each revenue, as well as by the Dock Company.

"The Export dock, which adjoins the Import dock, has so many unnecessary doors and entrances to it, that the Lords of the Treasury, after a personal survey and examination, ordered the Dock Company to pay the salaries of four of the Excise watchmen during the time that any ship remains in it, to take on board exciseable goods, which, however, has hitherto been but seldom.

"I do not think that there has been for many years, much smuggling from the East India ships, after passing Gravesend; at the same time the revenue must be better guarded in this dock (though rather objectionable from what is just stated) than in the river; the expense must be less, as employing fewer tidesmen, and that too for only about two-thirds of the time that they were employed in the river.

"The business is regulated by the Acts of 43 Geo. 3, ch. 126; 46 Geo. 3, ch. 113; 53 Geo. 3, ch. 155; and 54 Geo. 3, ch. 228.

"It was understood, that the Dock Company's charges were not to exceed those incurred by the East India Company, before the dock system took place. I have taken some pains to ascertain what the East India Company's expenses were, but cannot obtain any satisfactory information. Those who are the most competent to form a correct judgment, say, that the present are not so high as the former charges, and that the packages, particularly those of tea, are received into the Company's warehouses in London, in better order, and with less breakage than when discharged in the river. Certain it is, however, that heavy complaints are made against the dock charges, particularly that of tonnage imposed by the Act of 43 Geo. 3, ch. 126, sec. 91, of 14*s*. per ton, but which the Directors have lately reduced to 12*s*. and in some instances, to 10*s*. per ton.

"By a memorial of a numerous body of the shipowners, presented to the House of Commons, on the 13th of May 1818, it is stated, among other things, that this service of discharging the ships, would be better performed at other docks in the port of London, at from 3*s*. to 5*s*. per ton, and that those heavy charges are not only calculated to drive the Private East India trade from the port of London, but even from the country.

"The House of Commons hereupon appointed a Committee, who in June 1818, heard evidence in support of the complaint, but the late period of the Session in which the inquiry commenced, prevented it from making satisfactory progress; and it was suggested in the Report, that the investigation should be resumed at the earliest opportunity, but I do not find that it has yet been resumed.

"Although, as before observed, I have not been able to ascertain whether the charges under the old and the present system are the same, I fear that the present are high. I know, from undoubted authority, of a ship which arrived from the East Indies about twelve months ago, whose size and dimensions prevented her from entering the dock, and was therefore obliged to discharge her cargo, by lighters, in the River, the expenses of which amounted in the whole to no more than 120*l*.; but had the same ship's cargo been discharged in the dock, the charge would have been 527*l*.'

"And I think that the removal of the cargoes from the

dock to the Company's warehouses in London, must be greater by land carriage than by water carriage; those warehouses, too, being chiefly situated in the interior of the town, are objectionable on that account on the part of the revenue, for the reception of such goods as are imported for commercial purposes, or for re-exportation.

"I have annexed, for your honour's information, Tables of the rates on charges made by each of the Dock Companies.

"I am, honourable Sirs,
"Your most obedient humble servant,
"18th Dec. 1819. (Signed) T. GROVES."

Is sugar an article that is peculiarly liable to plunderage?—It has been, before the dock system took place; I believe there was no article that suffered so much by plunder as sugar and coffee, previous to the dock system.

Are they articles that afford a great degree of temptation?—From their being frequently loose in bulk, from their being loose in the hold, they were fair game very often.

Do they afford greater facility to depredation from being loose, than the average of articles in other trades?—I think they do; they put them into their small clothes pockets, and wherever they could, being valuable articles.

Are coffee and other articles, such as afford a greater temptation to plunder, and a greater facility?—Yes.

Is it not therefore worth while to submit to a more rigid system, for the purpose of protecting those articles, than the average articles of general trade?—I think it is, because they are more liable to pilferage and depredation.

The inconvenience to which the owner of the ship and the merchant submit, in consequence of the rigid system of exclusion, may be compensated in the case of the articles of sugar and coffee, which would not be compensated in articles of general merchandize?—Yes.

(*Examined by the Committee.*) Do you conceive that the very rigid system observed in the West India Docks, is essential to the preservation from plunder of sugar and coffee, or that it is not the necessary consequence of the dock system?—My opinion is, that if sugar and coffee were discharged from ships in the river, as they used to be formerly, before the docks took place, the same system of plunder would prevail.

The question is, whether the protection which you say is now applied in the West India Docks, to the sugar and to the coffee, is not in consequence of the dock system; that it must be so in any dock that had proper precautions, and that was surrounded by walls?—A dock properly constructed. I conceive there is a good deal in the construction of a dock; and that the West India Dock, having an import and an export dock, is very good, and in being so constructed, that no carmen, or people of that description, are allowed to go in.

Supposing the trade now received by the West India Docks were to be admitted as an additional trade to the London Docks, do you think, that according to the system which at present prevails in the London Docks, the same protection would be given to the revenue, and to the property of the proprietors?—I should have some doubts of that; as I have already observed, instances have occurred where the empty ships have been allowed to remain in the docks, and they have received goods from the laden ships, with a view, as I suppose, of taking them out, and smuggling them, when they got into the river. I do not speak from my own knowledge, but I have heard of such cases.

Your opinion is, that the same security could not prevail as does at present by the classification; the West India Docks being exclusively confined to the reception of West India produce?—No: at the same time I have stated in that Report, I believe the smuggling in the London Docks is very trifling indeed; but if it is compared to the West India Docks, the West India Dock system approaches as nearly to perfection as any system can do.

George Hibbert, Esq.

Appendix, No. VII.—Statement of the Loss sustained by Plunderage upon West India Produce in the Port of London, in the years 1799, 1800, and 1801.

Sugar imported:

1799 - - 2,362,572 cwt.
1800 - - 2,012,688
1801 - - 2,721,876

7,097,136 equal to 525,713 hhds. at 13½ cwt. each.

Plunderage thereon at - - 28 lb. per hhd. before landing.
at - - 16 ditto - - after landing.

44 ditto on 525,713 hhds. of 13½ cwt. each.

	£.	s.	d.
Makes 206,530 cwt. at 71*s*. per cwt. -	733,181	10	—

Of which the duty amounted to about - - - £123,213 15 —

Rum imported:

1799 - - 1,689,768 gallons.
1800 - - 1,904,256
1801 - - 2,177,928

5,771,952 { equal to 54,452 puncheons at 106 galls. each.

Plunderage thereon at $2\frac{19}{15}$ galls. per puncheon, makes 156,093 galls. at 4s. 6*d.* per gallon - - - - - - - - -	35,120 18 —
Excise and customs on do. at 11s. per do.	85,851 3 —

Coffee imported:

1799 -	- 165,780 cwt.
1800 -	- 359,128
1801 -	- 386,533
	911,441

Plunderage thereon, at the rate of $2\frac{1}{2}$ per cent. on the quantity imported, being 22,876 cwt. at 120*s.* per cwt. - -	136,716 — —
Excise lost on do. at 8*l.* 17*s.* 4*d.* per cent.	202,035 17 4
Other goods (cotton excluded) value together 720,000*l.* each year, is 2,160,000*l.*	
Plunderage thereon, at 1 per cent. on the value of which to the revenue about 5,000*l.* - - - - - - - - -	21,600 — —
Total - -	£1,214,505 8 4

Being the total value of produce plundered in the said three years, including a loss to the revenue of	£411,100 15 4
To the proprietor or ship owner - - - - -	803,404 13 —
	£1,214,505 8 4

And being upon the three years importation equal to an annual loss to the revenue of - - - - - - - - - -	137,033 11 9
To the proprietors, &c. - - - - - -	267,801 11 —
Or, to a total annual loss of - -	£404,835 2 9

Mr. John Drinkald.

Are there the same legal quays and sufferance quays now, that there were before the establishment of the West India Docks?—Nearly so, there are; some of the sufferance wharfs have been done away by the commissioners of the customs, as well as the whole frontage of the new Custom House, for which I offered 2,800*l.* a year.

Generally speaking, the accommodation is the same?—With that exception.

Was yours a legal quay or a sufferance wharf?—A legal quay.

Could you have admitted any of the West India trade?—At Sabbs' Quay, certainly.

Till within two or three years?—No: that which I speak of, till within the last two years, was the Custom House quay.

If the trade had not been taken away from you, you could have accommodated it?—Yes; previous to the West India Dock Act.

And in accommodating the West India trade, you could have taken proper care of the goods?—As far as I was concerned; but I could not be responsible for my servants, nor for the coopers who were allowed to come in.

Is it not usual for a wharfinger to be responsible for his own servants?—For my servants, perhaps; but not for the coopers who have power from the merchants to come in and sample the sugars.

You were also a lighterman?—Yes.

You could have accommodated the West India trade with your lighters?—Yes; I did.

You could take due care of their goods?—As far as I was concerned.

And as far as your servants were concerned?—The system was this; that there was a watchman appointed by the captain of the ship, over the sugars.

Then there might well be plunderage, if the goods were entrusted to a lighterman who had not the responsibility of taking care of them, and then were delivered to a wharfinger who did not consider himself responsible?—When they were received, the wharfinger, after they came into his warehouse, was answerable, as far as it could be ascertained.

The lighterman was not responsible?—No; they were considered in the charge of the watchman of the ship.

The lighterman not being responsible for the goods while they were on board his craft, they were shockingly plundered?—No: I do not admit that.

They were not plundered?—I have no doubt they were, sometimes; and they were plundered before they went into the lighter, by being exposed upon the decks.

In your custody, on board the lighters, the goods were not safe from plunder?—No, they were exposed, certainly, to plunder, if the watchman who had charge of them allowed it.

In your custody, upon the wharf, the goods were not safe from plunder?—For the reasons I have stated, the coopers being admitted to take the samples and to do as they pleased, by the order of the merchant.

Do you not think that if the lighterman was responsible for the goods in his custody, and the wharfinger responsible too, the goods might have been protected from plunder?—From the time that they came into the lighterman's possession, if he was to be charged with the deficiencies, they would have been safe; and the same with the wharfinger, if no person was to be allowed to come into the warehouses but the wharfinger's people.

Therefore, if you, as a lighterman and a wharfinger, had taken as much care of the property as the West India Dock Company did, it would have been equally safe in your hands?—We had not the power, because other people were allowed to come and to act according to the custom of the port; the system was completely different.

In short, till the West India Docks were established, there was an unvaried usage for plunder, from all quarters, of West India produce?—From a great number of quarters, there is no doubt, West India produce was plundered; it was very different, the West India cargoes were stowed differently from what they are at the present time; hogsheads of sugar were cut in two to admit the stanchions of the ship into the middle of them; and hogsheads, if there was not height under the beams to admit of a tierce, the tops were taken off, and the tierces let in; sugar was put into provision casks, hammocks, and every thing else, and then the sugars were brought upon deck in that state to be coopered, and of course were very much exposed to the plunder of the lumpers on the river.

While that improper system of plundering prevailed, the people concerned used to consider it rather as perquisites?—If the question alludes to any particular trade, either lightermen or coopers, I can answer it: coopers were paid a low price, and, taking as persons do tithe, in kind.

In plunder?—No; they were paid 6*d*. a hogshead for coopering, and were allowed to take a certain quantity of sugar, that was the system; therefore they considered it as a matter of course, and known to the merchants, who, every market day, had an opportunity of seeing the samples on their boards in the shops.

Were any other descriptions of persons paid in the same way?—Lumpers, they were paid by the ship-owner, at as low a price as they could get; some of the men, and the master lumper, used to think they had a right to take sugar.

They all helped themselves to make up for short wages?—Yes.

Any other description of persons?—I do not mean to say, that the journeymen lightermen that were employed, were immaculate, though they were paid full wages: but some of them were not paid full wages. Wharfingers at the legal quays were allowed to have lighters, which they employed solely in the West India trade, and they employed a description of men, that a lighterman would not, and therefore they certainly were very much in the habit of plundering, which they have done to my knowledge.

The Committee have been informed, that a considerable proportion of the West India cargoes went in plunder of this description; do not you understand that in all those calculations, the plunder or perquisite you have been speaking of is included?—Yes, I believe it was taken into the account; there were a variety of other ways as well.

From thirty to forty pound a hogshead?—I forget what the allowance was now.

Therefore this, which used to be called plunderage, was at least, in a considerable degree, a mode of paying wages?—It certainly was an understood thing.

So that it was not so much actual loss to the West India merchant?—There was certainly another way with the revenue officers; they took their share, for the conniving at the gauging and weighing, which they have not an opportunity now of doing.

Upon the whole, it may be taken, that under the present regulations, there is not the same danger of plunder, that there was twenty years ago?—Certainly not; nothing like it.

If the monopoly of the West India trade, which the Dock Company at present possess, should expire next year, there is no reason to apprehend that the same bad habits would all recur?—I have very little doubt, if the monopoly was done away, the West India Dock would have the exclusive business of the whole of the trade, after a short time.

If the monopoly of the West India trade, which the Dock Company at present possess, should expire next year, there is no reason to apprehend that the same bad habits would all recur?—Not to such a degree certainly; merchants would now know more of their business, than they did at that period; they would employ those persons they could depend upon.

For instance, on board your lighters, according to your present system, the property would be safe?—Yes; but there are some lightermen I would not trust with my property now.

If a man had the good fortune to employ you, his property would be safe?—Some of the merchants of London have had that good fortune, and have found it so; I pay my men well, and am careful in their selection.

The King has a good many honest lightermen in the kingdom?—I am certain he has.

And many honest wharfingers, no doubt, at the legal quays?—No doubt of it; very respectable men, certainly.

Would it not be possible for a wharfinger to employ his own cooper?—If the owner of the cargo thought it proper, but it is not very likely that the wharfinger would like to have the responsibility of the loss, if a merchant chose to step in with any person.

The question refers to a merchant not stepping in, but leaving the responsibility with the wharfinger?—If they should return to the legal quays, there would be no room for them.

Would there be any insecurity in discharging at one of the legal quays?—It would not be so safe as the West

India Dock, where a ship goes alongside and delivers the cargo into the warehouses.

The question supposes the goods in your lighters?—They would be more subject to plunder than they would be in the London Docks, and much more than in the West India Docks.

Would they not be as safe at the legal quay, or in the London Dock?—Not so safe as in the West India Dock certainly.

Used there to be much drainage, as it is called, at the wharfs from the sugar casks?—A good deal.

Whose perquisite used that to be?—The wharfinger had the scraping of the warehouse from drainage.

That loss also is included in the calculations of the loss that used to take place?—There is no doubt of it; allowance was made for that and for sampling.

That falls to the lot of the West India Dock Company now?—That would of course fall to them, unless some regulation to the contrary has taken place; I believe they have no sweeping off the tops of the heads as was the case formerly.

Mr. Charles Stuart.

Were you acquainted with the trade of the river before the West India Docks were established?—I was.

And with the West India trade?—Yes, and with the West India trade.

West India produce, the Committee understand, was much plundered at that time in the river Thames?—It was.

Plundered on board the ships?—Yes, and plundered in the lighters, and plundered upon the quays, all of which I have been an eye-witness to.

Thomas Tooke, Esq.

Do you consider that a general system of landing cargoes in wet docks in warehouses, and surrounded with high walls, has given greater security to the revenue and the property of individuals?—I conceive it has.

Do you consider that if this system is carried on at a moderate rate of charge, it will be very conducive to the improvement of the commercial interests of this kingdom?—Yes; I conceive that if the charges of the navigation of the Port of London could be materially reduced, it would tend, in a very great degree, to restore the business of the Port of London to the utmost it has ever been at.

Do you not believe the converse of the proposition to be true, that if the charges of the Port of London are much higher than those in the neighbouring continental ports, the effect will be to drive the business from this country over to other countries?—That is undoubtedly the tendency of the high relative expenses of the Port of London.

No. II.

CONVENIENCE OF SITUATION.

John Tilstone, Esq.

"An expense has been imposed on the trade, (compared with what it might have been under the former system,) in consequence of the distance of the West India Docks from London, the cartage of goods being more than it was from the legal quays; but this, we conceive, is counterbalanced by the excellent condition in which the goods are now delivered to the purchasers; formerly they were exposed to the weather, from the time they were unshipped to the landing at the quays, and consequently delivered to the buyer in a deteriorated state."

George Hibbert, Esq.

If West India ships were permitted to come as high up the river as Wapping, do you think the securing the hatches would afford adequate means of protecting the cargo from plunder?—It would be a very useful precaution, but it would not be sufficient.

Has it been found so on former occasions?—As far as my experience goes, it certainly has not.

Was it not the practice to lock down the hatches before the establishment of the docks?—Yes, it was.

Did that precaution afford sufficient security against the plunder of the cargo?—It did not.

Was your house, among others, a sufferer by the plunderage which took place at that period?—We were less so than others; we had accommodations at the port, which were very uncommon; we were possessed of one of the legal quays.

In your judgment, is the principal loss to be apprehended from plunderage before the ship arrives at the quay at which she has to discharge, or afterwards?—I think, with the present accommodations of the port, the principal apprehension is of a loss before the goods have passed the King's beam.

You mean, taking the present mode of discharging at the West India or other docks?—Yes; I do not mean to say that formerly that was so great as the subsequent plunderage; the total plunderage was so great then, I cannot readily form a judgment upon it; at present, I chiefly apprehend the plunderage before the goods pass the King's beam.

At the time there were no docks at all, the principal plunderage might be after they arrived at the legal quays, but now it would be before they arrive at the docks?—Yes.

The question then is, whether if West India ships, instead of being compelled to go into the West India Docks situate at the Isle of Dogs, were to be permitted to go up to Wapping, whether the property would be so well protected as it is at present?—Unquestionably not.

Frederick Bowman, Esq.

Do you conceive that if sugars were deposited at any docks situated on the Surry side of the river, the refiners would sustain considerable loss?—Very considerable loss and inconvenience.

That loss must generally fall upon the buyers of sugars?—At all times.

And to that extent lessen the consumption?—Or raise the price.

What loss are you speaking of?—The loss would be in the lighterage, which we must necessarily have; they must be put into lighters to be taken across the river, we being to the north, the Commercial Docks to the south.

Therefore this is more convenient to your premises than the Commercial Docks?—Yes, and that would also be twice the distance.

If the sugar refiner was on the other side, it would be the other way?—Yes, but there are none.

What is the difference of distance from the London Docks, and from the West India Docks, to your premises?—To the West India Docks it is two miles.

What is your distance to the London Docks?—Half a mile.

It would be still more convenient to you, to have to convey it only from the London Docks?—In respect of cartage, certainly.

Mr. Charles Stuart.

Is it not a very great convenience to importers, and to

dealers also, to have commodities near at hand?—Certainly it is.

For the facility and convenience of having access to them from time to time?—Certainly.

What distance may the London Docks be from your residence in Tower-street?—Not above a mile, I should think.

Do you think that it much exceeds half a mile?—From a half to three quarters.

Did you never hear it observed that the dock gates are exactly a quarter of a mile from Tower-hill?—I never did.

What distance do you suppose the West India Docks may be from your residence in Tower-street?—I suppose from two miles and a half to three miles.

Would not you give a higher price for commodities that were warehoused in the London Docks, than for those warehoused in the West India Docks, you being able to have access at all times to the one, and being precluded due access to those in the other?—I should certainly give the preference to having them where I could always go and have access to my goods, most assuredly.

Supposing the trade of the Port of London was to undergo a change something similar to this; at present, foreign sugars when imported are deposited at the London Dock, which is much higher up the river, and more centrical as connected with the Port of London, although those sugars are generally, if not altogether, again exported; supposing those sugars were to be deposited at the West India Dock, in preference to the London Dock, would it not be more convenient for the importer if they were so deposited at the West India Dock, in place of the London?—I should think it would be certainly preferable for them to have them housed at the West India Docks.

Why do you think it would be preferable to have them housed at the West India Docks?—From the greater facility which would be given, I think.

Do not you think, that from the fact that the West India Docks are lower down the river, and therefore more accessible from sea, it would be more convenient to have the foreign sugar which was to be exported deposited there than brought higher up the river?—I should certainly think so.

Are you not also inclined to be of opinion, that as West India sugar is chiefly and almost wholly taken out, either for refining or for home consumption, if it was deposited at the London Dock rather than the West India Docks, a very considerable expense of cartage would be saved which is now incurred, owing to the distance of the West India Docks?—There certainly would be an expense of cartage saved.

To that extent, would it not be advantageous to the owner of this sugar if it were so deposited?—No, I do not think that it would be any advantage *to him*, it might be to the *buyer*, there might be a little expense saved in the cartage.

Supposing you were going to purchase sugar, and that one parcel was offered to you lying at the West India Docks, and the other lying at the London Docks, and that the cartage from the West India Docks was a distance of three miles, and the cartage from the London Dock only a distance of half a mile, would you not consider the additional cartage in the price of this sugar?—No, I should not consider it in the price of the sugar; but it stands to reason that I should give the preference to the nearest place, if they were of equal quality.

You would prefer to that extent the sugar lying in the

London to that at the West India Dock?—To that extent, but it is very trivial.

John Inglis, Esq.

State to the Committee the advantage resulting from the use of the London Docks in respect to the convenience of trade?—The convenience is certainly very great, from their vicinity to all the public resorts of business, and especially to the Custom-house; it would be utterly impracticable to do the business of the London Docks at a much greater distance, from the sort of attendance of the persons connected with them.

For those persons, are you not of opinion that the situation of the West India Docks is disadvantageous and inconvenient to the trade?—No doubt of it.

Are you not of opinion, that in the extent of land carriage which is necessary, the property is exposed to plunder?—I am not aware that instances of that have taken place; I have heard of them, but I cannot state it as a fact; but I can state as a fact, that I had certain goods myself, which when re-weighed in London, coming from the West India Dock, had been plundered, but I cannot charge that to the Dock Company; because I must presume the goods left the dock in a state of security.

To whom would you be inclined to charge it?—Probably to the carman, or to some other persons who had the care of them during the transit.

Is the road between the West India Docks and the City built upon generally?—It is now very much built upon.

Still are there not conveniences for plundering the property in the transit from the West India Docks to the

City ?—That would depend entirely, I think, upon the person having charge of it; he might very conveniently take an indirect line of road, to give an opportunity for plunder, if he was so inclined.

Are the carmen who convey the produce from the West India Docks to the purchasers in the City under the direction of the purchaser, or of the West India Dock Company ?—I apprehend, the West India Dock Company have nothing to do with the carmen, they are either under the direction of their masters as public carmen, or belonging to the grocers themselves, who employ their own people.

Is there not a considerable expense incurred by that cartage ?—Yes, a very considerable expense.

Upon whom does the expense of that cartage fall ?—It falls in the first instance upon the purchaser of the goods; but in the end, like all other charges, it must fall upon the vender.

Has it an effect upon the price ?—I have not the least doubt of it; it had an effect upon the price before the docks were opened, for sugar was obliged to be landed at other places than the legal quays, and whenever sugar was sold lying at a warehouse on the other side of the water, the buyer always stipulated for an allowance for the extra cartage between the custom-house quays and wherever he lived.

What is the difference in the expense of cartage from the London Docks to the City, and from the West India Docks to the City, or other general place of consumption ?—A hogshead of sugar, from the West India Docks to Whitechapel, would be three shillings and sixpence; to Mark-lane, or Mincing-lane, is four shillings; and from five to seven shillings to greater distances: the same hogshead of sugar, I apprehend, would be carried from the London Docks for a shilling, to the nearest places.

That which costs four shillings from the West India Dock, would cost one shilling from the London Dock?—Yes.

In your opinion, the expense of cartage from the West India Docks is nearly four times greater than that from the London Docks?—I think so: there would be as much cartage, in process of years, as would build another dock.

Is not all the produce of the Brazils sold here for re-exportation, not being admitted for home consumption, excepting cotton?—Cotton excepted, I believe it is.

Then can any possible advantage be derived in the sale of this produce from its being brought so much higher up the river as to the London Docks?—I believe the consignees and the proprietors uniformly wish it to be brought nearer town than the West India Docks.

Have you ever heard any West India proprietors complain of the distance of the docks?—I do, for one; I have heard almost every merchant who has to do business there, uniformly complain of the distance; every person connected with the establishment, complains that the distance is a great inconvenience; I feel it myself, for I do not import sugar only, but articles that are wanted to be looked at: when business requires me to go there, it spends me a forenoon; and it is very inconvenient to persons, especially at the west end of the town, such for instance as cabinet makers, who want to look at a log of mahogany; they lose the greater part of a day in going down to look at it.

Mr. Dennis Chapman.

Do you know of any thing to prevent West India ships

from receiving their outward cargo in your dock?—I am not aware of any thing that could prevent it.

Is it not as convenient as the West India Dock for the purpose of exportation?—I certainly consider it much more so, being much nearer the seat of commerce, and the places from which the goods are sent.

Mr. Beeby Eilbeck.

What distance are your docks from the wharfs where coasters usually load for the outports?—I should suppose from a mile and a half to two miles and a half; I refer to Cotton's wharf, and other wharfs on the Surry side.

What do they load there principally for the outports?—They take in sugar and dye woods, and a variety of articles to go coastwise.

What distance are the West India Docks from those docks?—They would send them by craft; probably in that case, they would not be much further than we; but if they send them by carts, round by the bridge, it would be twice the distance.

Supposing they were sent to London-bridge, what would be the comparative distance between the West India Docks and the Commercial Docks?—I should suppose that we are nearly the same, the third mile-stone stands at our gate, from the Surry side of London-bridge; and I believe the West India Dock is very little more; I think they call it three miles to their dock-house, which is very little more.

Is it not intended to make a new road, by which the distance will be very much decreased?—There is one in contemplation that would shorten it, I should think, three quarters of a mile, when it is made.

In that case, would the distance be considerably shorter from the Commercial Docks to Lower Thames-street, than from the West India Docks ?—If they should make a new road, I think we should be nearer even to Thames-street than they would be from the West India Dock.

Do you know any thing of the different tolls of cartage from the West India Docks and from yours?—I think they would be much more round the Commercial-road than from our docks.

Do you conceive the cartage would be more expensive from the West India Docks than from yours ?—I should conceive, if the distance were about equal, the tolls there would be rather more ; but I am not acquainted with what the tolls are.

Could you not afford facility and dispatch to the West India traders in the discharge of their cargoes ?—We could afford it ; for when we took in the sugars, we adopted the same mode as they did in respect to their sugars.

Do you not know that many sugar refineries are established in the neighbourhood of Thames-street, such as Old Fish-street, Distaff-lane, College hill, Garlick-hill, and all the streets in that vicinity ?—There are a great many sugar refineries there.

Are not your docks as near to those sugar refineries as the West India Docks ?—I should think nearly the same ; we are at the same distance to the foot of London-bridge as they are.

Thomas Tooke, Esq.

In speaking of the charges at the London Docks, do you mean to speak of the charges on that description of produce which you are in the habit of importing and warehousing there ?—Yes, I confine myself to that; I have an impression that the charges are in proportion to those other kinds of produce, but I cannot speak of the others.

Those articles, being the produce of Russia, are not the subject of monopoly?—No, they are not.

They may go into any other docks as well as the London Docks?—I believe they may.

In the choice of docks for discharging cargoes consigned to you, would not your house consider other circumstances besides the charges; would not they consider the convenience of separation where the goods were lodged, the proximity to the places of their consumption, and the facility of access that might be given there to the buyers to see and examine them?—We include all those considerations, and independently of those, we do find their charges are as low as at any of the sufferance wharfs.

If a cargo of tallow, for instance, were landed at the West India Docks, do you consider the buyers would give the same price for it at that great distance that they would if it were to be delivered to them from the London Docks?—That would be decidedly an objection in the sale; and in a great number of instances there would be some sacrifice to be made in the price, in consideration of the inconvenience of the distance.

Would not the buyers expect an allowance in the price for the increased expense of cartage, and the inconvenience of having to attend their business at so much greater distance?—They would, undoubtedly: besides the still greater objection to the distance, from the circumstance that the buyers would not be able so readily to inspect the bulk of the goods, and therefore they might, on some occasions, at the same price, prefer articles which were lodged in a nearer situation, which they could consequently inspect with more convenience. There are some goods in our line where the buyer could not judge of them at all by sample, such as hemp and flax; the inconvenience of a greater distance would be therefore very considerable.

Francis Kemble, Esq.

Have you any means of informing the Committee what would be the difference in price in the cartage of a hogshead of sugar from the London Docks and the West India Docks to Limehouse, Ratcliffe, or any of those districts? —I live in the heart of the city, and do not know what the Limehouse or Ratcliffe people pay at all.

Take it to the heart of the city, what would be the difference?—The actual difference, I suppose, would be about half-a-crown, or at most, three shillings; for it makes this difference, that a waggon could generally make two turns to the London Docks, when it can rarely make more than one to the West India Docks.

F. Wilson, Esq.

Have you had any occasion personally to notice the regulations that are observed at the West India and the London Docks?—The West India Docks are so far from our counting-house, that I have not been there half a dozen times in my life.

No. III.

SAFETY AND FACILITY OF ACCESS.

John Tilstone, Esq.

"Again, if ships, with West India produce, were allowed to enter the London Docks, and there to land and warehouse the whole of their cargoes, I am humbly of opinion, it would be extremely injurious to the revenue; for ships *drawing* 15 *feet water*, I am *credibly informed*, would not generally be able to enter the London Docks the same tide that they passed the West India Docks; and *ships of 17 feet draught of water* (the average draught of West Indiamen) could not, on any tides, get up to the London Docks in time to be taken in the same day.

"The depth of water requisite for a ship of 17 feet to lie afloat at low water, is confined to so small a space at Union-stairs tier, as to make it hazardous to take a ship of that draught so near the London Docks, unless they were sure of the ship being taken in immediately."

W. Mitchell, Esq.

You have stated that the responsibility of the Dock Company on ships, commenced on their arrival at their moorings near the dock gates; do you imagine that when the rates on shipping were established, they were settled as a compensation for that responsibility, as well as the accommodation to which the ships had been entitled?—Speaking without the smallest knowledge upon the subject, not having any thing to do with settling the rates and the duties of the Company, I should say, certainly, that ought to be taken into consideration, as well as every thing else; because I know the Company have been called upon to make good some very serious losses upon shipping.

Do you not know that when the directors were called upon for losses of that description they denied their responsibility?—I am not aware that they denied their responsibility in fact; although I know of cases of their having paid some very considerable sums of money; I do not know the grounds upon which such applications were made.

Did they not resist the payment for the ship Resolution and her cargo, till compelled to make it by a court of law ?—I was not in the direction then ; I know nothing, but the fact of the loss having been finally settled by the Company.

You have spoken to circumstances of a much earlier origin, to the manner in which ships discharged their cargoes when the docks were first established ; surely you must be supposed to know something of a transaction of a much later date, which makes so conspicuous an item in the account of the Company ; it appears in five succeeding years ; in the year 1809, there is an item of £17,219, and a charge in each of the four subsequent years, amounting altogether to £21,138 ; one would imagine that a circumstance of this kind could hardly escape your notice ?—When the question was asked me as to my knowledge of the situation of the West India shipping, as to the discharge of their seamen previously to the formation of the docks, I distinctly answered, I was not acquainted with West India shipping at that time, but that I have been informed that it was the practice of the owners of West India shipping to discharge their seamen as soon as ever their ships got to their moorings in the river ; but I did not speak as to my own knowledge on that subject, and I am afraid I can only speak to the facts here as they appear upon the account ; I am not aware of the grounds upon which the claim originated ; I am not aware of the grounds upon which the directors of the Company resisted those claims, if resistance was made to them ; but I gather from these accounts the fact, that the Company did ultimately pay the loss.

Whatever the grounds were on which the resistance was made, did not the verdict of the jury show that they considered that resistance improper ?—It certainly showed that the Company were liable.

In the year 1809, the Committee perceive charged the

loss of the ship General Miranda, £10,857; was not that a loss of the same description?—I should suppose so.

Was not the ship Hope, of Liverpool, lost in the same way?—I am totally ignorant of the fact.

Have you never heard that the Princess of Wales, from Jamaica, and other ships, have been in very imminent danger in entering the dock gates?—I do not recollect the names mentioned.

Are not these accidents owing to the improper construction, or rather position of the dock gates?—I can only state that since I have been a director, no accident of the sort has occurred.

George Hibbert, Esq.

It appears that in the course of the years 1808 and 1809, the Company paid certain losses respecting two ships, of the names of Resolution and General Miranda, to the amount of £30,000 or thereabouts?—Yes.

Do you recollect what gave occasion to that?—Accidents which happened to those ships, upon their entrance into the dock.

And the owners brought actions?—The owners brought actions against the Company for the loss, under the plea that it was by the negligence of the Company that those losses happened.

And the juries before whom those causes were tried, decided that it was the negligence of the Company?—They decided against the Company.

Samuel Turner, Esq.

Does the system adopted at the West India Docks appear to you to give at present perfect security to the merchant and planter?—Most decidedly.

Do you consider that that security might be endangered

in the transit of vessels from the West India Docks to the London Docks?—If the system was confined to the docks, under chartered companies, I do not know that there would be any great danger; because docks under companies, having pretty nearly the same security as the West India Docks, it is certainly possible the business might be done without any danger to the planter or the revenue.

The question refers to the passage up the river from the West India Docks to the London Docks?—I can see no danger between the West India Docks and the London Docks.

Supposing a vessel were detained by the tide before it arrived at the London Docks, do you consider that the cargo would be in any danger?—I should conceive the police must be very defective if there was much danger in coming up those few miles.

Mr. John Clippingdale.

You are a river pilot?—Yes.

How long have you been so?—Ever since March 1797.

You are well acquainted with the navigation of the river Thames, and with the draught of water which vessels using the West India trade require?—Yes.

Have you had an opportunity of observing the facilities with which vessels using the West India trade enter the West India Docks?—Repeatedly.

Is it common to enter those docks the same tide that they come up?—More frequently than not.

Do they often get into those docks without dropping anchor?—Repeatedly so.

Is it your opinion, that the passage round the Isle of Dogs, and the additional distance of the London Docks, would make any difference to vessels of the burthen necessary in the West India trade?—A considerable difference, independent of the risk and danger attendant upon it.

Have the goodness to state your reasons for that opinion?—In the first place, it is nearly the top of the tide when a ship comes to Blackwall, (within half an hour or three quarters) then we have just time to sheer the ship to, whereas it would take at least two hours more to go up to the London Dock with the ship, under the same regulations, admitting that the wind was fair.

What are the winds which it is necessary you should have, in order to get up the same tide?—From the south-east and by south to the east; that is, five points out of thirty-two.

Are you to be understood, that there are only five points in the wind, out of thirty-two, with which you could get up the same tide to the London Docks?—Yes, without tacking the ship.

What is the state of the river sometimes, as far as regards the vessels there, and the inconveniences ships might suffer by the crowd of vessels?—From Blackwall to the London Dock considerably crowded; the pool is in a very awkward situation.

Is it as much crowded now, as it was before the establishment of docks?—I think, at times, much worse.

Is the navigating of a large vessel to the West India Docks attended with considerable danger?—Not any at all.

Is the navigation up to the London Docks attended with danger?—Yes, considerable.

From what circumstance?—The draught of water.

Would a vessel find any difficulty in respect of its moorings, in entering the London Docks?—After leaving the lower tiers, off Deptford, no ship of more than seventeen feet can get a place of mooring with safety.

What depth of water does a West India ship draw?—From sixteen to twenty feet six, some few under that.

Could such a vessel enter the London Docks in one tide, do you conceive?—No.

What course must she adopt, in the event of her not being able to enter in one tide?—If her owners determine she shall go to the London Docks, it will be necessary to stop her at Deptford, till an opportunity suits.

Would the stopping at Deptford, and mooring and unmooring such a vessel, be attended with any considerable expense?—Yes, certainly.

With much increased risk?—The risk is beyond expression, to any one acquainted with it.

Do you know any thing about the vessels resorting to the London Docks?—Yes, I do.

What is the draught of water of the largest vessels resorting there?—I think very few exceeding seventeen feet.

You have heard of vessels exceeding seventeen feet going there?—I believe there have been, but very few to my knowledge.

Any Brazil ships?—I do not recollect any myself.

You never heard of any risk or danger to those ships in going there?—I do not recollect any; I remember a Portuguese ship coming out of the London Docks being nearly lost on the opposite side of the water.

How long ago was that?—That was, I think, about twelve or fourteen years ago.

That might have been from mismanagement?—Very possibly.

Have you never heard of any ships being lost in going into the West India Docks?—Oh yes!

Do you know the depth of water at the entrance of the Commercial Docks?—I should suppose at the dock gates themselves there may be nineteen feet water; but there is a mud bank to get over, which rises at least five feet.

What is the depth of water in the dock?—That I cannot take upon myself to say.

Ships drawing more than fourteen feet water, would not find it convenient to enter the Commercial Docks?—Yes, I should think in spring tides a vessel of sixteen feet might enter.

But not more than that?—I think not.

You have stated the average draught of West Indiamen is eighteen feet and a half?—Thereabouts.

A ship of the largest size you have mentioned, drawing twenty feet six, might get into the London Docks?—I think, with a very fair opportunity indeed, she might.

It would require very favourable circumstances to enable her to enter?—With a wind at about south-east and by south, which is nearly a straight wind up the river, she might.

You are in the habit sometimes of piloting vessels from Gravesend to the London Docks?—I am.

Can you state the ship of the greatest depth you have navigated into that dock?—Eighteen feet; but then it was under the most favourable circumstances, with a spring tide and an easterly wind.

Is the proportion of the West India trade, drawing so much water, considerable?—That I cannot take upon myself to say.

Would not you be struck with a ship of that size, as above the usual rate of ships?—There are not so many as there are of the lower draught, but there are several ships of that draught.

How large a ship can go into the West India Docks?—I think drawing as much as twenty-one feet and a half; I have repeatedly taken ships there drawing above twenty,

I think a ship belonging to Mr. Plummer, in Fen Court, the Sir Godfrey Webster.

That ship is of 540 tons?—Yes.

What depth does the teak ship Anne, belonging to Mr. Hibbert, draw?—I think twenty-one feet.

It requires no particular circumstances to enable you to enter the West India Docks?—No; and nine times out of ten the vessel is able to enter the same tide.

Mr. John Drinkald.

You are a ship-owner and lighterman?—I am.

How long have you been a ship-owner?—Upwards of twelve years; a lighterman thirty-five; and till within the last two years and a half, I have been a wharfinger, renting property under the Crown.

Have you acquired during that time a knowledge of the accommodation in the port of London, and the system pursued at the West India and London Docks?—I have; one fifth of the produce of the West India trade went through my hands as a lighterman, before the establishment of the docks.

Has a great deal since gone through your hands?—A great deal.

You have a knowledge then of the West India trade, and the accommodation it requires?—I have.

What depth of water do the West India vessels generally draw?—Various depths; from fourteen feet to upwards of twenty-one, and more I have known.

Do many of them draw as much as seventeen feet water?—Very few of the West Indiamen that do not draw as much as seventeen.

Is there any advantage, in your opinion, in the West India vessels entering at once from sea into the West India Docks?—I conceive, as a ship-owner, very great indeed.

State your reasons for that opinion?—On Sunday last only, I had a vessel weighed out of the Queen's Channel, and entered at once into the West India Dock basin; she weighed just before the making of the flood, and entered in one tide into the basin; that same vessel made a voyage from London to the West Indies without letting go her anchor, and returned from the West Indies into the West India Docks without letting go her anchor. I have another vessel which has done the same.

Independently of there being advantage from their entering so rapidly, is there any disadvantage as far as respects the navigation of the river from the West India Docks to the London Docks?—It is impossible to say what time it would take for a vessel to go from the West India to the London Docks; it is very seldom that we can make from Gravesend into the London Docks with certainty; no person would think of running into the pool without ascertaining the state of the pool, whether there was a passage up. I am in the habit of going backwards and forwards, and it frequently happens that we cannot get a passage for a Gravesend boat without difficulty and risk, much more for a West Indiaman.

Be pleased to state what the circumstances are which prevent or inconvenience the passage of a vessel from the West India to the London Docks?—In the first place, the want of sufficient water to navigate; in the next place, the bad state of the pool almost constantly; which I think is now worse than it was when the whole of the West India trade passed through it.

Do you mean that it is more crowded?—Yes, from the increase of colliers and coasting vessels since that period, and the bad arrangement of the mooring of the vessels by the harbour masters.

Do you think that any arrangement of the manner of

mooring the vessels now using the pool, by the harbour masters, would render it inconvenient to the West India trade to come up?—There is not sufficient water; there is less water now than there was formerly.

If West India vessels arriving in fleets should use the London Docks to any extent, would that create any great inconvenience to the general trade of the Port of London? —It is with very great difficulty now that the trade of the Port of London is carried on, particularly on the Sunday, with so many coasters going away, and East country ships coming in; it would not be safe for the West India ships to be added to that number. There is a great deal of damage constantly done at the present time; there would be much more with an increase of shipping.

You are understood to say, that it would not be safe to the other trade frequenting the Port of London?—It would be as dangerous to them as to the West India vessels.

Could a West India vessel enter the London Docks the same tide as she leaves Gravesend?—It would depend on circumstances; it must be a very favourable opportunity, and even then, if they were prudent, they would send up from Deptford, to ascertain whether she could pass through the pool.

What are the other circumstances, on which you would say, that that favourable opportunity depended?—There must be a certainty that the pool was clear, and it must be a spring tide; very few West Indiamen draw less than sixteen, seventeen, or eighteen feet water, some more.

What wind must she have to get in?—From the southward and eastward.

In the event of her not being able to get in the same tide, where would she find moorings?—I am sure I should be afraid myself there would be no place to lay with safety; and to drop a large ship down, with a wind to the eastward, after not being able to get into the London Docks, would be madness; there would be no place at all for her to go to.

What number of mooring places are there, at which West India vessels could be moored?—I know of no place where they could be moored with safety, excepting at Union Stairs tier, where there would be water for two vessels drawing about fifteen or sixteen feet water; and the same at Princes Stairs; but those places are generally occupied, as being the only places where there is any water to be found.

Even supposing they could find places for mooring, would not the mooring and unmooring such a vessel be attended with great expense and with some risk?—It not only would be attended with expense, but with risk, for they could not get the mooring chains up; if, after high water, a vessel should be obliged to drop down, she would be obliged to drop her anchor, and shear alongside the tier, and then they would have to take the moorings up, even admitting there were no vessels there; but I have never seen those places without having vessels placed in them.

Would it be attended, do you think, with a risk of grounding?—I have no hesitation in saying that it would.

Being acquainted with a West India cargo, can you say whether the grounding of such a cargo is not of more consequence to a West India cargo than to any other?—The danger to a West India cargo is in this way, if a vessel heels over, if she has ever so trifling a quantity of water in, it will naturally be on the bilge, consequently the sugar will sustain damage; that was a very common thing before the docks.

Have the goodness to explain that?—A vessel standing

upright when she takes the ground, she naturally takes the ground on her keel, till the bottom, which we call the bilge, catches her; say there are ten or twelve inches water, that will naturally come over on the flat part the casks are stowed upon, and of course the sugar must get damage, which is a very common thing in vessels coming from the West Indies, if a captain is not very particular in attending to his pumps.

You think a West India vessel using the London Docks would be subject to that?—I have no doubt of it.

Are you acquainted particularly with the Commercial Dock?—Yes, it was formerly called the Greenland Dock, now the Commercial Dock.

Are its conveniences, as it respects warehouses and wharfs, adapted for the reception of West India goods? —There is one large stock of warehouses, but they have no wharf in front of the warehouse; there is a small platform to the principal warehouse.

Is there sufficient depth of water for large vessels to go in?—I do not know what water they have there; there have been a variety of different arrangements made at that place; I should consider it a very improper place for the deposit of West India produce in the present state of it.

Supposing the dock system were to be thrown open, and that the result was competition, is it your opinion that the Commercial Dock could enter into that competition?—No, I think not; they have not the ability, in my opinion, to enter into competition, either with the London or the West India Docks; it was adapted to the oil trade and the timber more than any other.

Are you acquainted with the precise trades which were contemplated at the time of the construction of those docks?—No; I understood it was for the oil, timber trade, and the East country trade.

What difference do you imagine there may be in the distance to London Bridge between the Commercial Docks and the West India Docks?—I should think there is two miles difference, independently of the stoppages in coming through the Borough, and over London Bridge, and Fish Street Hill, and including the distance down to the sugar refiners, I should think there would be two miles, or two miles and a half to the sugar refiners.

Is there not a very large consumption of sugar on the Surry side of the water, in the Borough, and in those counties which are supplied from the Borough, by the wholesale grocers residing there?—There are very few wholesale grocers, I believe, on the Surry side; I do not know of any one.

Would not the local situation of those docks, being on the opposite side of the river, preclude, in point of convenience, the West India trade from going thither?—Certainly; the shortest way would be for them to have their sugar by water; the carriage would be so far by land, and not very good roads; the sugar refiners would not give the same price for the sugar laying at the Commercial Dock, as they would at the West India or the London Docks.

As you say that the consideration of the locality of the dock would influence them as between the Commercial, and the London, and West India Docks, do you think there would be any difference in their estimate if the sugar were lying in the West India or the London Dock?—I think there would not; being both on the same side of the river, it would make very little difference of time; they can get the cartage done at a very little more.

Nathaniel Domett, Esq.

You are a ship owner?—Yes.

In how many ships are you and your partners interested? —In sixteen or seventeen ships in the Jamaica trade, and two or three in the private trade to India.

Have you yourself formerly commanded a ship?—I have.

Are you interested at all in the West India Docks?—Not at all.

Are you interested in the London Docks, or any part of your family?—Part of my family are, not myself.

Of course, from your situation, you are acquainted with the navigation of the river Thames?—I am.

Will you be good enough to state the draught of water which West Indiamen generally require?—A ship of 350 tons will generally average about seventeen feet, when sugar loaded.

How many will the largest vessels, those of 500 tons, require?—About nineteen feet and a half.

Some of the largest of all draw twenty, and a few inches above twenty, do they not?—There is one of them draws near twenty-one I have seen.

Very few of the Jamaica vessels are under 350 tons, are they?—Very few.

Nor many above 500?—No.

Are there any above 500?—Yes, the Ann and the Coromandel; we have one ourselves of 490, she draws nineteen feet and half when she comes home; the Sir Godfrey Webster was of 548 tons.

May the Committee take the average draught of water of West Indiamen, at between seventeen and twenty feet?—A little more than seventeen; Jamaica ships from seventeen to twenty.

Have you had opportunities of observing the facilities with which vessels using the West India trade, can enter the West India Docks?—Frequently.

Do they frequently enter the docks the same tide in which they come up the river?—Very frequently.

And that without dropping anchor?—Very often without dropping anchor.

Do you consider that, as a ship-owner, a considerable advantage to those docks?—It is an advantage certainly; a great deal of time is saved by it.

Is it an advantage with respect to risk as well as time?—Yes, it is an advantage in every respect, undoubtedly; as soon as the sails are clewed up, they run a rope out to one of the West India Dock buoys, and then sheer them in, and if it is at the top of high water, there are convenient moorings, and sufficient depth of water to remain outside till the next tide.

Is the entrance of any other dock so situate as to enable you to come up, and run into the dock the same tide?—There is no one above the West India Dock which has the same conveniences; the East India Dock is similar to it in some respects.

Is the Commercial Dock similar to it in those respects?—I have never had a ship in there; the London Dock certainly is not so, it is higher up and crowded with ships.

Is the passage between the entrance of the West India Dock, and the entrance of the London Dock, attended with considerable delay?—I think it is attended with great delay, and the risk is also considerably increased.

Should you think it advisable to bring a large West Indiaman, properly laden, round the Isle of Dogs into the pool, for the purpose of entering the London Dock, when you can enter the West India Dock lower down?—I should certainly not think of doing it.

State in what respect the risk is increased?—The depth of water is decreased upwards, and along the whole of Limehouse Reach; on the Surry side, a shoal extends nearly half way across the river, and if a ship does not reach the London Docks in one tide, I do not know above one or two places where she can lie afloat during low water.

There are but one or two places where she could lie afloat at low water, if she was not able to enter the London Dock?—Just so.

From the nature of the navigation, and the circle taken round the Isle of Dogs, would it, in your judgment, frequently happen, in particular winds, that a vessel might not get round, and get into the London Dock the same tide?—Certainly, I should think so, a West Indiaman.

What extent of accommodation do you conceive is afforded for vessels between the two docks, in which you say a loaded West Indiaman might lie afloat, in the interval of her not being able to get into the dock?—At Deptford she might lie afloat, I think, in Hanover Hole, and I believe at Prince's Stairs there is room for a ship or two.

How many vessels could lie conveniently at Deptford at low water?—I think I have seen twenty or thirty lie afloat there, before the construction of the docks.

Do West Indiamen arrive in considerable numbers, at particular periods of the year?—Yes, fifteen or twenty of them at the same time.

The one place you have described as affording accommodation for only two or three ships, and Deptford for a larger number; supposing both those places crowded, what should you do with your ship, provided you could not get accommodation for her?—I would keep her below at Blackwall.

Supposing you had passed Deptford, what should you do?—There is no choice but to lay her where she will take the ground.

Is that a circumstance you would subject a loaded West Indiaman to, if you could help it?—It certainly ought to be avoided if possible, for there is risk of its injuring the ship.

Is there not risk as to the cargo?—If she lies a little down, the water would get into the lee bilge, and would not be got at by the pumps.

It would of course injure the part of the cargo that it came into contact with?—Yes.

Is a West India cargo more liable than any other to injury from such a circumstance?—Sugar in hogsheads is very liable to injury from such a circumstance.

From all those circumstances, you state your conviction that there is a great increase of risk in coming round from the entrance to the West India Dock at Blackwall to the London Dock?—I have no doubt upon that.

You have mentioned that considerable delay might arise?—Yes, it is very probable delay might arise, if the wind was westerly, in getting the ship up to the dock.

Can you enter the West India Dock, coming up the river with a flowing tide, with many winds which would not enable you to go round the Isle of Dogs and go into the London Docks?—A ship would get to the West India Dock much sooner.

Are there not winds which would enable you to enter the West India Dock, coming up the river, that would not enable you to go round the Isle of Dogs?—I am not aware of that, for Limehouse Reach and Bugby's Reach are nearly the same; and what would be a foul wind in Limehouse Reach would consequently be a foul wind in Bugby's Reach.

What is the length of Bugby's Reach?—It is about a mile; it commences some distance above Woolwich, and terminates at Blackwall.

The depth of water is sufficient in Bugby's Reach, at

the time the vessels are coming up, to enter the dock?—It is.

What is the length of Limehouse Reach?—About two miles; the two reaches together are three miles.

Is there the same water for working a vessel in Limehouse Reach that there is in Bugby's Reach?—Bugby's Reach is not a deep water reach, but at the time ships are coming up, it is generally two-thirds flood, there is therefore water enough then.

Supposing the wind was one that was either adverse, or what you would call scant, to come up Bugby's Reach, the risk would be increased by the additional length?—Yes, and there are always a number of ships in Limehouse Reach; but in Bugby's Reach you may stretch from one side to the other in beating up.

You state that you are an underwriter, and that you should require a higher premium on a vessel which was to go into the London Docks, than on one going to the West India Docks?—Yes, a West India ship.

Do you think you could get a higher premium?—No, very probably not.

Have you ever known such higher premium given?—I have not.

You say there is great risk in coming round from the West India to the London Docks?—There is.

Can you explain how, if that is the case, there is no difference in the insurance?—I cannot, except that there is a great deal of competition between the underwriters.

Do you know of any vessel drawing seventeen feet water, coming to the London Docks?—I should imagine there may have been several, but I do not know it myself.

Could a ship drawing twenty-one feet water navigate the river, and enter safely into the London Docks?—I think it would be attended with very great risk, because a ship of that draught of water must necessarily move nearly at the last quarter of the flood.

Could a ship, drawing nineteen and a half feet water, enter with safety?—She could enter the dock with safety; there is a great deal of water there.

Could she navigate with safety?—That would depend upon the state of the river; neither a ship of nineteen and a half, or twenty and a half, could lie afloat any where between the London Docks and Deptford at low water, except at one or two places, where they might lie, if not pre-occupied by other ships.

Must not such a vessel enter the docks at the height of the tide?—She ought to do, or at the rising tide; I believe they do not open the docks after the high water mark.

Is it your opinion, from what you know of the capacity of the London Docks, that they are well adapted to receive the generality of the West India trade?—Not except they were to alter their system.

The question refers to the navigation only?—The navigation is considerably increased, by the difficulties I have stated already, by there being less water, and by the shoals extending a good distance from the Surry side there, across Limehouse Reach, and by the passage being, generally speaking, extremely narrow, from the immense number of colliers extending from the north side three-fourths of the way across the river.

Do ships entering the London Docks, generally arrive there the same tide?—I do not know; ships of any draught of water, coming from Long Reach, if they get up to Long Reach at nearly high water, it is necessary they should stop there, and then it is necessary for them to stay there from half to two-thirds flood, on the following tide, to enable them to sail over the shoals, in Erith Reach and on Barking Shelf; that being the case, it is nearly high water, or always in the last quarter of flood, before a ship of sixteen feet water and upwards can get to the West India Dock even, consequently the chance is still less of her reaching the London Dock on that flood.

In point of fact, ships coming from sea hardly ever enter the London Docks the same tide?—They may do it with an easterly wind.

You are not aware whether the fact be one way or the other?—I am not.

Are there not harbour masters appointed by the corporation of the city of London?—Yes.

Is it not their duty to regulate the mooring of ships in the pool?—I believe it is.

Might not better arrangements be made as to the mooring of colliers, than in your opinion are now acted upon?—I think it might be done, by stopping the colliers further down; I do not think room can be found for them, between the place where they now lie and London Bridge.

John Inglis, Esq.

What is the average tonnage of vessels resorting to the London Docks?—I cannot speak precisely to the average tonnage, but I should suppose something like 150 tons. There have been ships there as high as 700 tons, a number of the short traders are small vessels.

The London Docks are quite capable of giving accommodation to ships of 350 tons, drawing seventeen feet water?—Undoubtedly, as capable as any dock whatever.

In your opinion, would the West India ships going from the West India Docks up to the London Docks be exposed to any considerable danger?—There has been no instance of any accident taking place; in the year 1821, 1,271 ships entered the docks; I should suppose the average of ships entering the docks during the whole time since they have been opened, would be about 1,000. I have never heard of any accident happening between Blackwall and the London Docks, nor of any ship being prevented there that could not enter the dock. I should state a circumstance that possibly may happen, and which sometimes does happen, that a ship, if she is late in the tide coming up, must bring up at Blackwall or somewhere in the Pool, and remain a night for the next flood, which is the only difference I know of between the two docks.

Do you think the ship would be exposed to the danger of plunder in that passage from Blackwall up to the London Docks?—I think not; I am not aware of any danger; if their hatches were locked down, there would be no danger;—it would be only waiting another tide, as before stated.

You are aware that by locking down the hatches, the property would be secured from plunder in that passage?—Perfectly so.

If, as you have stated, twelve hundred sail of vessels come annually into the London Dock, if the whole of the West India trade came into the West India Dock, the East India trade, both regular and private, to the East India Dock, the timber both from the Baltic and the British American colonies into the Commercial and East Country Docks, must not the establishment of wet docks in the river Thames have relieved the pool from a far greater number of ships than any increase of trade in the port of London can be supposed now to bring into it?—No doubt of it.

If there is any great risk, such as has been stated of passing through a crowded pool, or danger of not finding a sufficient draught of water to come to the London

Docks, is it likely that those large Brazil ships of which you have spoken, would still persist in coming there to discharge their cargoes?—I can only answer to that, that experience has shown that they do come there, and that we have never had an accident in any ship coming to the London Dock, or entering the London Dock.

You have also a considerable number of American ships, which are generally sharp built ships, and of course draw a considerable draught of water; have any of them ever met with any accident coming up to the London Docks?—None whatever, and I believe we have the whole of the American trade, not only of tobacco, which is restricted to us, but the rest of the trade, which comes to us in preference.

Do you know whether those ships come through the canal, by which they might avoid coming round the Isle of Dogs, or whether they expose themselves to the hazard and difficulty of making that passage?—I believe very few of them come through the canal; it is possible, I think, at a certain season of the year, that they may adopt that passage, but certainly they do not generally.

If the danger and difficulty of going through the pool is great, is it not likely they would make a point of going through the canal?—The present canal is below the pool, but the river is so cleared now by the conveniences and the accommodation that the docks afford, that they do not find the obstructions in it that used to be experienced on former occasions.

As the Brazil ships are not confined to any particular dock, if the charges of the West India Docks were lower, or as low as those of the London Docks, and all the disadvantages and difficulty of coming up the river could be avoided by going there, is it not likely they would give the preference to the West India Docks?—They certainly have not done it, for I believe we have had the whole of the Brazil trade.

Mr. Dennis Chapman.

Do you recollect any ship being lost in the pool coming up to the London Docks?—I do not recollect a circumstance of the kind.

No such circumstance has ever occurred?—Not to my knowledge.

Do you recollect any ships having their cargoes plundered coming up through the pool?—I have never heard of any thing of the kind to my knowledge.

If ships were plundered in the pool, coming up to your docks, would not that be noticed on landing the cargo?—If any part of the cargo happened to be plundered, it would certainly be noticed at the time of landing; it could not escape notice.

Frederick Gibson, Esq.

How large are the largest of the Brazil vessels?—We have had some of 600 tons.

They are Portuguese vessels?—Yes, they are; the trade is chiefly carried on now in British ships.

Mr. B. Eilbeck.

You went into the service of the Commercial Docks in 1809?—Yes.

You speak of the depth of water at the entrance of the docks; what do you state the average depth of water to be?—About eighteen feet six inches, I should think.

That is the average?—Yes.

Do you speak of high water?—Of course; at low water the tide is entirely away from the docks, as well as from every other dock.

You speak of the average depth at high water?—Yes.

At neap tide the depth is not more than fourteen feet? —From fourteen to fifteen.

The average depth which a West Indiaman draws, you state to be about sixteen feet?—Yes, I conceive it is; when I was in that trade it was so considered.

Of course, at neap tides the average of West India ships could not come into your docks?—No, they could not for a day or two; but when I say that the average of the ships is sixteen feet, there are some at twelve feet; I do not believe any of them in the West India trade draw more than seventeen feet.

You consider sixteen as the average?—Upon the largest ships; if I may take the small and the large together, I should suppose that about fifteen feet and a half would be the average.

You think you stated it at six inches too high?—Yes.

The word average was your own word?—Yes; I believe it was.

It is necessary that there should be some more water than the number of feet precisely which a ship draws, in order to enable her to go into the dock?—There ought certainly.

About how much would you allow more than the ship draws?—I never hesitate in taking a ship in there, if I have four inches to spare, we are so well provided with every facility to take her in.

You would not hesitate at any time to take a ship into the dock, if there were four inches of water more than the ship actually draws?—I would not.

There is a bank, is not there, at the entrance of this dock?—No, I believe not any that is not lower than the sill of the gates.

Is there a bank or not?—There is a small bank by the washing out of the docks; but it is taken away every year.

You speak of the area of the docks being fifty-three acres?—I believe it is thereabouts.

What may be the average depth of them?—They vary in depth; No I. is, I think, twenty feet.

What is the size of that dock?—I believe it is eight acres; I must refer to the map; I see it is nine and three quarters.

Are there twenty-one feet of water in that at all times?—At all times, nearly; for we do not let the water off: the water is deeper there than outside in the lock to the dock.

It sinks below the sill, does it?—Yes, it does; about fifteen inches.

There is ordinarily about twenty-one feet?—Yes; it varies sometimes; it may be as low as twenty feet.

That is called, in your plan, nine acres and three quarters?—Yes, it is so.

Of course, if the water in the dock is twenty-one feet, and the bottom of the dock is lower than the sill, there must be less water in the lock than there is in the dock?—Yes.

What is the average of water in the lock?—The lock is the same as the sill outside; we call eighteen feet six the average spring; we have sometimes had twenty-one feet.

That is the average spring tide?—Yes.

And the neap tides about fourteen?—From fourteen to fifteen, the average neap tide.

What is the average mean tide?—I should suppose, if we add the two, it would be about the half; about sixteen feet.

Then the average depth of water, at high tide, taking in spring tide and neap tide, is about sixteen feet?—Yes.

How many days do each of the tides last?—The neap tide is only two or three days, the outside; the spring tides last the same; and the average tides last about a week.

Three days in a fortnight they cannot go in at all?—Yes, just so, if they exceed that draught of water.

Those Commercial Docks are situate nearly opposite to the Limehouse entry of the West India Docks?—They are a little below it; not much.

They are situate on the south side of the river?—Yes.

If West Indiamen, instead of coming to the Commercial Docks, had occasion to go up through the Pool to the London Docks, do you not think that would be attended with considerable inconvenience?—I do not think the ships experience any; they now go to the London Docks with as much facility as they did to the West India Dock; neither do I recollect any accidents.

What sized vessels do you remember going there?—The Union, East Indiaman, went in there before the East India Docks were opened.

What size was she?—Six hundred and fifty tons.

What draught of water?—I think nineteen feet.

Are they not liable to be detained a tide?—I do not know that they are; I had very little knowledge above that place; when I went to sea we used to consider it a very arduous thing to go up the Pool; but they do not seem to consider it so now.

The trade is more courageous now?—Yes; I believe the harbour masters keep more regularity now than they did formerly.

As far as your experience went, when you were a captain in the trade, it was attended with difficulty and inconvenience?—The pilots took the same money for taking a ship up to Deptford or Bell Wharfs, and they did not wish to carry them further; they used to find out more difficulties than there were, perhaps.

Have not the Commercial Dock Company applied to the Board of Customs for permission to unload ships in the river, because they could not enter, and to lighten them?—Yes, we have; quite at the neap tides, we have ships of 600 tons, some of the Dantzic ships; then if they are very anxious, we apply for leave to get them in, rather than lose the two or three days.

The application has reference to those ships of 600 tons?—Yes.

And to three days of tide?—Yes, they could have them in in two or three days.

Could you have taken those ships in at spring tides?—Some of those ships draw more than twenty feet; Norway ships draw an immense quantity of water, as much as our East Indiamen.

Was not the use of those very large vessels in the West India trade, introduced principally during the late war?—It was; before the war there were no very large ships; we considered then, a ship of 400 tons a very large ship in the West India trade.

For what reason were they introduced during the war?—A scarcity of shipping; most of the vessels were employed in the transport service, and they considered it was cheaper to sail one large ship than two small ones.

Do you consider that the same motives operate now, to induce persons to continue those large ships in the West India trade?—Quite the contrary, because there are now so many ships seeking for freight, that a man cannot load a large ship; he would lose the whole season before he could get sugars enough to load a large ship.

In your opinion, would the number of those large ships diminish from time to time?—It has done so, already; they are most of them gone into the free trade to India.

Is there any thing in the navigation that makes it more desirable to go to the West India Dock than the London Dock?—Certainly; the danger is less; for so much of distance is saved.

In what part of the river is there most danger?—I believe the chief danger is going round Cuckold's Point, that is near Limehouse.

That is avoided by going to the West India Docks?—Yes; but the harbour masters have moored the vessels so now, that they do not go near it.

The navigation by Cuckold's Point is not attended with the same danger it was formerly?—No; there is plenty of room now; the large American ships are going backwards and forwards every day, and we hear of no accident.

In point of convenience, is the London Dock more convenient for the landing of general cargoes than the West India Dock?—I think that there can be nothing more convenient than the London Dock; the West India Dock is furnished with every convenience; it is as convenient as it can be.

How does it happen that so few vessels go through the Isle of Dogs canal?—The pilots now, are so easy, they find no difficulty in going round; and while they are waiting, perhaps, to make a lock or two, the ship would be round.

Would they avoid the risk of Cuckold's Point by going through the canal?—I think they would.

And, nevertheless, they prefer going round to going through the canal?—Yes.

Have any accidents happened between the point of the

canal and the London Docks?—I have not heard of any; I do not recollect any.

Used they frequently to happen?—I recollect one or two West Indiamen lost on Cuckold's Point, before the West India Docks were made; but that was owing to the ships lying so far over; there was not room for a ship to pass.

Mr. James Walker.

What is the largest sized ship that can be admitted into those Docks?—The Dock is capable of receiving a light 1,400 ton ship, the largest class of Indiamen; but I should suppose a 600 ton loaded ship is its greatest capability in an ordinary spring tide.

Is the dock capable of receiving a ship of 600 tons at the ordinary tide?—Yes; there is from eighteen to nineteen feet water at the ordinary spring tide.

What depth does a ship of that size when loaded draw?—I think about eighteen to nineteen feet; but with regard to the draught of ships of different sizes, I do not pretend to be so intimately acquainted.

Then you would not have above an inch or two to spare?—Of course not; it would require a good spring tide to bring in a ship of 600 tons; we have had upwards of three feet more water, or twenty-one upon the sill, but that is an extraordinary tide.

The draught of water depends a good deal upon the construction of the ship?—Yes; very much so.

Are those docks, in your judgment, capable of accommodating any portion of the West India trade?—I should think they are, as far as their capability of entrance goes.

Are the docks capable of improvement for that purpose, if it should be necessary?—Very capable of improvement.

Are they capable of deepening?—Yes, they are; it would be attended with a considerable expense deepening the entrance or making a new lock, which is the only expensive part of it; if there is not depth of water enough in the docks now, that could be increased.

Without much difficulty or expense?—Yes.

The entrance you propose making is by Cuckold's Point?—No; the place at which the Commercial Dock Company have purchased property, with that intention, is higher up.

It is that point that is considered the most dangerous part of the navigation of the river?—I believe that Cuckold's Point was so considered, but not so now, since the tiers of ships opposite to it have been removed.

Thomas Tooke, Esq.

Have any of your vessels, going up to the London Docks, ever been lost coming up the Pool?—I am not aware of their having ever met with any accident of any kind.

Are you aware of their having been ever plundered in coming up the Pool?—No.

F. Wilson, Esq.

Have any of your ships been lost in going up to the London Docks?—Never.

Are any above 350 tons?—Yes, many of them.

Are they your own ships, or are you only alluding to ships in which your goods have come?—Vessels in which goods have come.

Not your own vessels?—We do not own one.

Have you ever had any ships of above 350 tons detained, for want of water to get up to the London Docks?—I do not recollect any.

You say that none of the ships that have brought goods

for you to the *London Docks* have either been lost or detained in coming up through the Pool; do you know whether any of them have been plundered in coming up through the Pool?—I do not recollect any instance; very large ships sometimes are detained coming through the Pool at neap tides.

But they have never been plundered to your knowledge in consequence of that detention?—I do not recollect any instance.

Did you ever pay any difference in the premium of insurance on account of a ship coming to the one dock or the other?—Never.

No. IV.

SOLIDITY OF BUILDINGS AND WORKS.

Henry Longlands, Esq.

The intention, if the canal had been taken, was to form that into an export dock, and to supersede the necessity of having another export dock?—The annexing it to the dock by a cut, a plan of which was submitted by Mr. Rennie. The Company have also been urged to execute a very considerable work, which would be necessary to supply outward bound ships with water for their voyage, that is still under consideration, the estimates not being complete; the Company have also, for a great many years, had the Blackwall entrance under their serious consideration; that entrance has been in a m st alarming state; within the last two years, the tide rose and fell within the walls of that entrance; but it has now undergone a repair, and may last one year or several, the time is uncertain; it was with a view to the danger of that entrance that the Company purchased the premises I mentioned, belonging to Messrs. Smith and Timbrel.

When you say the tide rose and fell within that entrance you mean when the gates were shut, showing a secret communication of some kind with the river?—I mean, that outside the gates, the tide rose and fell within the fence walls; and that there was hourly danger of the whole falling in and being destroyed.

Would the putting that into a perfect state of safety be attended with very considerable expense?—It has been attended with very considerable expense, but there is another subject connected with that entrance which would be a source of great expense, which has also been under consideration, and that is its faulty position; the direction of the entrance unfortunately is such, that the set of the tide throws vast quantities of mud into it; an item which swells the Company's expense for repairs is that of clearing the Blackwall entrance of the mud, which costs them nearly £2,000 per annum.

John Rennie, Esq.

In what state are the Blackwall and Limehouse entrances, as far as security is concerned?—At present they are in a tolerable state of repair; but it is extremely uncertain how long they may continue so; there has been a very considerable sum, amounting to about £15,000, already expended on the outer wing walls of the Limehouse entrance, which has added considerably to its security, and I should hope that that will remain some years without much further repair.

In the event, however, of their requiring a further and substantial repair, have you any estimate of the expense which would be required?—It would be extremely difficult to ascertain the expense of repairing them thoroughly; I can hardly ascertain the exact state they are in, without making perforations in the foundations and walls, which would almost amount to the making a new entrance.

What would the expense of such a repair as you have spoken of, almost approaching to a renewal, amount to?—Little short of £50,000.

Looking to the whole of this concern, and to the repairs which are occasionally required, what sum of money does it appear to you should remain in hand for those purposes? —I should think certainly not less than £100,000.

Do you think it would be safe to keep less than £100,000 for those purposes?—Certainly not.

Considering the situation in which the two entrances are, is it your opinion that it would be prudent on the part of the docks, presently to make fresh entrances there? —I think it might be.

You think they may last for a few years?—They may.

But their lasting beyond those few years you think doubtful?—I do.

Why doubtful?—Because they are subject to a great number of casualties.

Not more than other works?—They have not been so well executed as they might have been, and that is the reason.

The mahogany sheds have tumbled down, you say?—That proposed is in the lieu of one that is tumbling down.

How long has that been built?—I cannot say; I believe a long while; we are obliged to shoar it up to prevent its tumbling down.

Which shed do you speak of?—I speak of the old one that was built before my father had the direction of the docks.

Does it appear to you to be as much as ten years old? —I should think more.

Of what materials is it composed?—Entirely of wood.

Is the wood decayed?—Yes, it is decayed.

Is the extent of defective work considerable?—It is very considerable.

Is the whole of the work that comprises the entrance a defective work?—I should certainly not have built it in that way.

Considering the immense importance of those docks, do you not consider it a prudent measure to have a second entrance to them?—I should certainly think so.

There was at one period a most material accident occurred to the entrance of one of those docks, was there not; a coffee dam blowing up?—I have heard that such an accident did happen.

Were not the works at the West India Docks built under the direction of your late father?—No; he merely had the direction of them, I think, about the year 1817, when he first began to give his professional opinion upon them.

The original works were not built under his superintendence?—They were not, as far as I recollect.

And they are not, you say, substantially executed?—I think not.

Were the works at the London Docks built under the direction of your late father?—They were.

Are they substantially executed?—I have never heard to the contrary.

Have you ever examined them?—Yes, I have.

And they do not appear to have defects similar to those you have stated to exist in the West India Docks?—They do not.

Were the works at the East India Docks built under the direction of your late father?—They were.

Are they substantially executed and free from defects?—As far as I have been able to ascertain, they are certainly.

Were the works at the Commercial Docks built under the superintendence of your late father?—I believe not.

You cannot speak to their state and condition?—I cannot speak to their state.

You have stated that the West India Docks are defective in many respects, as to their construction; be pleased to state in what respects?—Principally in the execution of the work.

Do you mean with respect to the foundations?—With respect to the bricklayer's work and the foundations, and the work generally.

William Mitchell, Esq.

Are not those immense expenses incurred in repairs a proof of the very inefficient manner in which the works were originally executed?—Undoubtedly there were some of the works which were not executed originally in that substantial manner in which they might have been.

Mr. James Walker.

Have you a knowledge of the West India Docks?—I was in the engineer's department at the time of the formation of those docks.

You are well acquainted with the situation of their entrances?—Yes.

In your opinion, have the West India Dock Company good reason for viewing those docks with alarm, considering them in a dangerous state?—No, I do not see why they should; I think the wing walls of the Blackwall entrance are in a bad state.

Have you any idea of the expense it would be necessary to go to, to put them in a perfect state?—No; I have generally considered, that in a dock of that magnitude, the Dock Company should perhaps not be confined to one entrance, that in case of any thing going wrong with one, there should be another; and perhaps the question just put has reference to my having offered the West India Dock Company property to make another entrance at Blackwall.

At present you say they have good reason for considering the present entrance in an unfit state?—In speaking of that I go from report only.

If the entrance into the West India Dock unfortunately failed, the Greenland Dock or the Commercial Dock would be very convenient for the reception of West India ships?—In such a case, certainly; for the Limehouse entrance to the West India Dock is hardly wide enough to receive the largest loaded ships; I speak from recollection.

In case of an accident at the Blackwall entrance, it would be a great convenience to the West India trade to be at liberty to come to the Commercial Docks?—I think it would, to the Commercial or the London Docks; the Limehouse entrance of the West India Docks is considerably narrower than the Blackwall entrance.

Do not the vessels which enter at the Blackwall entrance go out at the Limehouse entrance?—If they do they are then empty, and then their extreme width is above the level of the walls; I believe the one is forty feet and the other thirty-two.

No. V.

MEANS OF ACCOMMODATION.

John Tilstone, Esq.

From the experience you have had, of more than twenty years, does it appear to you, or does it not, that the establishment of the West India Docks has answered the expectations that were then formed?—It does; my expectations of the system which was about being carried into execution at the West India Docks at that time, have been more than realized; in 1796, the trade of the port of London was in a very deplorable state; there was great want of warehouse room; the merchant's property was plundered to a very considerable extent; the ships were delayed in their discharge, and smuggling was carried on to an alarming degree: all of which has been prevented by the West India Docks, and the system adopted there.

Mr. Thomas Burne.

I believe you are surveyor of the Customs at the West India Docks?—Comptrolling surveyor.

During how long a time have you held a situation in the Customs?—As comptrolling surveyor of the customs, ever since the year 1804.

Were you before that time in the Customs?—I was.

Have you, during that time, had an opportunity of being acquainted with the system adopted at the West India Docks?—Yes, I have.

Have you found that system to afford full security to the revenue?—I consider, in every respect.

Do you consider it as affording security to the merchant?—That I certainly do, or else it could not to the revenue.

Do you consider it as facilitating the discharge of vessels?—There certainly is a greater facility in discharging them than there used to be.

In your judgment, would the revenue be equally well protected, if vessels were admitted into docks surrounded by walls, without reference to any particular system whatever, adopted in those docks?—I do not understand the question.

Is the admission of a vessel into a dock, surrounded by

walls, with warehouses in that dock, the only thing which, in your judgment, affords security to vessels?—Certainly, that is one security; but the system is the principal thing, in my judgment.

W. Mitchell, Esq.

Is there any thing in the extent or character, or peculiar nature of the West India Docks, which renders them in your judgment applicable to the West India trade, which would not be found equally applicable at other docks?—The West India Docks have been built for the West India trade, and the warehouses, the machinery and every thing has been applied to that particular trade, and therefore it certainly must be better adapted to that particular trade, than those docks which have applied themselves to the admission of ships indiscriminately.

Is there any thing in the capacity, or the nature of the accommodation there, that renders them peculiarly applicable to that trade?—I am not sufficiently well acquainted with the capacity or the peculiar nature of other docks, to answer that question, but I can state the capacity of the West India Docks, and what the West India trade requires; the import West India Dock will admit of 204, the export dock will admit of 184, and the basins 48, a total of 436 ships; the docks are not capable of unloading and loading at the same time conveniently that number, but the import dock is capable of unloading at one time about 50 ships, and the export dock of loading with convenience 130 ships.

Has the attention of the West India Dock directors been peculiarly directed to constructing the docks, the accommodation belonging to them, and all the machinery relating to them, so as to fit them for the West India trade in particular?—The directors of the West India Dock

Company have hitherto directed all their attention to the reception of West India cargoes; they have provided not only warehouses, wharfs and so forth, but machinery which is peculiarly adapted to that trade; they have portioned their dock for the reception of the different articles of that trade; one side of the dock contains sugar, coffee and other articles; another side of the dock is called the rum quay, where rum and wine are deposited by themselves; and other parts of the dock are appropriated solely to the reception of wood, each having the peculiar machinery necessary for the different description of articles.

You are aware that ships from the Brazils are permitted, by an Act of Parliament, to discharge their cargoes either in the London or West India Docks; can you state how many ships from the Brazils, since that Act has been in force, have discharged at the West India Docks?—I never heard of one being discharged at the West India Docks.

To what cause do you ascribe those ships going into any other dock?—I ascribe it principally to those checks and restraints which the Company preserve, in order, as I believe, to give due protection to the property entrusted to their care, and it may also arise from other circumstances.

Would not the Brazil ships have found their way into your docks, had the charges been as reasonable and the accommodations as great as in other docks?—I am not aware that Brazil ships are situated precisely as the regular ships in the West India trade are; I have stated that the ships in the regular West India trade, with few exceptions, make but one voyage in the course of a year, and that therefore the export dock or a dock to lay up for a certain time, is absolutely necessary for them; but the ships in the Brazil trade are under the circumstances mentioned, that is, ships merely chartered, and sent out to make only one voyage, and then they go into any other trade, and therefore the comparison is not exactly in point with West India ships.

Is there any other difference between West India ships and Brazil ships, than that the one is subject to the compulsory clause of going into the West India Docks and the other not?—I have been stating some points of difference, as they appear to me; but I am not so well acquainted with the nature of the Brazilian trade, as to say what other difference there may be to induce them to prefer the other docks.

Are not the West India Docks very short of being full, during a considerable part of the year?—They are.

John Inglis, Esq.

Are the London Docks fully sufficient for the accommodation of the trade now resorting to it?—They are.

Are they not more than sufficient?—They are more than sufficient for the present trade of the port that comes to them.

Could they not accommodate a considerable portion of the West India trade?—They could.

In addition to the present trade?—They could.

If it were necessary, have they not premises sufficiently large to increase their accommodation for the West India trade?—They have.

Could they not make a new dock upon the premises of which they are now in possession?—They certainly could extend their water by making another dock.

Have they not plenty of space now in their possession for enlarging their warehouses, and providing other accommodation for the West India trade?—They have.

You stated in your evidence that you could extend your water; to what extent could you give additional surface of water?—I really do not know; I could show it on a map, but I do not know the space.

Your present area of water is twenty acres?—Yes.

Can you state at what expense you could give an additional area of water?—No.

Or for what additional warehouses, if the West India trade should want them?—We have not had a special estimate for them, but we have the walls built, and one story of a range of warehouses, which are used as sheds at present; and by adding three stories more to them, they would become the same description of warehouses we have already, and that at a moderate expense, I apprehend.

But neither the extent of the water nor the land convenience can you give any precise estimate of?—I can give a general estimate that we could take into the London Docks, if no other merchandize was there but West India produce, equal to 200,000 hogsheads of sugar.

Are you speaking of warehouses only, or the dock and warehouses?—I speak of warehouses.

Then you could house in warehouses 200,000 hogsheads of sugar, if you had no other merchandize?—Yes.

Do you know how many ships can conveniently lie in an acre of ground?—No, I do not; but I know how many ships we have had in our dock at one time; I believe somewhat above 200 ships have been in the dock at one time.

When you say 200 were in the dock at one time, must they not have been lying side by side in tiers, two or three out from the wharf?—Probably in tiers in the centre of the dock, or some of them.

Be pleased to state to the Committee, in which particular parts of your wharfs and warehouses you consider that the accommodation could now be given?—There will be better evidence to that than I can give; but the warehouses adjoining to Pennington-street could be applied to that purpose, as well as several of our new erections, which are at present empty.

Do you mean that the system which at present prevails at the West India Docks, could be preserved by that accommodation which you suggest, as within the reach of the London Dock Company?—Certainly; I think they could do the business precisely, if necessary, in the same way.

Mr. Dennis Chapman.

How many ships can you discharge at one time along the quay of your dock?—About forty; we have had forty-seven.

What would be the average tonnage?—I suppose, about 180 to 200 tons, or about 200 tons.

You have said your vaults can hold 52,000 pipes of wine, do you mean with perfect convenience?—Yes; but I have understood, since I made that answer, that from the measurement of the vaults it appears they will contain 57,157.

If more business came into the London Docks, have you not facilities for making an export dock, and building more warehouses for the accommodation of that additional trade?—Our shed warehouses are only ground floors; the foundations are put in, so that they could be raised equal to the warehouses on the North quay; and two or three of the new warehouses lately built, have been built in the same manner, so as to be raised at any time.

Frederick Gibson, Esq.

If there was any considerable influx of business in the London Docks, have not the Dock Company space for building an additional dock and additional warehouses?—A very large space; they have a stack of warehouses called Pennington-street, which consists at present only of vaults and a ground floor, which are so built as to be raised whenever there is occasion for them.

Those warehouses might be so raised upon, as that carts could load on the outside, without coming into the dock gates, provided that mode of doing business was thought necessary?—I should think Pennington-street is wide enough for that purpose; the boundary wall is the entrance of the street, which I believe is wide enough for a cart to stand and take goods in; but that is a thing I have not turned my mind to.

Mr. William Sawtell.

Is there any thing, in your judgment, at the London Docks, to prevent the West India trade coming there?—I know of nothing.

Could the West India ships, in your judgment, be accommodated in the London Docks?—Yes.

And the West India produce in the warehouses?—Yes.

Do the Dock Company employ coopers?—A great number.

Sugar coopers?—They employ coopers on wine and brandy, and those kind of things.

Are the revenue officers at the West India Docks a superior class to those at the London Docks?—Not that I know of.

Have they higher salaries?—I am not aware that they have; the comptrolling surveyor and the principal surveyor have house-rent at the West India Docks; but generally speaking, they have the same salary.

They are, generally speaking, persons of the same description?—They are.

In your opinion, is a larger proportion of revenue officers necessary, with a view to the security of the revenue, to superintend the discharge of vessels in the one dock than in the other?—I do not see that it is.

Mr. Beeby Eilbeck.

When were the Commercial Docks established?—I believe, in 1807; they were originally docks a hundred years ago, as the Greenland Dock; but as a Commercial Dock not till the year 1806 or 1807.

They were established by virtue of some Acts of Parliament, were they not?—They were; but the Act of Parliament was procured some time afterwards; I believe a year or two.

What is the situation of the Commercial Docks?—It is a place upon the river; there is an entrance to the river; there is a place where there may be another entrance to it.

What is the extent of the premises?—It may be about sixty acres.

How many entrances have you into those docks?—We have but one.

Is it not in contemplation to make another entrance?—It is; the land is purchased.

Is the lock at that entrance sufficient to admit ships in the West India trade?—It is.

What is the depth of water at the entrance of the lock?—It varies according to ebb and spring tides; I should suppose at the average spring tide it is about eighteen feet six inches, and from that to nineteen feet; we have had twenty-one feet.

Do you mean that it would admit the West India trade at other periods than those of spring tides?—Yes, I should presume; we never could at the neap tides; we have never less than fourteen feet; but that is only for a day or two.

What should you average the draught of water in the West India trade at?—I should suppose the average is sixteen feet; we never have less than fourteen, and that is only for a day or two, then we get up to sixteen and eighteen.

You know of no impediment to West India ships entering the Commercial Docks?—Certainly I do not.

How many docks have you?—There are six altogether.

What extent of ground do they cover?—I think fifty-three acres; but I cannot charge my memory immediately without looking at the map.

To what purposes are those docks applied?—For timber, chiefly.

How many sail of vessels could they accommodate?—I think we could put three hundred sail of vessels in the whole of our docks.

Is there not an estimate made, and a plan prepared, for another entrance to the dock, if necessary?—There is; the engineer has the plan and estimate.

What warehouses have you?—There are eleven in number.

What is the situation of those warehouses with respect to the docks?—They are all so situated that a ship can lie alongside of them.

Are those warehouses sufficient for the accommodation of West India produce?—Several of them are; one in particular is equal to any in the West India Docks, indeed two.

How much West India produce could now be accommodated in your warehouses?—In the warehouses, at present, we could accommodate about 20,000 hogsheads; indeed we have had nearly as much as that.

State what you have had, and under what circumstances it came into your docks?—In 1811, the West India Dock could not accommodate the trade, and of course they applied to us, and sent their sugars to us; at that time we had 16,000 hogsheads, besides tierces and barrels, and so on.

How long did they remain in your warehouses?—More than twelve months, I believe, some of them probably two years; it was in motion, some going and some coming.

Were they not deposited in your warehouses with the approbation and consent of the revenue officers?—Certainly.

Did not the revenue officers consider your warehouses as perfectly sufficient to give accommodation and security to the revenue?—They did, certainly.

Did any instance of loss or plunder upon that produce arise to your knowledge?—None to my knowledge.

Mr. Jas. Walker.

You are the engineer to the Commercial Dock Company?—I am.

How long have you been in that situation?—From the year 1809.

Was that before the docks were opened?—Yes; I was employed on the docks from the time the Commercial Dock Company began their works in re-modelling and altering the docks.

When was the first time that they were considered as open for commercial use?—I think it was in the year 1808 that the new lock was formed; it was immediately the new lock was formed that they were opened for shipping.

Previously to your appointment to your office?—About the same time; but I superintended the forming of the new entrance previous to my being regularly appointed.

Were any of the docks constructed under your direction?—Yes; Nos. 4, 5, and 6 have been.

What is the largest sized ship that can be admitted into those docks?—The dock is capable of receiving a light 1,400 ton ship, the largest class of Indiamen; but I should suppose a 600 ton loaded ship is its greatest capability in an ordinary spring tide.

Is the dock capable of receiving a ship of 600 tons at the ordinary tide?—Yes; there is from eighteen to nineteen feet water at the ordinary spring tide.

What depth does a ship of that size when loaded draw?—I think about eighteen to nineteen feet; but with regard to the draught of ships of different sizes, I do not pretend to be so intimately acquainted.

Then you would not have above an inch or two to spare?—Of course not; it would require a good spring tide to bring in a ship of 600 tons; we have had upwards of three feet more water, or twenty-one upon the sill; but that is an extraordinary tide.

The draught of water depends a good deal upon the construction of the ship?—Yes; very much so.

Are those docks, in your judgment, capable of accommodating any portion of the West India trade?—I should think they are, as far as their capability of entrance goes.

Are the docks capable of improvement for that purpose, if it should be necessary?—Very capable of improvement.

Are they capable of deepening?—Yes, they are; it would be attended with a considerable expense deepening the entrance or making a new lock, which is the only expensive part of it; if there is not depth of water enough in the docks now, that could be increased.

Without much difficulty or expense?—Yes.

That must be done by excavation?—Yes.

One dock is deep, so that vessels may go round the sides, but shallow in the middle?—Yes.

Could that dock be deepened in all parts?—Yes; we are now deepening No. 1 dock; in taking the mud from it, which I think we are doing at 1*s.* 1*d.* a yard, and that is quite as cheap as it could be done if the water was out.

You mean 1*s.* 1*d.* a cubic yard?—Yes.

How much would it take to deepen an acre?—About 260*l.* deepening it a yard.

At that expense, you could deepen the whole of the centre of the dock No. 5?—Yes; or any part of our docks.

The question refers to that which is shallow in the middle?—Yes, I dare say if there was so much as that to be done, we could get it done cheaper by employing a steam engine; at present we are doing it by hand.

You say the docks are capable of receiving West India ships; are the warehouses capable of receiving West India produce with perfect convenience?—Some of them are; I do not think that all of them are; West India produce to a considerable extent has been already warehoused in those warehouses, and since that time the Commercial Dock Company have built others.

Could the warehouses be rendered sufficiently commodious for West India produce to a greater extent than they are at present?—Yes, certainly; and the building of warehouses is a work of very short time, if the order and the means for building them are found; the largest warehouse we have, No. 1, was built in six working months.

Could there be a new entrance made nearer London Bridge to those docks, if requested?—Yes, it has been in contemplation; and the Commercial Dock Company have purchased land with a view to it.

So that the Company have the land already for the purpose?—They have not purchased all the interests in it; they have purchased part of them.

You have area enough to erect warehouses to any extent for the accommodation of the trade which comes to the docks?—We have it to a very great extent.

What depth of water should you have at your new entrance, if you made it?—It would depend upon the trade for which it was intended; if any thing in regard to the West India trade was intended, we should make it deep enough to receive a loaded West Indiaman at all tides.

Have you the means of making it low enough for that?—Certainly; and we should require to deepen the river in the way to it, which might be done in the way I have mentioned. We have a steam engine and pipes laid into the docks, as they now are, for the purpose of deepening them, if we should find it necessary; that is, by letting off the water and keeping them dry.

By laying the sill of the entrance lower, and deepening the bed of the river leading up to it, you could, of course, make them convenient for receiving larger ships?—Certainly.

And ships that draw a greater depth of water?—Yes; one of the entrances is not begun yet; the upper entrance.

You say, that at an ordinary spring tide you have received vessels of 600 tons burthen?—Yes.

That three days out of a fortnight, you are capable of receiving such a vessel?—Sometimes three days, sometimes two, sometimes not at all; the tides are very various, as is well known.

Even in the case of a spring tide, it is uncertain whether you could receive such a vessel as that?—It is.

With your knowledge of those docks, do you think that in the event of an open system, they would be likely to become successful competitors for any part of the West India trade, as they stand at present?—I should think so; I do not see why they should not.

You think, at present, they have sufficient accommodation to become successful competitors for the West India trade?—Yes.

Which of the docks is it you think is most fit for receiving those vessels?—No. 1, the Old Greenland Dock.

How many of those vessels do you think it would contain?—The dock contains an area of ten acres; I suppose we may reckon four or five ships to an acre; that would be from forty to fifty ships.

In the event of your deepening the docks generally, making them more fit for the West India trade, have you fixed on any particular dock?—No. 1, would be first resorted to, as being nearest the entrance.

Into that you think they could enter with facility?—With the facility I have described.

Have you any estimate of the expense which it would be necessary to go to, to give it complete facility of entrance?—I have not; the principal difficulty would be in the sill of the lock.

In the event of your using No. 1, as a dock for discharging, what dock would you give them as a dock for laying up in?—I should think they might lie in No. 3, or No. 4, the one containing four acres and the other ten acres.

Is there water enough in those two docks for them to

lie in ?—Water enough for a light ship; No. 3 has, I think, sixteen feet water, and No. 4 the same nearly.

Have you made any general estimate of the warehouses which it would be necessary to build, in order to receive a considerable portion of the West India trade?—No.

There is no such estimate?—The estimate would depend upon the quantity.

Have you made any estimate of the expense of such accommodation in future?—No.

Would there be any accommodation at the Commercial Docks for ships loading for the West Indies?—Of course there would be; I mentioned No. 4, as being convenient for ships lying up, and of course they might be loaded there.

There is a canal also contiguous to the Commercial Docks?—Yes, the Grand Surry Canal.

What is the distance from the canal to your docks?—They abut quite close to each other, the entrance to the canal is considerably higher up than the entrance to the docks, but they are close to each other; a mile from the entrance.

Can merchandize be conveniently transferred from the Commercial Docks to the Surry Canal?—Yes, certainly; a communication might be made.

Are the Commercial Docks capable of receiving ships drawing not more than fourteen feet water, every tide?—Not every tide: there are some neap tides which are even lower than that.

Those are as rare as the flood tides of twenty-one feet?—Not quite so rare as that; the difference between an ordinary spring tide and an ordinary neap tide is about four feet, therefore, as we call eighteen feet six the ordinary depth with an ordinary spring tide, the ordinary depth at an ordinary neap tide is about fourteen feet six.

What is the ordinary mean depth?—About sixteen feet six.

Generally speaking, is the entrance of the Commercial Dock capable, every tide, of receiving vessels that do not draw more than fourteen feet water?—Yes, generally speaking it is; and the Commercial Dock Company have a capability of making another entrance into their docks at the same place, at a deeper level, when an opportunity offers for the purchase of property.

To what depth might that entrance be conveniently made?—We should make that as deep as the present entrance of the West India Docks, about six feet below our present entrance.

That is six feet below low water mark?—Yes; the Commercial Dock Company of course have not, in the present state of things, had serious thoughts of setting about the thing; but they have an idea of property in that neighbourhood, which if they have ever occasion for it, they would purchase, with a view to making a deeper entrance.

At present they have not the property enabling them to do it?—No, at present they have not.

Is it, in your judgment as an engineer, physically practicable?—Yes; and if the West India trade were opened, I have no doubt it would be done.

At what expense could you deepen the present entrance, so as to make it as deep as the entrance of the West India Docks?—It would amount quite to making a new entrance, every part must be taken up; I should suppose that would cost from 20 to £25,000.

Could you, for that expense, make an entrance that would admit ships at all times and of any size?—Yes, about that sum.

What additional depth could you get?—My recommendation would be to make it six feet lower.

If you made a new entrance at the other end, should you not be able to make it so as to admit ships of all sizes?—Yes, certainly.

Have you any estimate of the expense of making another entrance on the opposite side?—If the question refers to the place where property has been in part purchased, I suppose, to make that a complete entrance, altogether, would cost £50,000.

R. H. Marten, Esq.

Are you not a Director of the Commercial Docks?—I am.

How long have you been so?—About six years.

You are perfectly well acquainted with the Commercial Docks?—I certainly am acquainted with them.

Are you well acquainted with the Acts of Parliament by which the docks have been established?—I have perused them.

To your knowledge as a Director, have the Company the power, if it is necessary, of extending and improving their works and premises for the purpose of accommodating any future trade?—They have yet power by those Acts which they have not used.

What power?—The power of raising money.

They have not raised all the money they were enabled to raise?—No.

What extent remains to be raised?—I think, speaking from recollection, £40,000.

What is your present capital?—Our present capital is about £313,000, with about £25,000 out on debentures, which may be redeemed in 1824 or 1825.

There is a further power of raising £40,000?—Yes.

Have you expended the whole of that capital in your works?—Yes; I think we have very little floating capital.

Have you the means of making calls upon the Company to any extent beyond the £40,000?—No; I do not understand that we have, at present, the means of making calls on our present subscribers; but we have the means of raising money by subscriptions.

There is nothing in the Act to prevent your extending your works to increase the accommodation, if it should be thought desirable to give you the West India trade?—No; we have recently extended our works by means of debentures; the state of the trade being very low, and our shares reduced in value, instead of creating new shares at that depression, we borrowed the money on debentures, which are redeemable in the year 1825.

If the West India trade were laid open to you, you could give accommodation to a portion of it?—To a very large extent.

Mr. John Lampson.

You hold some office in the Customs?—Landing surveyor.

Where are you stationed?—I am at present stationed at the office of the legal quays.

How long have you held that office?—About a year and a half, the office of landing surveyor in the port of London; I have been successively through the different departments of the customs.

How long have you been employed in the customs?—About six and twenty years.

Are you acquainted with the Commercial Docks?—I am.

Have you been stationed there?—I was stationed there on the part of the revenue before it was called the Commercial Dock, or its entrance formed, and was there till some time after its completion.

Have a variety of prize goods been housed there?—Yes; they were entirely under my superintendence, the Danish prize goods.

In what year were they housed?—To the best of my recollection, in the years 1808, 1809, or 1810.

What species of goods?—A great variety; stock-fish, apparel, jackets, the Icelanders' jackets, and dress of various kinds; and general cargoes, such as are brought from Iceland.

Were those goods liable to plunder?—They were liable to plunder; because plunderage has taken place.

In the Commercial Docks?—Yes; but not in the state in which the Commercial Docks are now; they are in a different situation.

If those goods were deposited in the Commercial Docks, could plunderage take place?—I think not; I am confident it could not, in the same way; they are not now under the same circumstances.

Do you remember any sugars being deposited in the Commercial Docks?—Yes.

Were they plundered?—No; I believe not.

In your opinion, can articles of West India produce be deposited in the Commercial Docks with perfect security?—I have no doubt, that while deposited in the Commercial Docks, they are as secure as in any other.

Are their warehouses fit for the reception of sugar?—Some of them are.

Are their cellars fit for the reception of rums?—That I can speak less to.

In your opinion, the Commercial Docks could afford accommodation and security to West India produce, to the perfect satisfaction of the revenue officers?—I should think, perfectly so; I do not think that the revenue would be more in danger, when the property was once there, than at any other Docks.

Do you know that when vessels are in the course of discharge, a certain quantity of produce might be left on the quay from the night to the morning?—I should rather suppose not; if I was superintendant there, I should prevent that.

You would think the degree of security at the Commercial Docks such, that it would be necessary to prevent that circumstance?—As well there as at the West India Docks; I should conceive it was no more secure at the West India than the Commercial Docks.

Do you think a brick wall twenty-five feet high is a greater security than pales of twelve feet?—We have proof against that; for they have scaled the walls of the East India Dock, and taken out property, I have heard, to the extent of £8,000.

Are not the East India Docks surrounded with buildings, and has not that been made the subject of complaint? —The walls of the East India Dock were not connected with any building; there was no building whatever within a vast distance; in fact, not at all connected with where the depredation took place.

Whether their fences at the West India Dock can be scaled you cannot state?—I have no doubt they can be scaled, if a wall nearly twice the height could; I am not aware that any wall can be found that cannot be scaled.

You would not consider that with a fence of twelve feet high, the produce left in the course of discharge there would be safe?—I mean to say, that no produce can be safe, if left upon the quays after the legal hours.

Should you consider that produce, in the course of discharge, was safe, with no other protection than a fence twelve feet high?—That is a kind of question that I cannot answer, because it is not official; we do not leave things in that situation, and therefore I cannot answer that question, as it cannot occur.

Would not property be safe if, in addition to a fence of twelve feet high, there were revenue officers there?—I am not aware that revenue officers need be there; there are no revenue officers appointed to guard the West India Docks; it would increase the expense certainly; the other docks have not revenue officers there.

How do you mean that revenue officers are not at the other docks?—I mean in the night; I understood the question to refer to the night and not to the day; inevitably revenue officers must be there in the course of the day.

You conceive they are perfectly safe in the course of the day?—Yes.

If in addition to a strong fence of twelve feet high, the revenue were to employ watchmen to protect the goods, would not they be in your opinion safe?—Certainly; and undoubtedly there would be much greater protection than at the up-town warehouses, and the legal quays; there is not a tenth part of the protection there.

Mr. John Manning.

You are an officer of the customs?—I am.

What is the description of your office?—Landing surveyor.

How long have you been employed in that capacity, or employed as a custom-house officer, in the port of London?—Six and twenty years as an officer of the customs, and two years as landing surveyor in the port of London.

Where is your present employment?—At the Commercial Docks; at the wood docks generally.

Have you had opportunities of being acquainted with the London, West India, and Commercial Docks?—Very little, at either of the two former; I have been about fifteen months at the Commercial Docks, as a landing surveyor; at the West India, not more than three months, which was in the year 1802, and at the London Docks a short time, ten years ago.

Have you had opportunities of observing whether ships and cargoes are well accommodated, and effectually protected in the Commercial Docks?—Completely so; the description of vessels that go into those docks, since I have been on duty there, are confined to ships laden with wood chiefly, and foreign corn, and fish oils.

Have you heard of many complaints of plunder of corn that was brought to those docks?—Never.

Is the dock commodious for the reception of every description of wood?—Yes, perfectly so.

Could mahogany and dye woods be received there?—Certainly.

Could they be as well received and taken care of at the Commercial as at the West India Docks, in your opinion?—I think they could.

Are they as convenient also for the exportation of any description of wood as the West India Dock?—I have not been at the West India Dock since the first year of their establishment.

Are they perfectly convenient for the exportation of wood, as well as the importation?—Yes, certainly they are.

Has it ever come within your knowledge, that wood, destined for the West Indies, was necessarily conveyed from the Commercial Docks to the West India, for the purpose of exportation?—It is conveyed by lighters from the Commercial to the West India Docks for exportation, in all cases.

That is wood intended for the West Indies?—Yes.

Would it be more convenient, in your opinion, that that

wood should be shipped immediately, in the Commercial Docks, if the law would allow it ?—That is a question for the ship owner, whether the expense would be greater in bringing his ship to the Commercial Dock, or to take it by lighters from the Commercial to the West India Dock.

But supposing the expense would not be greater, would it not be more convenient to ship the wood in the Commercial Dock than to transfer it, and then ship it ?—Certainly; and with less risk to the revenue.

Is that a circumstance that frequently, or only rarely occurs ?—It frequently occurs.

Have you any doubt that that is attended with considerable inconvenience ?—No more than the exportation of other goods by land or water.

But the shipping it twice over is more inconvenient, perhaps, than doing it only once ?—Certainly.

And putting it first on board the lighters, and then on board the ship, is more inconvenient, perhaps, than putting it immediately on board the ship in the Commercial Dock ?—Certainly it is so.

Are the officers of your department, generally speaking, trust-worthy men ?—Certainly; or it would be my duty to represent them.

Do you consider the property of the merchants as free from plunder in the Commercial Docks as any where else ?—Yes, certainly.

Have you had any occasion to find that the revenue was not perfectly secured both at the London and Commercial Docks, as far as you have had intercourse with them ?—I never heard of any loss sustained to the revenue in either of those docks.

Perhaps it is not within your knowledge that sugars were formerly deposited at the Commercial Docks ?—I recollect it, but I was not on duty at those docks at the time.

Did you see it there?—I do not recollect that I ever saw it there; not officially, certainly.

Are the docks, wharfs and warehouses at the Commercial Dock, in your judgment, any of them fit for the reception of West India goods now?—Several warehouses are fit for the reception of West India produce.

Are the wharfs fitted for the accommodation of landing?—They are.

Is the accommodation for landing there as good as at other places, generally speaking?—I cannot make the comparison between the Commercial and the West India Docks; the Commercial Docks, for the accommodation of West India produce, certainly cannot be equal to the West India Docks, for they were never built for the purpose;—but it is possible to improve them; they are capable of every improvement.

Have you any reason to doubt, that if West India produce was deposited in the warehouses of the Commercial Docks, it would be perfectly safe there?—Under proper regulations, I think it would be perfectly safe.

And that the revenue would be secure?—Certainly.

If the regulations were as good, and the accommodation as great, they would do just as well?—Certainly.

And the people employed at the Commercial Docks, you believe to be just as honest as the people employed at other places?—Quite as honest.

Perhaps a great deal more so?—From what I have heard, certainly; I never heard of any depredation at the Commercial Docks; I have at other docks; but of course it is merely a rumour; it is only hearsay.

Every body supposes people employed by himself, to

be more honest than those employed by others?—They are not employed by me.

You have the superintendence of them?—Yes, I have.

Thomas Tooke, Esq.

You are a Russia merchant in the city of London?—I am.

How long have you been acquainted with the Port of London?—I have been seven and twenty years in business in London.

You were acquainted with the port before any of the docks were made, except the Greenland Dock?—I was.

Have you had occasion since the new docks have been opened, to send any ships or cargoes to the West India and London Docks?—The house in which I am concerned send the largest part of their importation into the London Docks, as furnishing the best accommodation.

Do you send any to the Commercial Docks?—We send articles to the Commercial that are not usually received in the London Docks; namely, linseed and bonded wheat, and oats and timber; and we send timber to the Surry Canal occasionally.

What description of merchandize do you send to the London Docks?—We send hemp, flax, tallow, and bristles.

Have you had occasion to bond merchandize either at the London or the Commercial Docks?—We generally bond all our goods, excepting flax, which pays so small a duty as not to be an object. The number of cargoes that we landed last year in the London Docks, consisting of hemp, flax, tallow, and bristles, was about thirty, and the value about £250,000.

Have you found the business of the London and Commercial Docks regularly transacted, as far as you have had any dealings with them?—With great regularity and dispatch, and accommodation.

In the London and Commercial Docks you say you have found the business transacted with perfect regularity; have you found that it has been perfectly consistent with the security of the property?—Perfectly so.

The loading and the unloading of cargoes?—Yes, it is conducted with very great dispatch and security, as far as I can judge.

Have you any reason to apprehend that there is a great deal of plunder going on in the London Docks?—No, I have not; I have known of only one instance some years ago, when there was a small deficiency in either some flax or hemp, I cannot say from memory which, but it was a very trifling object.

Have you happened to have any dealings at all with the West India Dock Company?—None; excepting a good many years ago we had occasion for a particular connexion to land a few cargoes of mahogany there; but it is so long since, I have no distinct recollection of any of the charges or circumstances connected with it.

From your long acquaintance with the port of London, are you able to form any judgment, whether West India produce could be as conveniently accommodated either at the London or the Commercial Docks as the West India Docks?—I see no reason why the London Docks could not, in proportion to their extent, give the same accommodation as the West India Docks.

Is their vicinity to London-bridge, the head of the port, a circumstance that would render it as convenient for the purpose?—I should conceive that to be a very great advantage.

Have you ever considered the amount of the rates and

duties at those docks, or any of them?—I am not acquainted with the proportion of the charges as between the West India Docks and the London Docks; but as between the London Docks and the sufferance wharfs, I believe that the whole of the advantages, in a pecuniary sense, preponderate in favour of the London Docks; at least so we think, and we act accordingly, in directing by far the largest proportion of our business to those docks.

In your judgment, must the landing of West India cargoes at the West India Docks frequently be attended with a great deal of additional expense in land carriage?—I should imagine that the difference of expense would be in proportion to the difference of distance, or nearly so.

The West India Docks, the Committee understand, are three miles from London bridge, and the London Docks one?—I should conceive the difference of expense would be very considerable, so far as relates to the conveyance.

No. VI.

MACHINERY.

John Tilstone, Esq.

Have not the West India Docks the advantage of very valuable machinery, which does not exist elsewhere, and which enables the Company to perform several operations of landing cargoes with much less expense to the proprietor?—Yes; I have no doubt of it.

Might not other dock companies have the same machinery, and afford the same facilities to the landing of goods?—They might have the same machinery, if they chose to go to the expense of it.

William Mitchell, Esq.

What are the peculiar characteristics of the warehouses

necessary to make them fit for the reception of sugars?—That they have all been adapted for the purpose of housing in a proper manner that article.

Is not strength a great requisite?—Certainly, most material.

What machinery is employed in warehouses for sugars and coffee?—There are cranes and jiggers employed.

And trucks, I believe?—Yes; for the conveyance from the side of the ship into the warehouse, and in the warehouse.

Is any other machinery necessary in warehouses for those commodities?—I am not aware of any, except those implements used in the stowing casks.

Are not those implements used in warehouses for goods of any and every description?—The Dock Company keep very much distinct articles of different denominations; in the same floor with sugars they never house coffee, I believe.

Must you not have cranes and jiggers, and trucks, whatever commodity you house in the warehouse?—Certainly.

Then no extraordinary machinery is necessary for warehousing sugars and coffee?—I am not aware that any extraordinary machinery is requisite.

The extraordinary machinery in the West India Docks is, as to the landing and stowing wood?—I understand the machinery as to wood is different from that of other articles, owing to the immense weight of the mahogany and many other descriptions of wood.

Mr. John Manning.

Are there at the Commercial Docks the means of putting mahogany under cover, if it was brought there at present; are there covered sheds for the purpose?—There are.

For this purpose?—Not for the purpose, for they never had the power of having it there.

Are they furnished with machinery for the purpose of moving logs of five or six ton weight?—Yes, I think we have; we landed some cargoes of teak-wood from Sierra Leone, which is very heavy wood, and they have machinery for that purpose.

What description of machinery?—Cranes.

Have you machinery for the purpose of landing that?—Yes.

You have not examined that at the West India Dock, so as to draw a comparison?—No; I have not been there officially since 1802.

No. VII.

SECURITY AGAINST PLUNDER.

John Tilstone, Esq.

In your judgment, could the advantages you have mentioned be equally obtained, if the West India trade was permitted to go to various docks, or various places in the river, instead of being confined, as it now is, to one?—Certainly not; in a dock of promiscuous trade, such as the London Dock, for instance, I think it would be impossible. I think that the West India merchant's property could not be protected from robbers and from smuggling: ships are unloading inwards and taking in their outward bound cargo, lying alongside each other; that is not the case in the West India Docks; when the ships have discharged their cargoes inwards, they are removed to the Export Dock, or to a distant part of the dock, so that there is no communication between the vessels unloading and loading.

You do not know of any plunder, in fact, taking place

place at the London Docks more than at the West India Docks?—I have not any duty at the London Docks, therefore I cannot say what plunder has taken place; but I have reason to suppose there must be more there than at the West India Docks, because I know there is none there. But in the London Docks, where ships are discharging inwards and loading outwards, lying alongside each other; and where the ship's boats are allowed to be used in the dock, there is a greater opportunity for smuggling and plunder.

Is the revenue defrauded there, to your knowledge?—Not to my knowledge; I cannot mention any particular case, but I think it is very liable to that.

Upon the whole of your evidence, the only advantage essentially or necessarily peculiar to the West India Docks, is, the limited variety of articles allowed to be imported there?—From the limited number of articles, certainly greater protection is afforded.

That is the only advantage necessarily peculiar to those docks?—There are many advantages arising from the regulations.

That is the only advantage necessarily peculiar to those docks?—Certainly.

Mr. Thomas Burne.

Be so good as to state to the Committee, what was the result of your investigation at the London Docks, as far as the security to the revenue was concerned?—I was appointed by order of the Board, in consequence of some irregularities that were discovered; and, in consequence of that order, I went to the London Docks, and the first thing I did was, to see in what manner the business had been conducted, on the part of the revenue. It was very evident, that the business had been conducted there in a very improper manner, I believe, from want of knowledge in the official department of the Customs, for want of attention; they appeared to me to have misunderstood the system altogether.

The system appeared to you, to have been misunderstood?—Yes; and I as reported to the Board.

Was there any considerable loss to the revenue, in consequence?—The first thing I did was, to place the different officers in that situation that the business might go on regularly and correctly; I did that by adopting the same means we had at the West India Docks; the same means of security, so far as it was possible.

Is there access to all the warehouses in the London Docks, without carts coming upon the quay?—No; the carts come upon the quay, and take the goods in there.

There is no access otherwise?—I believe there is not.

That is not the case at the West India Docks?—No; they are excluded totally.

Could the point of security to the merchant, then, be made precisely the same?—I conceive not.

The Commissioners for the investigation of the Customs and Excise, having stated, in their Fifth Report, that irregularities arose from the number of articles being so great, and the facilities thereby created to the commission of frauds; do you concur in that opinion?—No, I conceive not; that the irregularities arose from the system being a bad one, with respect to the Crown.

You are not of opinion, that the system is less intricate at the West India Docks?—It is certainly less intricate, for the number of articles is less numerous.

Are you of opinion, that fewer facilities are afforded to the commission of fraud in consequence of that circumstance?—I should think so.

If the regulations in any dock appeared to the revenue

officers stationed there, to be incompatible with the security of the revenue, is it not their duty to make representations upon the subject?—Most certainly.

Had that been done in the case of the London Docks previously to your being called in to make the Report to which you have alluded?—It appeared that they did not understand the business; the system was wrong from the beginning to the end, in respect of the revenue.

Then it appeared that the frauds on the revenue, in the London Docks, were owing to the remissness or the ignorance of the officers stationed there?—Principally so.

Was any opposition made by the Directors of the London Docks to the introduction of the system proposed?—Not the least; they gave me every facility in examining their accounts; without their assistance, I could not have done any thing.

Are individuals, who come into the London Docks to taste wines or other articles, permitted to have access to all the warehouses, without being attended or superintended by any revenue officer?—There are revenue officers stationed at every warehouse, who are called lockers.

Have individuals, who are so disposed, the means of plundering the articles deposited in those warehouses?—They might drink a glass or two perhaps, but they would not let them take any quantity away.

Thomas Groves, Esq.

Would the sugar, remaining on the quay to be coopered, be safe with such an indiscriminate admission of persons as prevails at the London Docks?—I think we have had so much proof of things being safe, that there is no reason to apprehend pilferage or depredation; I think that the West India Dock system approaches as nearly to perfection as any imperfect system can do.

Part of the benefit of that system you consider to be, the exclusion of carts from the quay, and the exclusion of persons who resort to the London Docks?—Yes; but those surrounding walls have been found to answer beyond the expectation of any one; they have afforded that sort of protection that cannot be had in any detached warehouse whatever.

Do not you conceive the great security to arise, both to the revenue and the merchant, from the surrounding walls, and the disposition of the officers within the dock?—The surrounding walls certainly afford very great protection; but I think there is besides something in the construction of the dock, which adds to the security of the West India Dock; being constructed as it is, with an import and an export dock, as soon as a ship is cleared, she is obliged to go out into the export dock, and that prevents the possibility of putting packages on board her.

Thomas Turner, Esq.

Have you found the system adopted at the West India Docks afford security to the revenue?—Very great.

Do you consider that the export and import dock being different, is a circumstance that affords a greater security?—Undoubtedly.

Do you consider that the turning out the crews at night affords greater security?—Yes.

Do you think that the fact, that the crews do not remain on board there, assists the revenue?—Yes.

Do you think that the not permitting carts upon the quays at the West India Docks affords also security?—Yes.

Then in any dock where those circumstances do not take place, will the security be as great as in the West

India Docks?—I think the security at the West India Dock is preferable to that at others, in consequence of those circumstances which have been referred to.

W. Mitchell, Esq.

Are the owners of the produce who come to superintend it very likely to plunder their own property?—Certainly not; but they cannot always be present.

Are the buyers who come to view the produce likely to plunder?—Certainly not; but they cannot be supposed to be always present either.

Are persons who have no business in the wet docks admitted within the gates without an order from one of the directors or secretary?—Not in the West India Docks.

Are they in the London Docks?—I am not sufficiently acquainted with the regulations of the London Docks to answer that.

Supposing such a regulation to exist, is there any danger of property being plundered from the parties whom you describe to be entitled to admission there?—Not being aware of any act of plunder at the London Docks, I cannot speak to it; but I can only state what appear to me as the precautions which would prevent plunder taking place.

Do you not think that carts being loaded at the back of the warehouses may furnish opportunities of plunder rather than prevent them?—I think not, at the West India Docks.

Have you never heard of bags being thrown into carts while so loading?—No, not since I have been a director; and I am not aware that ever I did hear of it; that such a thing might not have occurred I do not mean to state.

George Hibbert, Esq.

Do you think the regulation adopted at the West India Docks, by which the crew are all taken out of the ship, and the cargo discharged by means of labourers under the direction of the officers of the Dock Company, is necessary to the protection of the cargo?—I have always thought it was the only means of entirely securing that great object; that it was one of the necessary means for preventing the great evil of plunder, and I think so still.

Has it been found to be adequate in the West India Docks?—Not in every instance; the system of protection of the West India Docks has been gradually perfected; in the first year, with all our precautions, we found now and then that fraud had been too ingenious for us; but as we went on, I do think that we have cut up the evil by the root. I will mention, for instance, that we have found sugar secreted in ships when they have been going out of dock, which has induced new precautions; it had been secreted, probably by some of the inferior officers of the ship previously to her coming into the dock, concealed in such places as were most likely to escape the observation of those that delivered the ship out.

Would the means of plundering a ship, by contrivances of that description, be materially increased, if the ship was permitted to navigate five or six miles higher up the Thames?—I think they would.

Would they not be materially increased, if the crew were permitted to remain on board?—I wish to add, by way of explanation, that it would be more difficult to detect them; I think the system of the West India Docks complete, to detect every contrivance of that kind.

There are two docks, an import and an export dock?—There are.

The ships which are outward bound are not permitted to take in any of their outward cargo in the import dock?—No; except that some have been permitted to take in ballast, and some bricks, which have been considered as ballast.

If ships coming from the West Indies were permitted to come into a dock where there were ships receiving their outward bound cargoes, do you think the facility of plunder would be increased?—No doubt it would.

Do you think the same facilities could be afforded to the trade, by a dock which received both the outward and the homeward bound ships?—Of course not; not consistently with my last answer.

Do you think the security which is afforded to the West India trade by the West India Docks could be afforded by any other establishment that had but one large dock?—I do not.

Do you think that the admission of trades of different descriptions into the same dock would render it more difficult to carry into execution the system which now prevails for the protection of the property at the West India Dock?—In my own belief it would be impossible to apply the system to a dock of that kind.

Have the goodness to state your reasons for that opinion?—It was a full conviction of that, that led me to encounter all the difficulties of establishing the West India Docks; and my reason is this, that our system is unquestionably a very rigid one, bearing hard, in some respects, upon the ships that enter our dock; and nothing could excuse these hardships, and these restrictions, but that they were necessary for the protection of the cargo, and of the revenue, and of the planters; I conceive them all to be so; they are easily proved to be so; they are all grounded upon abuses which did exist, to a very considetable degree, under other systems; and this system was devised to remedy the evil.

Are they, in your judgment, so necessary for the protection of other trades besides the West India trade, as to make it reasonable to adopt them in those trades?—I am not quite a judge upon that question; I know my own trade best; I am quite sure that they are necessary, to put an end to the abuses and the evils which afflicted the West India trade; and I should imagine they are inapplicable to any other trades.

You are understood to say, they are of a rigid description, and therefore such as it is not reasonable to adopt, unless it is necessary?—Yes.

They do not appear to you to be applicable to other trades, in the same measure as they are to your trade?—No; certainly not.

Is it not your opinion, that if the West India trade did resort to the Commercial Docks, there would be as great a security from plunder, as at the present West India Docks?—I am so far from believing that, that I do most firmly believe the direct contrary.

Supposing the ship to be ordered by law to have her hatches locked down at Gravesend, and revenue officers put on board, and this ship brought up to Wapping, and there put into a dock surrounded by walls, as the London Dock is, and then subjected to the precautions the law provides, are you of opinion the cargo would be exposed to plunder before it arrived at the King's beam?—Yes, I am.

Do you think it would be in danger of it?—I think plunder would, to a certain degree, take place.

Samuel Turner, Esq.

Do you recollect the system which prevailed before

the establishment of the docks?—I cannot say that I do, perfectly; I was a very young merchant at that time.

The question refers to a comparison between the London and the West India Docks; did you so understand it?—No; I conceived the question to be whether there was additional danger to the West India merchant or planter, by the vessel going higher up the river.

Were you acquainted with the system which prevailed before the establishment of the docks?—I was, to a degree; I was a very young merchant in those days.

Is it consistent with your knowledge, that at that time the hatches were locked down from the arrival of the vessel at Gravesend, till her arrival at the legal quays?—No; that was not within my recollection.

Is it consistent with your knowledge, that revenue officers were on board during the whole of that passage?—That is not within my own immediate knowledge; I believe both facts to be so; but my concerns in the counting-house did not go into those immediate details of the deliveries from ships.

Is it within your knowledge, that a considerable part of the plunderage which then took place, took place between Gravesend and the arrival at the legal quays?—I rather believe that the greater part of the plunderage did not take place exactly in that situation, but in the delivery of the ships; putting the cargoes from on board the ships into lighters; and that it took place afterwards, in the warehouses; the warehouse keepers themselves plundering to a very great degree.

Have you any knowledge of a fact which was laid before the Committee in the year 1796, that out of the plunderage which took place upon a West India cargo, consisting in the whole of forty-eight pounds upon a hogshead, thirty-two pounds of that took place before it arrived at the King's beam?—I am not aware of the circumstance.

If that be so, will it materially alter your opinion as to the risk of plunder between Gravesend and the legal quays?—No, it will not; I think that the system is considerably altered, that there is not the same easy mode, perhaps, of disposing of plunder, even if it was obtained, at the present moment; I should say that the question, so far as it goes merely, is between the London Docks and the West India Docks; but the same danger must attend the transit from Gravesend to the West India Dock; it is only a few miles difference between the one and the other; the danger must be equal in both cases, as far as to the gates of the West India Docks.

Andrew Colville, Esq.

You were understood to say, that you consider the West India trade should be carried on in a dock exclusively appropriated to that purpose?—I certainly do.

And that the West India Docks are peculiarly adapted for carrying on that trade?—They have been constructed solely for that object.

Do you think that it would be injurious, if ships in the West India trade were allowed to go to what dock the captain of the vessel chose to select?—I conceive it would be injurious to the revenue, and that it would also be injurious to the planter who has property on board those ships.

Have the goodness to state your reasons for thinking it would be injurious to the planter and merchant, to allow the ships to be carried to any dock the captain chose to select?—My principal reason for being of that opinion is, that in any other dock in the Port of London, the crews would not be excluded; there would also be other ships loading and unloading in the same dock, all of which circumstances would afford great facility to plunder; another circumstance which induces me to be of that opinion is, that the other docks in London, being higher up the river, the ship would be, in the course of that passage, detained one, two, or three tides, which would give a greater opportunity to plunder, before the ship got into the dock.

Then from those circumstances, a certain portion of the security which is now given would be lost?—I certainly conceive, from those circumstances, that the same security would not be obtained by the planter and merchant, as is at present obtained at the West India Dock.

Mr. John Clippingdale.

Do you know whether it is the habit of the London Dock Company to open their dock for the receipt of vessels at night?—I rather think not; I am not competent to answer that question.

If such a vessel as this, using the West India trade, and with a West India cargo aboard, were detained in the stream at Deptford, is it your opinion, that the risk of plunder would be increased to any consequence?—No doubt of it.

Mr. John Drinkald.

Does the system adopted at the London Docks appear to you to be such as is adapted to the West India trade? —Certainly not; for they could not keep one set of ships clear; the crews of the foreign ships in the London Docks, such as the American, other foreigners, and Hamburgh ships, are allowed to remain on board; therefore the West Indiamen would be liable to plunder from those people in the night.

Are there any grounds on which you think the same system could not be introduced?—They have not the power of carrying the system into effect; in the first place, they have not the room; they have not another dock to put the empty ships into; they could not carry on the business in the London Docks, on the system on which it is conducted at present in the West India Docks.

Mr. Charles Stuart.

In your judgment, is the confining of the West India Dock to the West India trade advantageous to the planter and the merchant?—Perfectly so; because every thing is secure, the revenue is secured, and the property is perfectly so.

Do you think the same security could be afforded, and the same expedition obtained, if other trades were admitted promiscuously into the same dock?—Certainly not.

You have stated that it is your opinion, that the practice which prevails at the London Docks, of permitting the purchaser to resort there for tasting wines particularly, is in your mind a disadvantage, in so far, that at the West India Docks that practice is not permitted; have the goodness to inform the Committee, the reasons you are of that opinion?—It is very accommodating to the trade to have to come down to taste the wines upon the quay, and is likewise a great convenience to the importer; but at the West India Dock they do not suffer any thing of the kind, they keep the goods entirely to themselves, and will not suffer any other person to come in and molest them in the least.

As the purchaser is permitted to go to the vault at the London Dock, and is not permitted to do so at the West India Dock, is not that a facility which the importer or seller possesses at the one dock, and not at the other?—In the article of wine; gentlemen that are in the habit of having choice wines, would rather like to go down to taste them themselves than have them up by sample, therefore it is the accommodation afforded to the trade which has rendered that custom so general.

You are in the wine and spirit trade?—Yes.

Supposing a parcel of wines were offered to you for sale, and you were told that at the one dock you could go down and taste them in the cask, and that in the other you must be satisfied with a sample; which system would you prefer?—I should like to taste them out of the cask.

To that extent you think the system at the London Docks preferable?—As to wines, certainly.

Have you ever known any inconvenience arise to the revenue or the merchant from permitting them to be so tasted?—No.

John Inglis, Esq.

Are not the docks and premises of the London Dock Company surrounded by walls?—Yes, they are obliged to be so by the Act of Parliament.

What do the London Docks consist of; you have an import dock?—They consist of two basins and a dock; they are used for export or import, according to the circumstances, for both purposes.

Do this dock and those basins and all those premises, being surrounded by walls, in your opinion, give security to the property landed there?—Security as great as can be given.

Do you not think that a wet dock surrounded by walls, is of itself of importance to give security to property?—Yes, with the checks established there at the gates.

What means are taken to give security to the property which is deposited there?—The means of security are being surrounded by walls and keeping a regular watch night and day; there are a body of watchmen who remain there all night, together with certain officers belonging to the excise, and no article of merchandize is suffered to be carried out of the dock gates without being inspected, and no man is suffered to depart without being examined also; I speak of the persons belonging to the establishment.

Are all the persons belonging to the establishment who go out at the dock gates regularly searched?—Yes.

The crews of the vessels are allowed to remain in the London Docks?—They are.

Do they remain there generally?—The crews of all foreign ships, part of the crews of British ships, sometimes the whole, but that depends upon the master; the masters and officers of the British ships generally remain.

Do the masters of the British ships generally discharge the crews on entering the London Docks?—I cannot say they all do, I believe the short traders generally do not.

Are the generality of crews discharged?—No; of the generality of British ships making long voyages, the crews are discharged at the end of the voyage.

In the generality of ships in the London Docks, in your opinion, are the crews generally discharged or not?—No foreign ship, I believe, discharges her crew; the generality of British ships probably do, but I cannot speak to that decidedly.

In your opinion, does the circumstance of the crews remaining on board the vessels, expose the property in the docks to plunder?—I think the contrary.

State to the Committee your reason for that opinion?—My reason is, that the master and officers of the ship and the crew have an interest in preserving and protecting the cargo.

Will you explain why the officers and crew have an interest in protecting the cargo?—Because if any plunderage takes place on board the ship, the owners would be liable for it.

Whilst remaining in the docks?—Until it is discharged from the ship, it does not come into the possession of the Dock Company until it is landed upon the quay.

Are not the crews of foreign vessels under the controul of the masters and owners of those vessels?—Under the controul of the masters certainly, the owner may reside abroad; they are under the controul of the master and the person to whom they are consigned in this country.

Have not masters the means of preventing the crew committing plunder, by using a proper degree of vigilance? —It is their interest to do so, and their duty.

Are the crews of vessels remaining in the docks searched on going out of the docks?—The seamen are always searched on going out of the docks.

Are not the dock gates shut every night?—Yes.

After the shutting of the dock gates, are the crews of the vessels therein allowed to come on shore?—No; after a certain hour in the evening, they are never permitted to come on shore.

And they remain on board their vessels during the night?—Yes.

Do you not think that the keeping the crews on board is a very great advantage to them in point of morals?—I certainly think so, it is a great advantage to the British ships in the protection of their seamen who do remain, and of their apprentices especially in their morals and habits.

Upon the whole you state your opinion to be, that the remaining of the crews of foreign vessels, instead of being the cause of plunder, rather turns out to be the means of protecting the property from plunder?—I think so; I should state that I know of no instance of plunder on heard any ships in the docks; I do not recollect to have heard of any instances.

Do you take such a part in the direction and management of the dock affairs, that, if there had been instances of plunder in the docks, they would have come within your knowledge?—They certainly would, especially for the first fourteen or fifteen years of the establishment, because I went weekly to the dock and attended the committee during that time.

In your docks, persons who want to purchase articles of course have access to them by sight?—Certain articles; others are sold by sample.

Are carts admitted upon your quays?—Yes.

They go there to take away produce?—Yes.

Do they come in front of the warehouses, between the warehouses and the water, or have you access for carts behind the warehouses?—There is one class of warehouses where there is a passage between the warehouses; it depends upon where the goods are.

Have you any warehouses which give access to carts behind, so as to enable the Dock Company to load the carts from the warehouses, in places to which other persons have no access?—No, certainly, there is no cart loaded where those connected with the dock cannot have access to it.

The question is not whether persons connected with the docks have access, but cannot other persons who go to the docks for business also have access; any person wishing to look at wine or tobacco, for instance?—A person may stand upon the quay, but he cannot have access to the place without an order on special business.

A person may stand on the quay where the goods are loaded?—Yes.

Are certain articles left upon the quays?—Certainly.

What articles are deposited occasionally, and left for some time on the quays?—Articles are never left upon the quays but where it is required by the proprietor or the revenue officer.

Are they occasionally left upon the quays for want of room in the warehouses?—We have no instance of that now; we have had it, upon former occasions.

You have been asked whether your warehouses are so constructed that you have the means of discharging into carts at the back of them without the necessity of their coming into the docks; do you conceive there is any advantage in discharging into carts at the back of the warehouses in the manner described?—I am not aware of any advantage; at the West India Docks it is necessary, for they have not quay room in their front; I am not aware of any disadvantage there is in loading the sugar at the docks.

If any advantage were found in so constructing warehouses, might not your new warehouses be so constructed?—If there is any advantage, the Pennington-street warehouses could be so arranged, but it is not what I would recommend, certainly.

When carts come into the London Docks, are the carmen admitted to range about among the produce, or are they permitted to leave the carts and horses?—I believe they are subject to a penalty if they leave their carts and horses.

If they were found to have left their carts and horses and to be ranging about, would they be subjected to that penalty?—The constables would prevent it.

Do you consider property exposed to any danger in the London Docks from proprietors being admitted to have access to their own property, either by themselves or their clerks?—Certainly not; I consider that it is very acceptable to the proprietors to have that admission into the docks to see their own goods, at certain periods of time; there was inconvenience from the wine being tasted by the merchants' clerks and others who came down there; but there is a remedy provided for that, that no person is permitted to taste wine without an order for that purpose.

Do you consider that the system adopted of giving both buyers and proprietors access at certain periods for buying or tasting it, does really expose that property to plunder?—I do not think it does.

Do you not conceive there is some advantage in the prevention of an indiscriminate access to the produce before its reception into the warehouse?—I am not aware that any persons have access to it in the London Dock, but those persons who naturally must.

For instance, the carmen?—The carman cannot have access to it in the London Dock, except to that which he is going to load immediately.

They are admitted to the quay where the produce is landed, and therefore the Committee presume, in a state of exposure to plunder; is there any advantage in preventing the access of those persons who are merely coming to receive goods, or whose attendance is not required by business?—No doubt, generally, the access of idle persons to the docks is an inconvenience, and it is restricted as much as possible at the London Dock.

Do you search the carmen when they go out?—Always; the carts are searched and the persons of the carmen also; no person can go out of the dock without a pass.

Mr. Dennis Chapman.

Is there much plunder?—I do not consider that there is any thing in the dock that is worthy of the name of plunder, being so very trifling.

What does happen which you think not worthy of the name of plunder?—Sometimes our gatekeeper discovers a man with trifling things; such things will occur once in two or three weeks, perhaps.

Nothing beyond that has come to your knowledge? —No.

Have you reason to believe, that plunder to any extent has ever been carried on at the London Docks?—I am certain it has not, for the packages themselves would show if they had been plundered, by their loss in weight.

You have said that the most perfect security exists at your docks, and that no plunder whatever takes place from the crews; do you know whether the quays at the London Docks are permitted to be considered as bonded warehouses?—Certainly not.

Do you happen to know why that is?—I do not.

You never open your docks at night, either for craft or to receive any vessel?—Agreeably to the Act of Parliament, no vessel can go out of the dock into the basin after four o'clock; nor can any vessel be received from the river into the basin before or after day-light; there is an Act of Parliament that specially appoints the hours.

Frederick Gibson, Esq.

How many gates are there at the London Docks at which people may go out with goods?—There are only two gates that they can go out in common; one at the East Smithfield end, and the other at the Wapping end; there is a third entrance to the tobacco warehouse.

Is that third entrance exclusively devoted to the tobacco?—Nearly so; officers of the revenue are permitted to pass in and out there.

There are only two entrances at which persons and goods can come in and out of the London Docks besides that?—Only one public entrance for goods to be carted out, or brought in; the other must be by special leave, which is very seldom granted.

Who are stationed at that entrance during the day?—The gate-keepers; there are five revenue gate-keepers and police officers appointed by the Dock Company, some of their own men.

Do the revenue officers search persons coming out of the docks?—If they observe any thing bulky in their pockets, and they frequently take their hats off and examine them.

Do they examine the sailors?—Only in the way I have spoken of; the labourers, when they leave off work, are examined; they often make them take off their shoes.

You know something of the system of the London Dock Company?—I do.

And the officers employed by them?—I have some general knowledge, having been there so long, and the observations I have made.

Are there not watchmen appointed every night in the London Docks?—There are, appointed by the Company.

Are there not watchmen during the day upon the quays?—What they call rounders; I believe they walk about with their staves in their hands; they are superior officers; when packages are opened, they attend very much to them.

Are there always officers of that description on the quays during the day?—Constantly.

Are there always officers of the Company in the warehouses during the day?—Constantly.

Together with some revenue officers?—Yes.

Are goods either tasted or examined either on the quays, or in the warehouses of the London Dock Company, without the presence of a revenue officer and some officer of the Company?—It is hard to answer that question;

the revenue officers are close to the spot; but a person might taste a cask of wine, and perhaps a revenue officer may not be within four or five, or three or four yards; there cannot be an officer placed to each package; they cannot have a cask bunged up but by the Dock Company's cooper.

Is it possible, in your opinion, that any of the goods that are tasted, or examined under those circumstances, can be easily plundered?—I think not; I think it is next to impossible.

Is it impossible that those lying on the quays can?—I think not; there are so many persons present, that I think it next to impossible.

Do you know that the goods are plundered, or made liable to plunder, in consequence of the admission of persons to the quays and the docks?—I do not think they are at all.

Do you think the system established at the London Docks now perfectly sufficient for the protection of the revenue?—I do.

To your knowledge, the revenue suffers no loss from fraud under that system?—None.

Are goods delivered out of the warehouses without an order being signed by the proper revenue officer?—No.

Was not that one of the great evils which existed before the investigation by Mr. Burne?—I think it was.

Has not that been completely remedied by his investigation?—It certainly has; the system that was adopted before Mr. Burne came to those docks was not in itself defective, but the officers who were entrusted with the administration of it neglected their duty, owing to a variety of causes.

Some of the officers were discharged in consequence, were they not?—None that I am aware of; but there was one superseded: if an officer is dismissed, by the standing rules he cannot be received into the service again; but he was superseded, and put into a lower situation, which he now holds.

Do you think it would be safe to allow packages of West India produce, which are landed in a broken state frequently, to remain upon the quay, while a number of persons were swarming about in all directions?—Yes; I should not think any person dare take any of that sugar; it is not like a grocer's shop, when a cask is empty, poor boys are scraping and getting the sugar out; in the docks they would not permit any person to do it.

You are acquainted generally with the system of the West India Dock; with the crews being discharged when the vessel comes in, and not allowed to remain on board; with no persons being permitted to remain upon the quays while they are landing the cargo; and all lighters and craft being excluded at night?—Yes.

If you had your choice of the one system or the other, which would you prefer?—I think where there are no persons of course there can be no plunder.

You would prefer a system in which all those people were excluded, if you had your choice?—Yes; if it were left to me I should say that I should prefer it.

In your opinion, without that degree of perfection, the system of the London Docks is sufficient?—Yes.

And that upon the West India trade the revenue would be sufficiently secured at the London Docks?—I cannot have a doubt of that.

If a man wished to plunder a cask of wine or spirits, must he not bring tools and implements with him in order to get access to its contents?—To any extent he must; a man might just make an incision into a cask, and suck a little out by means of a reed pipe, but he could not draw a quantity of it out without being furnished with proper materials to do it.

Could he make an attempt either with a reed to take out a small quantity, or to take out a larger quantity, with implements, without being noticed among so many bystanders?—It is hardly possible.

Then so far, the circumstance of so many people entering the London Docks, rather prevents than gives additional opportunities of plunder?—I think that an additional security.

Having had great experience of the system of the London Docks, as a merchant, should you require greater security for your property than is afforded by the regulations of those docks, and the manner in which those regulations are generally executed?—No; I think it is perfectly safe.

Mr. Beeby Eilbeck.

You say the docks are surrounded by wooden pales twelve feet high?—Yes.

Are you to be understood to state, that in your judgment that was a sufficient protection of the property?—I believe I observed that the revenue approved of it.

In your judgment, is a fence of wooden pales, twelve feet high, sufficient to protect property of this description, speaking particularly of sugar, from plunder, so as to secure both the revenue and the trader?—Equally so; because if a man is resolved to take down a fence, he can take down a brick wall; we have watchmen in our docks as a protection.

But in your judgment a wooden fence affords equal protection?—I consider it equally so, with the watchmen we have.

R. H. Marten, Esq.

How should you propose to afford a greater security than in the West India Docks?—I do not know that I could say greater security; but there should be as great security as is possible.

Would you exclude other trades?—Not if I needed them.

That would be too great a sacrifice to make to do it?—That is a question which I do not think it is necessary to consider; I do not think they have had temptation enough yet to lead them to that.

How would you prevent plunder to some extent, unless you excluded other trades?—By such vigilance that plunder should be next to impossible in that trade as in any other.

Do you not think the danger of it would be increased if other trades were admitted, and the crews of ships were permitted to remain in?—No, very little more; the difficulty would be to get their plunder away.

The Commercial Dock may be almost said to be completely open, may it not, there is a paling only?—That paling is twelve feet high.

There is no wall in any part of your docks?—There is a wall along the south side.

There is a part of this dock where there is neither wall nor paling, is there not, nothing but a ditch?—At the timber dock; they wanted no paling there; because they could not get the timber over the ground.

One dock opens on into another?—Yes, but they are all wallable.

You contemplate the possibility of erecting a wall all round, when you speak of security?—I do not know that we contemplate getting the trade yet, but the same security might be obtained, as I do not think there is a great deal of security in the walls, when I know they have got bales of muslin over the great East India Dock wall; that they have not only got over that wall themselves, but have got whole bales out; and it is the regulation and good attention which, in my opinion, form the best security.

Should you establish the same system of police?—We have watchmen every night now.

How many?—As many as are thought to be sufficient to be all round the dock; the number is not in my recollection at present, I think somewhere about five or six.

In each dock?—No, on the premises generally; I beg to be understood, as not speaking to the number from my knowledge.

You think there is the same sort of security against plunder, as is afforded at the West India Docks?—I think there would be that security, but if we did not find it to be sufficient, it would be made to be sufficient immediately, if we had the trade; at present we have security sufficient for the trade we have, and if we had other trade that would give a profit, we should provide accordingly.

Alex. Glennie, Esq.

Have you had occasion to land any cargoes at the London Docks?—Yes, but not of sugars; I have landed barilla and coarse articles.

Any other articles?—Wines.

Have you been satisfied with the protection afforded to your property at those docks?—O yes, certainly; and there is another very great satisfaction we have at the London Docks; the directors do not prevent our going and looking at our goods, to see that they are in good order; in the West India Dock, they will never suffer any person to go and inspect his own goods.

Do you consider that a great advantage?—I think it is a great advantage.

Do you think it is calculated to lead to great fraud and depredation?—The advantage of it is this, that we can more certainly speak to the buyer with respect to the condition of the article; if I go and look at the article with my broker, a buyer cannot then say, "Sir, these goods were delivered in bad order;" my broker can speak to the state of them.

Have you ever heard any complaint of the privileges or facilities allowed by the London Dock Company to the merchants with respect to their goods, as having led to great depredation?—No; not within my knowledge. In obtaining their charter, the West India Dock Company laid a great stress upon the saving of plunderage; those very sugars which have been the topic of conversation, were landed in their warehouses on the 14th of September, and delivered on the 25th, and lost, in that time, one of them only three pounds; one of them none; but some of them had lost ten pounds weight in the course of eleven days.

In the West India Dock?—Yes.

That was in the year 1804?—Yes.

Mr. John Lampson.

Do you think that in a dock where the crews of shipping are permitted to remain constantly on board, there is not more liability to plunder than where they are not so permitted?—I do not know from what cause.

The people being there at night?—Unless they remove it out of the ship there can be no plunderage, and I do not know where they can take it to.

Cannot it be put into lighters and other ships?—I am not aware that lighters would be alongside; precautions might be taken to prevent all that in a dock, to prevent the cause of all complaint.

Ships and lighters are near them in the London Docks, are they not?—In the London Dock there are general articles, they are mingled all together.

In the London Docks, ships and lighters remaining there all night, would there not be greater danger than if the crews were excluded?—It could not be conveyed out of the docks, I should imagine; I was never there at night, but I suppose the dock gates are shut.

Could they not be secreted in pockets, and subsequently conveyed out?—By no means; for the dock gates are guarded during the day-time, and persons searched on going out.

Do you know whether lighters are searched?—I cannot speak to that.

Is it not possible to secrete plundered goods in lighters or vessels in the London Docks?—If the same precautions are not used in lighters that pass out of the docks as are in the persons of men and women that pass out, certainly there is a probability that depredation may be committed; but if they have a strict search at the dock gates, in the same way as there is on the land, I think it cannot be done without detection.

Do you, in point of fact, search the carmen at the London Docks?—I never saw them pass any person, with a suspicious appearance, that was not searched; it is not supposed that they search every one, a person could not carry a bulky article without its being seen.

Do they search the carmen?—I never observed that; I have passed in and out, but I do not think that carmen are allowed to go in beyond the dock gates, except with their carts, or to have access to the vessels or the warehouses.

In your opinion, are the cargoes of ships discharging in a place more exposed to plunder when their crews and officers remain on board and work them out, than they are when they are discharged by the day labourers hired by the Dock Company?—That is a question I can hardly speak to with any degree of precision; I am not aware that there would be any great difference.

Mr. John Manning.

Do you consider the property of the merchants as free from plunder in the Commercial Docks as any where else?—Yes, certainly.

During the time you have been an officer of the customs, have you been on duty in the London Docks?—I have, about ten years ago, but very little.

How long a time have you been there?—Perhaps six months or a twelvemonth.

In what situation?—As a landing waiter.

Have you reason to think that the general system of the London Docks afforded sufficient security to the revenue?—It afforded every security, as far as my knowledge went; the goods were invariably landed from the ship, and we consider that the revenue is secured when we have got the contents of the packages at the time of landing, and they were immediately conveyed to the warehouses, if bonded goods, or taken away by the owners of them, if duty paid.

You have nothing to do with the goods till after they have passed the King's beam?—We have to do with them till they have passed the King's beam, if duty paid, and till delivered from the warehouses, if they are bonded goods.

Either before or after their passing have you reason to think that any considerable plunderage has taken place?—

I have never heard of any, and I have no reason to think that any existed to any extent; a little pilfering will exist in all docks, and no doubt it does.

You think there was ample security for the revenue in those docks?—Yes; I am of that opinion certainly.

Thomas Tooke, Esq.

In the London and Commercial Docks you say you have found the business transacted with perfect regularity: have you found that it has been perfectly consistent with the security of the property?—Perfectly so.

Were the articles you have been in the habit of importing into the London Docks, articles of a description that were liable to plunder?—They were liable to plunder; and we had frequent occasion to complain of deficiencies, which we could ascribe only to plunder, previous to the erection of the London Docks.

You have had no such complaints to make in respect of those articles that were imported into the London Docks?—None; so far as I have heard.

Do you conceive, from any knowledge you have of the London Docks, that the regulations of those docks are such as to give sufficient security to the merchant, and protection to the revenue?—I have heard of no complaints; and my house has not experienced any deficiency, with the trifling exception before mentioned, to justify the supposition of any plunderage in the docks.

You have been in the habit of landing your cargoes in those docks ever since they have been erected?—Yes, ever since; some years ago, indeed, there was a small deficiency of flax, as before mentioned, that we had reason to conceive might have been plundered; but it was to a very small amount.

Is that the only deficiency, that in the course of that time you have had reason to observe?—Yes, it is.

Your house is in very considerable business?—We are, I believe, by far the largest importers of Russia goods into the port of London. I mentioned, I believe, that the gross value of goods we landed in the London Docks last year, would exceed £250,000.

Fletcher Wilson, Esq.

You are in the firm of Thomas Wilson and company?—I am.

What is your business?—General merchants.

What trade do you carry on?—We carry on a great deal of American trade, Foreign, West Indies, Baltic trade, trade from Italy and Africa.

In the course of carrying on that trade, have you been in the habit of importing very extensively into the London Docks?—Very.

Are the articles of which any part of that trade consists peculiarly liable to plunder, either from their nature or their value?—We import a great deal of silk into the London Docks, which is a very valuable article, and liable to plunder.

Among that variety of articles, are there not many which from their value afford great temptation to plunder?—Some, very great temptation to plunder.

Are there any which from their usefulness to the lower order of individuals, afford temptation to plunder in the way that sugar and coffee do?—I do not know of any particularly.

Have you had reason to think that merchandize imported by you, of any particular description or quality, has suffered much from plunder at the London Docks?—I do not know of any.

Do you import on commission or on your own account?—Sometimes the one, and sometimes the other.

Which in the greatest degree?—On commission.

Have you had occasion to make complaints on the subject of plunderor loss ?—I do not recollect any.

During what period of time have you been in the habit of importing ?—I have been in that department in the house for about fifteen years.

Have you imported into the West India Dock ?—Frequently.

Have you had any occasion personally to notice the regulations that are observed at the West India and the London Docks ?—The West India Docks are so far from our counting-house, that I have not been there half a dozen times in my life.

As far as you have had occasion to know or observe, has the same protection to your property been given in the London Docks as at the West India Docks ?—I have had no reason to find fault with either.

Are you as much satisfied, in point of convenience, with the regulations of the one as the other ?—In large establishments there are always some inconveniences, but the London Dock regulations are very good ones; I think that both docks are well-regulated establishments.

In point of protection, if you were to draw a comparison, which should you say afforded the greatest, or have you full and adequate protection at both ?—I should think in both we have very adequate protection.

No. VIII.

EXCLUDING CREWS AND APPRENTICES.

John Tilstone, Esq.

At the West India Docks the crews are removed from the ships, and all the goods are discharged by the servants of the company ?—Yes; I have stated in my report, that the crews are taken out on the ships entering the dock.

The West India Docks, in my opinion, have a decided advantage over all the other docks, inasmuch as the ships enter those docks directly from sea; then the ship's hatches are locked down, and only opened during the time the landing-waiter is in attendance; and when the ship is unloaded, the Dock Company, at their expense, rummage the vessel most completely, taking up every particle of sugar or other goods that have been spilt in the discharge of the vessel, all which is charged with duty; that is not the case, I believe, elsewhere. I do not think that it is practicable elsewhere. Then there is another very great advantage which the West India Docks have over the other docks, and that is, all their goods for home consumption are delivered at the back of the warehouses into carts or waggons; so that no carmen or other people can come upon the dock quays, consequently, the merchant's property is not exposed to plunder, nor the revenue to loss.

In your judgment, would that system be practicable, paying due regard to the convenience of the public and the merchant, at other docks to which trades in general were admitted from a distance?—Certainly not; the warehouses are so constructed that they do not admit of such convenience of delivering the goods in the way they are delivered at the West India Docks.

At the London Docks, for instance, what is the course?—The carts and waggons are admitted on the quays, and consequently, there is an influx of people upon the quays.

Persons are also admitted there during the hours of business, for the purpose of a market; it is in fact a market?—Yes, the West India goods are sold by sample.

The samples are brought up to the sugar market?—Sent up to the West India Dock-house.

There is no concourse of persons on the West India

Docks during the hours of business, except those in the immediate employment of the Dock Company ?—In the immediate employment of the Dock Company, or of the revenue.

In your judgment, does that tend materially to protect the property from plunder ?—I think it does most materially ; that is an important regulation.

Would such a rigid system of management as this be practicable, consistently with the fair convenience of the public in general, at the place where trade was admitted promiscuously ?—Certainly not : it could not be practicable in any dock but such as the West India Dock, where the crews were excluded, and the ships' hatches locked, and no person suffered to remain in the docks during the night.

If you enforced such a rigid system of management, with respect to trade in general, would it not operate very injuriously to the ship where there was not that risk, so as to counterbalance the advantage to be derived from this state, which requires special protection ?—Certainly.

In a place confined to this particular species of trade, can you, with advantage to that trade, adopt this system of management, without imposing that rigid restraint on other branches of trade which do not require it ?—Certainly.

You have stated, that the cargoes of ships discharged in those docks, are discharged by persons employed by the Company, and that their crews are not permitted to remain on board the ships ; will you inform the Committee, what description of persons those are who are employed for the discharge of the cargo ?—Common labourers, who are searched on their leaving the dock.

Might not the crews of the ships be employed for that purpose, equally well with common labourers ?—They certainly might be employed in discharging the ships.

Would they not be also liable to be searched, on leaving the docks?—Yes.

Then what advantage, do you conceive, arises from employing the labourers in preference to employing the crews?—I do not know that there is any advantage in employing the labourers instead of the crews.

Are you not aware, that there is the disadvantage of the crews being sent adrift, and exposed to idle habits in the mean time?—Certainly, they must be exposed to idle habits during the time they are out of employ.

As the crews, if retained in the ships, must be entitled to wages, although thus thrown idle, would it not be a considerable saving to the owners, if they were employed in discharging the ships?—If they have to pay them, certainly it must be an advantage to the owners, to be able to employ them.

Mr. Thomas Burne.

In your judgment, is it safer to the revenue to lump that sugar out by means of the labourers of the docks, than it would be by means of the crew?—I should suppose they would get it out in much less time; I have no doubt of that.

Would there be any difference as to plunderage, in your opinion?—Probably not, in the dock, there are so many officers always superintending.

Are you of opinion that seamen, under the direction of their captain and officers, would be more likely to plunder, than the individuals who are employed as labourers by any of the Dock Companies?—That is a question I cannot answer; there may be honest sailors as well as honest labourers, and I have no doubt there are; but there certainly is not the same controul.

Are persons going in and out of the West India Docks liable to search?—Yes; and also at the London Docks.

Thomas Groves, Esq.

Does the exclusion of the crew from the ship, during the time the ship is in the West India Dock, produce any inconvenience to the owner of the ship, which is not more than compensated by the advantage to the revenue, and the security to the merchant?—I should think the turning the crew out of the ship, in the West India Docks, is no inconvenience to the owner; the ship is guarded, the merchant's cargo is guarded and protected. I am not aware of any inconvenience that ensues from it.

Does the exclusion of the crew from the ship and from the docks, tend to the security of the ship against fire?—I should think so, there is no fire allowed.

There is no fire allowed to be on board the ships at night?—No, none at all.

In other places, where the crews are not excluded, is there fire permitted on board those ships at night?—Yes, there is.

That is of necessity?—Yes.

In those cases also, where the crews are permitted to remain on board the ship, is it necessary to have revenue officers on board the ship at night?—Certainly.

Is that necessary at the West India Docks?—Not at all; all are excluded.

Is that a saving of expense?—Certainly, it is a great saving of expense.

Is it also a saving from the risk of plunder, by the persons who might be themselves the watchmen?—I think it is.

Do I understand you, that the exclusion of all persons, except those in the employment of the Company, from the docks, is a material circumstance towards the security of the revenue, and of the property of the merchant?—

Yes, that added to its surrounding walls; the surrounding walls afford a great protection, and preclude the possibility of getting to the warehouses privately.

In addition to that, do you consider the exclusion of persons not in the employment of the Company, as a material circumstance, tending to the security of the revenue and the merchant?—Yes, I think it does increase the security.

Henry Longlands, Esq.

Is not the pay of the seaman responsible for any plunder that may take place during the discharge of the cargo? —I do not know.

If so, is not that a strong security for the integrity of his conduct?—I should think it would not operate as any restraint upon him, especially in the plunder of spirits, for instance.

You think they would plunder though they were liable to pay for plundering, and have their wages mulcted for so doing?—I certainly do.

You have stated the number of persons who are regularly employed by the West India Dock Company, they limit the number to those for whom they have regular and constant occupation as nearly as they can?—As nearly as they can, they do; but I do not mean to say that the whole of that number are so fully occupied at particular seasons of the year as they are at others.

But at particular seasons of the year, when you have the greatest number of ships discharging, do you not find it necessary to hire a number of occasional labourers?—We do; and there are persons connected with the establishment that have been so hired, as extra labourers, for fifteen, sixteen, and seventeen years continually; persons that are well known in character, and in every respect.

Do you not hire men occasionally by the hour?—No; the shortest period of time for which we take any man, is for half a day.

Will any respectable man hire himself for half a day, at a certainty of being unemployed the other half day, if he can possibly avoid it?—I am sorry to say that I see frequent instances of very respectable men, and I am still more sorry to say, of well-educated men, who are happy to get half a day's work at those docks.

Do not the most respectable labourers find constant employment, and the least respectable ones submit to this kind of extra occupation?—That does not follow; in the case of coopers, for instance, there are periods when we employ 300 coopers; we cannot afford to keep a permanent establishment equal to that, or to a tenth part of it; but there are among those 300 coopers as good workmen, and as respectable individuals as any in the trade; and as I before stated, there are an immense number of those extra coopers who have regularly served the Company, season after season, for sixteen and seventeen years.

The question applied to common labourers; what do you pay them for a half day's work?—Eighteen pence.

Do you mean to state that you are able to ascertain the good character of all those labourers employed in this manner, and at those rates?—Certainly not; but I mean to state this, that I think there are at least 200 and more of those extra labourers who will be known to our officers, both as to honesty and industry.

Do you think those men, whose character you say you cannot always know, are more to be depended upon for integrity than the seamen and apprentices of vessels, under the superintendence and control of their proper officers?—I do not know that they are; but I think they are much more competent, under the control and superintendence of the experienced officers the Company place over them, to do the duty required in those docks.

Would not the Company's officers have the same superintendence over the crews and apprentices on board vessels, as they have over those men whom they now employ?—Certainly not; they would not know them.

William Mitchell, Esq.

Do you consider one of the restraints upon which part of that security to the property of the planters is founded, to be that of excluding the crews of the vessels from the docks?—I do.

Do you think that the extra men employed in the West India Docks, who take the chance of being hired for half a day, are less likely to plunder than the crews and apprentices of the ships would be?—I should think so; because these men are almost the whole of them known at the different departments at which they work: and they know, in cases of misconduct, that they are never employed again; and there is that system of check and search going on, which you could not exercise with irresponsible persons, that must certainly produce greater safety.

Is that a proof of your confidence in those persons, that you have them all searched twice a day?—It is not a proof of our mistrust; certainly it is one of those regulations which must be submitted to, whether you know a man to be an honest man or dishonest one.

Do you mean to state that you do know the character of many of those extra men whom you employ?—I should think from the length of time that a great number of them have been employed at the docks, it is quite impossible but that the principal officers of the docks must be, in a great measure, acquainted with their characters.

Do you not take men by chance when you want them,

who when they rise in the morning do not know where they shall dine at noon, or sleep at night, but merely take the chance of being hired at the dock gates?—During the period of war, or even during the period when an easterly wind has kept a great number of West India ships out, they arrive in considerable fleets, we are only then obliged to take persons we are not in the habit of constantly employing, or giving occasional employment to, and so far we cannot know the character of those persons.

Do you think property safer in the care of those people than it would be in the care of seamen, whose future employ depends upon the character they receive from the master of the ship whom they last served, who would be under the control of their own officers, and the superintendence of the dock officers and revenue officers?—Judging from what I have heard, with respect to the seamen on board West Indiamen, and also from what is the practice, of what would be the benefit to the owners of West India shipping, I should certainly say, in the first place, that that description of seaman is not the person I would rely upon in preference; and in the next place, that I think, if the owners of West Indiamen were to be allowed to lump out their own ships, they would not do so with their own crew.

Is not the pay of the seaman, being responsible for any plunder he may commit, a security you have not with your labourers?—I believe the crew are bound to remain on board the ship till she is finally discharged; but I understand the owners of West Indiamen are so fully convinced of the impolicy of keeping their seamen on board their ships, that they get rid of them immediately upon their arrival, and that therefore there can be no possible tie between the seamen of the ship and the owners.

Is it likely that the owners of ships, who complain of

their crews being turned out, would not employ them if they remained on board ?—If I may allude to the conversations I have had with several ship-owners and brokers in the West India trade, it is my opinion they do not now complain.

Is it not likely that the crews of ships who load the cargoes would break them out and discharge them more expertly than common labourers ?—I should certainly think not; because those seamen do not at all times load the ship; when the ship gets out to the West Indies it very frequently happens that many of those men leave the ship, and it also very frequently happens (I see it in my own accounts) that charges are made for the hire of persons to load the ship, or assist in loading; and when she arrives in the West India Docks, the vessel is then unloaded by persons who have had experience in unloading ships for a number of years, and therefore I think it must be done much better by such labourers than the seamen of the vessel. I am speaking only as to West Indiamen.

George Hibbert, Esq.

If the crews were permitted to remain on board the ship, and to assist in the discharge of the cargo, do you think the risk of plunder would be increased ?—I beg to say, that having at different times been the owner, or part owner, of eight ships in the West India trade, I never did yet discharge a ship by means of the crew.

What was your reason for that ?—In many cases it was impossible; in war time, for instance, it was quite out of the question; in peace, it was not the practice; the homeward crew in general left the ship upon her coming to her moorings.

Then you are understood to say, that in the West India

trade, it has not been the practice?—I know nothing of such a system: but I should not have thought it eligible.

But if the crew were permitted to remain on board the ship, after her arrival in the docks, do you think the cargo would be protected from plunderage?—Am I to understand the question as to discharge in a dock or in the river.

The question is meant to apply to discharge in a dock? —I should think the risk of plunderage would be increased by suffering the crew to remain on board.

Mr. John Drinkald.

You consider the discharge of the crew as a measure of importance?—Certainly.

Do you, as a ship-owner, consider that it would be impossible to adopt that in the general trade of the port? —I do.

Do you know whether the fact, that the London Dock keep the crew on board, is the reason why they will not open their docks at night?—I suspect it to be that and nothing else, and that they are fearful of plunderage from those they might let in, in the night, in the craft.

Would the officers of the docks have a control, do you conceive, over the crew, if the crew were to discharge the vessel?—The crew generally leave our vessels; the short trade is very different from the long voyages, there are some two or three men might remain by the ship, and then the London Dock Company find men themselves: and they charge so much per day for them; in the ships I had formerly in the Portugal trade, we had no command at all over them.

The officers of the London Dock Company have no control over the crews?—Certainly, none at all.

Have the officers of the ship any control over the labourers ?—None; the dock officers are their masters; I paid once for the neglect of the London Dock officers for nearly two pipes of wine, for neglect by men that were employed by them.

John Inglis, Esq.

Have you such an item of expenditure as a naval school ?—No, certainly, we have no occasion; our apprentices are kept on board ship, and sent by their masters to school in the neighbourhood, in the day-time.

Is not that an expense incurred by shutting out the crews from the docks ?—Yes, certainly; I consider that of the crews being kept on board the vessel to be of very great importance to the protection of the seamen and the apprentices, and to the nursery of the seamen for the navy. The school is a very good institution, I believe; but I fancy the maximum of persons embracing the benefits of that school, at any one time, has not exceeded above 350; I get my information from masters of ships. The West India ships are compelled by Act of Parliament to carry an apprentice to every hundred tons; and if five hundred ships enter the docks in a year, of 300 tons average, that would be 1,500 tons, and there must be 1,500 apprentices attached to that tonnage by Act of Parliament. The school can give accommodation only to 350; the remainder are turned loose upon the public during the time they are at home, and exposed to every sort of mischief that can happen to young men in such circumstances.

You have never heard of an instance of plunder taking place at all by the crews or persons connected with the ships, in consequence of their being permitted to be on board ?—I am not acquainted with any.

Are you now of opinion, from that circumstance, that

the masters and mates, and men, and the carmen and lightermen, are men that may be trusted?—Masters of ships certainly may be trusted, and the mates of the ships I consider as confidential persons, but the carmen can have nothing to do with the unloading of the ship; the seamen may, but they have no opportunity of disposing of their plunder; if they were to make it, they cannot carry it out of the dock.

Your dock is both an export and an import dock?—Yes.

And vessels discharging cargoes, and vessels loading to go away, must frequently lie close by the side of each other; a vessel loading for exportation must lie alongside of a vessel that is discharging an imported cargo?—That is not the practice; the outward bound vessels are put in one part of the dock, and those delivering their cargoes in another part of the dock; it is possible, when empty, they may lie alongside each other, but the empty vessels are generally removed from the quay.

Do you mean to state, that no vessels loading for exportation, ever lie alongside of vessels discharging imported cargoes?—I am not aware of it.

Are you able to state distinctly that there is any regulation which prevents its taking place?—I can only state generally, that the convenience of business would prevent it; the practical officers at the dock would state the fact, but I cannot.

If custom-house officers, one of whom has the superintendence of all the docks, have stated that that has taken place, are you so well acquainted with your own docks as to state that he is mistaken in that?—I rather think so; but the Committee will have better evidence upon that than mine.

The crews in the foreign vessels, and in the short voyages, remain on board?—Yes, no doubt.

Of course, in the day-time, they may pass backwards and forwards from one vessel to the other?—There is nothing to prevent it.

Then, what is to prevent a seaman, belonging to a ship, carrying with him any thing that he may have pilfered from the vessel to which he belongs, to any other vessel that may be in the dock, outward bound, empty?—There are always custom-house officers on board to prevent any thing being removed out of the vessel.

Do you mean to state, that every man who goes in and out of a vessel is searched every time he goes in and out?—Certainly, it is the duty of the custom-house officers to see that he carries nothing out of the ship.

If he had any thing in his hand that belonged to the ship the custom-house officer would of course prevent his removing it?—He would examine what it was.

But if a man has plunder concealed about him, do you mean to state that the custom-house officers can, by any care they can take, prevent men plundering, and carrying plunder off with them of a variety of articles?—I do not see that it is practicable, I do not know where they are to go with it, they cannot go out of the dock gate with it.

May they not carry it to an empty ship?—There has been an experiment tried to see whether it could be done, the officers of the customs have been let in to examine all the ships in the night, on a suspicion that it might exist, but nothing of the kind was discovered.

You have stated that you think there is a great advantage to the morals of the crew in their remaining on board?—I have, and I have no doubt of it as a ship-owner.

Being acquainted with West India ships, was it the

practice before the docks were created, or at any time since, for the crews to remain on board after their return?—The officers and the apprentices always remained on board, the crews were generally discharged.

Mr. Dennis Chapman.

Have you reason to believe, that plunder to any extent has ever been carried on at the London Docks?—I am certain it has not, for the packages themselves would show if they had been plundered, by their loss in weight.

It is not the practice to exclude the crews from the London Dock?—They are permitted to go in and out if they think proper.

There it is optional to discharge the crews, or to continue them on board?—Yes, certainly so.

If the ship-owner chooses to discharge his crew, the Dock Company can always furnish him with labourers to unload his vessel?—Yes, we can furnish them with men to unload under the direction of their officer.

Those who like to employ their own crew do so, and those who prefer discharging by the Company's servants have that option?—Just so.

After the gates are locked at night, are the crews allowed to go in and out?—Not after the wicket gate is shut; there are certain hours appointed by the Lords of the Treasury for shutting the wicket gate, at this time it is eight o'clock, after that time no person is allowed to go in or out.

Have you any reason to believe that the revenue is sufficiently secured at the London Dock?—I believe perfectly so, in every respect.

Do you recollect any cargoes being plundered by the seamen and crews of the ships in your dock?—I do not recollect a circumstance of the kind.

In that case can you suppose plunder would be prevented by constantly employing labourers to discharge, instead of employing the crew?—I should certainly think the crew as honest as the labourers; I should consider one set of men as honest as the other.

Do you not think that labourers, if disposed to plunder, have greater facilities than seamen for so doing, in consequence of the connections they naturally have in the neighbourhood where they reside; that they can find receivers more easily than the others?—I should consider it impossible for a labourer in the employ of the Dock Company to get any thing out of the dock, for they are very strictly searched by the officers before they leave the warehouse; and if any thing escapes the officer, which sometimes occurs, but very rarely, the gate-keepers are able to find out, and have found out even so small a quantity as two or three ounces of produce.

Frederick Gibson, Esq.

In your opinion, does the permission of the crews to remain on board, give rise to any plunderage of the goods brought into the docks?—If it does at all, it is to a very trifling extent; a man cannot carry out a package, merely a little, in his pocket.

In your opinion, does a system where the crews, together with the revenue officers, remain on board, they not being allowed to leave their ships at night, and watchmen being employed on the quays, fully protect the property?—Fully, in my opinion.

How long have you been employed in the London Docks?—From the first opening of them to the present time.

Is the opinion you have expressed derived from the experience you have had from the beginning of the establishment?—It is.

You are acquainted generally with the system of the West India Dock; with the crews being discharged when the vessel comes in, and not allowed to remain on board; with no persons being permitted to remain upon the quays while they are landing the cargo; and all lighters and craft being excluded at night?—Yes.

If you had your choice of the one system or the other, which would you prefer?—I think where there are no persons of course there can be no plunder.

You would prefer a system in which all those people were excluded, if you had your choice?—Yes; if it was left to me I should say that I should prefer it.

In your opinion, without that degree of perfection the system of the London Docks is sufficient?—Yes.

There are some ships that may either come into the London Docks or the West India Docks?—Yes, they may; and the ships from the Brazils always.

Do you know any reason why those ships should prefer coming to the London Docks, rather than the West India Docks, unless there was some preference in point of security, or charge, or convenience?—I imagine it arises in a great measure from the convenience; if they went to the West India Docks, they must part with their crew.

Mr. William Sawtell.

Are you acquainted with the system at the West India Docks?—I have acted there as landing-waiter.

You are aware, that in that dock, the crew are discharged from the vessels, and that there are some other differences between the system adopted at the London and at the West India Dock?—Yes.

To which of those two systems should you give the

preference as a revenue officer?—I do not see that I could give the preference to either; I think great accommodation is afforded in each; I do not see how I could give the preference to either.

Should you not say that the discharging the crews at the West India Docks was a means of giving greater security to the property deposited there?—No.

Mr. Beeby Eilbeck.

Having commanded a vessel in the West India trade, is, in your opinion, greater security given by discharging vessels in the docks by means of common labourers, than would be given by discharging them by the officers and people on board?—I should think that the common labourers are so closely watched there, they could do it with the same security as other people; they are searched on going down and coming up again.

By subjecting the crews to the same mode of search, do you think any additional risk of plunder would be incurred by suffering them to discharge?—I do not think they could, for every hatch is locked down after the legal hours.

As a master of a ship, if all the docks were opened, that you might go into each of them, by what should you be led to prefer one dock to another?—I do not know that it would make any difference with me as the master of a ship, except at the West India Dock the turning the boys ashore, which I consider affects their morals a good deal; no master of a ship likes that; in the London Docks you keep them on board.

Are there any conveniences attending the West India Docks that would induce you to prefer them to the London Docks?—That of being obliged to send all the apprentices to lodgings would induce me to prefer the London Docks to them, for there I could keep them on board.

Mr. John Lampson.

You consider that the keeping the crews on board is a security for the preservation of the cargo, but you do not consider it necessary?—No; I do not consider that they preserve the cargo.

What effect would it have in making the cargo more or less safe?—If they were allowed to pass in and out of the dock, after a certain hour, they might carry away small quantities, which might in the whole be considerable.

They are not allowed to pass at the London Dock at all hours, are they?—I do not know the night regulations; we are never on duty after four o'clock.

Not at the London Docks?—Not as belonging to the landing department; we have nothing further to do with the regulations after that.

Generally speaking, do you think the security to the revenue is as great in the London Docks as it is in the West India Docks?—I have no reason to think otherwise.

No. IX.

CLASSIFICATION OF COMMODITIES.

John Tilstone, Esq.

Is it not necessary for the convenience of the docks themselves, and various other reasons, that in every dock whatever, a certain degree of classification should take place?—Yes; which is the case at the West India Docks.

Is it not equally necessary in every dock, that that should be the case?—Yes; I think it is.

That is applicable to different warehouses; that is,

that goods of different descriptions are distributed in different warehouses?—Yes, or in different floors, parts of the same warehouse.

Supposing that same classification to take place in other docks, does it not afford all the security to the revenue, that can be afforded by the West India Docks? —It must afford similar facility under equally strict regulations.

Then the same description of goods, in any other dock to which the same regulations are applied, would be equally secure as they are in the West India Docks?—Yes, if similar regulations were adopted.

Mr. Thomas Burne.

In a dock where there are a great variety of articles, as in the London Dock, is not a certain degree of classification in the warehouses necessary?—I should think it would be of advantage to have them always classed.

Classed in different warehouses?—There are articles of the same kind in almost every warehouse.

In every dock in which there is an importation of a great variety of articles, must not a degree of classification be necessarily observed, with a view to a regulation of the conduct of the business?—I should think so.

Would that classification naturally take place, by placing goods of different descriptions in different warehouses?—Certainly; the greater number of one article in one warehouse, the better.

If that were the case, might not the regulations be such, with respect to these particular warehouses, as to give the same security to the revenue or to the merchant, as he could obtain by classification in particular docks?—I do not understand the question.

One of the advantages of the West India Dock, is,

that it produces a classification of different articles?—Yes.

Is not a greater degree of classification necessary in every dock in which there is a variety of articles?—Yes, I should think so.

If they were placed in those warehouses under proper regulations, does not that classification give the same security to the revenue, that the classification in docks would do?—The only objection is, that as the duties are not paid on the deficient quantity, they may plunder to any extent, and there may be no means of preventing it.

Might not the same security be obtained, by classification in different warehouses, as in different docks?—I suppose it might, if the regulations were good.

W. Mitchell, Esq.

Are not East India sugars landed in the East India Docks?—I believe they are.

Are not Brazil sugars landed either in the London or the West India Docks, at the option of the importer? They are confined to those two docks; but I do not know how far it is in the option of the importer.

Is not East India coffee landed in the East India Docks?—I believe it is.

And Brazil coffee in the London Docks?—I believe so.

Is not cotton landed in the East India and London Docks?—I believe so.

Then none of these staple articles of West India produce are landed in the West India Docks exclusively?—The East India cotton and coffee is not from the West of course; the Brazil coffee, which may be considered to be from the West Indies, is landed in the London Docks.

All these commodities are to be found in more docks than one, sugar, coffee, and cotton?—Cotton may be found in more docks than one; coffee may be found in more docks than one.

And sugar in the manner described?—Yes.

Then the classification of none of these commodities is complete as being in any one particular dock?—Certainly not; only the classification from particular countries.

Is not the object of classification answered as well by keeping them in separate warehouses as it would be by keeping them in separate docks?—I should think hardly as well; it might be done in separate departments of the same docks certainly, but then it would require that those docks should be adapted for that purpose.

Do you not keep separate commodities in separate warehouses in the West India Docks now?—We do.

Do you find that answer every sufficient purpose of classification?—We do; but I should state also, that the different articles of West India produce are subject to different duties, these are the British plantation duties; with respect to cotton, coffee, and sugar, housed at other docks, they are subject to a different description of duty from those articles housed at the West India Docks.

But those articles, not the produce of the British plantations, are kept in your docks in distinct warehouses?—Yes, they are.

And that answers every purpose of classification?—I have heard no complaint of any sort.

Mr. Charles Stuart.

Does not the practicability of keeping commodities separate, depend upon the number of warehouses any set of docks may have upon their premises?—I should think so.

Then if a greater variety of commodities came, for instance, to the London Docks, it would only require a greater number of warehouses, in order to give every requisite accommodation?—Perfectly so.

If sufficient warehouses were not already built, others

might be built, upon the premises of the London Dock Company, might they not?—Possibly they might; and if the same system was adopted, as at the West India Docks, the same facility might be afforded.

John Inglis, Esq.

Is not a system of classification of articles admitted into the London Docks, adopted there?—Certainly, that is studied by the persons who have to take care of the goods, how to classify them; but we probably have come into the London Docks from one hundred and fifty to two hundred different articles of merchandize; they are classified in the warehouses, as well as they can be, to the satisfaction of the merchant.

You could classify sugar and other articles, if admitted into the London Docks?—So far as we have a portion of that trade at present, the Brazil trade, we do do it.

In your opinion, does your mode of classification answer all the purposes of classification?—I never heard a complaint of it.

Frederick Gibson, Esq.

Articles, in general, in the London Docks are classified?—As nearly as they can be; but they are so miscellaneous it is impossible to separate them entirely, Russian goods by themselves, and German goods by themselves, and cochineal in a place by itself, and opium, and so on.

Is that classification sufficient for all the purposes of the revenue?—Quite so.

In your opinion, such goods as are imported into the West India Docks could be classified, sufficiently for all the purposes of the revenue, equally well if brought into the London Docks?—There are so few there, I dare say they keep them separately; there is no doubt coffee could be kept by itself, if in our docks, and the Brazil sugars by themselves, and so on; there are some warehouses entirely filled with cotton, others entirely filled with sugars.

No. X.

DISPATCH IN LANDING CARGOES.

John Tilstone, Esq.

Has the system adopted there, in your judgment, protected the revenue?—Most completely.

Has it protected the merchants?—Certainly.

Has it facilitated the discharge of cargoes?—Most assuredly; ships are now discharged, as stated in my report, on an average in five days; formerly the average might have been taken at a month at the least; consequently the expense was very great then, in comparison to what it is now, to all parties.

You have stated to the Committee, that the dispatch, in discharging ships at the West India Docks, is remarkably good; have you not known instances of ships being detained there, waiting for their turns to be discharged?—Certainly I have, some years ago.

Have you not, within the last two years, known such to be the fact, at particular periods?—If the entries were complete, I am not aware of any detention which has occurred; sometimes application is made for ships to begin to discharge when their entry is not complete, and then, by law, the ship cannot break bulk.

Have you not known instances in which the ship was ready to discharge, but she had to wait for her turn so to do?—Not for several years. I am not aware of any such occurrence, except during the combination of the coopers last year.

You have known such instances in former years?—Certainly; during the war, when the ships came in in fleets, there was such a glut they must wait for their turn.

If such a state of things should arise again, would it not be advantageous to the trade, that other docks should be provided?—In such times, fifty ships have been discharging the same day.

If other docks had at that time existed, where those ships could have been discharging, would it not have been a convenience and advantage to their owners?—It would have been a convenience, but I am not sure how far it would be for their advantage, or the safety of the property.

In the present state of the West India trade, are the accommodations provided such as afford immediate dispatch to all ships as they arrive?—Yes; complete dispatch is afforded to all ships whatever.

Supposing the accommodations now provided had existed during the war, at the period to which you have referred, would they have been sufficient to provide for the immediate discharge of all ships as they then arrived, without detention?—I cannot say that they would.

Then, if such a state of things were again to arise, the accommodation provided at the West India Docks would not be sufficient to meet such an exigency?—The accommodations are certainly much greater than they were; and, as fifty ships can be discharging at the same time, greater accommodation can be afforded now than formerly.

If the accommodation now existing, had existed at the period to which you refer, would that have met the exigency of that time?—It would.

Have you not known, during the war, that such a number as about three hundred sail of West India ships have arrived within the short period of ten or fourteen days of each other?—No, not so many.

How many have you known arrive, within such a period?—I cannot speak with any degree of certainty; perhaps from an hundred and fifty to two hundred ships; then they were daily coming in; constantly arriving.

How many can be discharging, at the present time, at once?—Fifty ships.

You have stated the exact time now employed in discharging a cargo at the West India Docks; can you state how that is, as compared with the same in any other dock?—No; because the cargoes are of so very different a nature, that no comparison can be drawn between the two.

Mr. John Drinkald.

Are the dispatch and the care at the London Docks at all equal to the care and dispatch at the West India Docks?—I generally find, that I can get as much done in one hour at the West India Docks, as I can in three at the London Docks.

In the present state of the London Docks, do you conceive that they could generally receive, cooper, discharge, and house the West India trade?—They have not the accommodation, certainly; a very small portion indeed would throw them into confusion; I have experienced it in ships going to the Baltic that have come from the West Indies; a vessel that I have had discharged in two days in the West India Dock, has gone into the London Dock, coming from the Baltic, and they have been eight or nine days, in the way they have conducted it there.

Mr. Charles Stuart.

Are you acquainted with the course of business at the West India and London Docks?—I am, with the course of business at both of them.

You have been so from their first establishment?—Perfectly so.

Be so good as to state what your opinion is, with respect to the facility with which cargoes can be unloaded at those two establishments?—I think the West India Docks, from the vast extent of ground that they occupy, and the system that is adopted, has brought the whole to a state as near perfection as it is almost possible; I should give the preference, certainly, to the West India Docks for expedition.

Do you think cargoes are more expeditiously discharged there?—Most assuredly.

What is the nature of the system adopted at that dock?—It is very peculiar, and I do not think it can be surpassed.

Do you think they could be discharged with equal facility and dispatch at the London Dock, or a dock constituted as that is?—I do not, because the property is not kept separate.

Nathaniel Domett, Esq.

Did any vessel, of which you were master or owner, ever discharge in the London Docks?—Several; I had a brig that delivered in the London Docks, ten or a dozen years ago.

Did you command her at that time?—No.

From what authority do you speak of the dispatch given in discharging vessels in the London Docks?—I have been down there, as an idler, for an hour or two, and I see that they do not discharge the ships so quickly as they do in the West India Docks; we had a brig belonging to us, in the summer of 1820, that entered the West India Docks, and from the time they commenced unloading her, till she was entirely cleared, did not exceed nine hours and one quarter; she had three hundred casks in her, two hundred and seventy hogsheads of sugar, and thirty tierces or puncheons.

That answer proves that very great dispatch is given in the West India Docks, but proves nothing as to the want of dispatch in the London Docks; the question refers to the dispatch given there?—I can only repeat, that from what I have witnessed, they do not use so much dispatch in the London Docks, as in the West India Docks.

John Inglis, Esq.

You are of course perfectly acquainted with the system upon which the London Docks are conducted?—Yes.

Does that system tend to promote dispatch in the discharge of the cargoes?—Yes, it does; but I must observe that, in consequence of the variety of articles which are landed at the London Docks, from the attendance that is required of revenue-officers, and other circumstances, it cannot be compared to the sort of dispatch given to a single article or two at the West India Docks.

Still the dispatch given at the London Docks is a benefit to the trade?—Certainly it is.

Mr. Dennis Chapman.

The Committee have been told, that, on some occasions, you do not unload ships with the same dispatch they do at the West India Docks?—That will depend entirely upon the cargo of the ship: if the ship comes from America with rice and cotton, which are articles of the same kind as those which are discharged at the West India Dock, we can discharge them fully as quick as the West India Dock Company can; if the cargo consists of great varieties, such as hemp, flax, tallow, bristles, and things of that description from the Baltic, it requires a longer time; ships in the Mediterranean trade, with silk and things of that description from Leghorn, would require still longer time, for they require more strict examination.

If you were to dismiss the crews, as they do at the West India Docks, and uniformly employ your own labourers in the discharge of ships, could you in that case discharge them with more dispatch?—In some cases I think we could do so.

The Brazil ships have pretty generally used your docks?—I believe invariably; I do not believe there has one gone from us.

Can you state what particular circumstances there may be about your docks, which have induced the Brazil ships to come there in preference to any other?—From the facility afforded them by the docks, their crews remaining on board the ships, and they find, I conceive, more dispatch than in going to the West India Docks.

Do you take upon yourself to say, that they find greater dispatch at your docks than they would at the West India Docks?—I consider so, or they would give the West India Docks the preference; if they could get better dispatch any where else, they would not come to us, or pay us more than they do at the other docks.

What is the average time you take to discharge a Brazil ship of 300 tons?—About five days.

You mean to commit yourself to that being the average time?—It depends upon what the cargo is; there are a great many circumstances arise in our dock that do not in the West India Dock; in the first place, the King's duties are not ascertained in the same manner as in the West India Dock; in the West India Dock, if a hogshead of sugar comes up, the lowest weight is a four pounds weight used at the West India Dock; in ours they weigh with a one pound weight, they try it two or three times first with a two pound weight, and then another one pound, and probably they will take four or five minutes in weighing a cask.

Do you think that there is greater means of accuracy at your docks in weighing than at the West India Docks?—Yes, they weigh a large package only with a four pounds, and a small package with a two, in the West India Docks; they invariably use a one pound weight in our dock.

Are there any other circumstances which you know of that would make a difference between the discharging of a vessel at your dock and at any other?—That is the principal one, the slow weighing; we can certainly discharge a vessel as quickly as the West India Dock people can.

Is not the circumstance you have mentioned, a means of delay?—Certainly, very much so.

Then what means have you of stating that you can discharge so quickly as the West India Dock?—I stated that there are particular causes of delay, and this I stated as one.

Do you mean to state that you can discharge as quickly at your docks, notwithstanding this cause, as they can at the West India Docks?—No, I stated that we could discharge as quickly at our dock as they could at the West India Dock, provided the revenue was ascertained in the same manner.

But the fact is, you do not discharge so quickly?—We cannot, in consequence of those circumstances.

Are you aware what is the average time in which a vessel of that burthen would be discharged in the West India Docks?—I suppose they would not be above five days in discharging it; five or six days.

Have you any means of knowing that by personal observation?—No.

When you say you can discharge as quickly at the London Docks as they can at the West India Docks, you are merely speaking as an officer of the London Docks, without any particular means of knowledge?—I have not the least doubt in the world upon it; prior to my entering the service of the London Dock Company, I had for twenty-four years the management of the largest water-side concern there was on the legal quays.

When was that?—From the time of the riots in the year 1780, to the time I entered the London Dock Company's service.

You conceive the experience you had of the discharge at the legal quays, before the opening of the docks, is a fair criterion of your knowledge upon this subject?—Certainly.

Then if you derive your knowledge from those two circumstances, will you state whether you know any thing of the dispatch with which a West India cargo is at present discharged in the West India Docks?—Only from what other persons have told me, not from my own knowledge; I have heard Mr. Groves of the Excise, and other gentlemen speak of the dispatch.

When you say that greater dispatch is given in landing the cargoes of vessels by labourers than by the crews, do you not take into consideration that a greater number of labourers are employed on board a ship than the crew of that ship would consist of?—I certainly do, because we should not spare labourers; we should put as many men as could possibly keep at work on board, that we may keep our own men well employed; the object of a couple of men on board a ship is nothing to the loss of time on shore, it would more than pay.

No. XI.

HOUSING AND SAMPLING SUGAR.

Wm. Mitchell, Esq.

Have you never read or heard of a complaint made to the directors, that originated in a general meeting of the wholesale grocers of this metropolis, about the year 1810, as to the mode of warehousing and sampling sugars?—There was a representation upon the subject made, and which received, as I have been informed, the mature consideration of the directors.

What was the result of that consideration; did they redress the complaint made?—I am quite unable to speak to more than the fact of the representation having been made.

George Hibbert, Esq.

Is it not far more convenient to the West India Dock Company, and attended with far less trouble and expense, to draw the samples of the sugar at once, when they are landed, and are most conveniently situated for drawing, than to postpone the drawing till they are all housed in your warehouses?—I am confident that was not the consideration which led to the law.

Is it not a fact?—I do not know; I am confident that was not the consideration which led to the enactment; the consideration which led to the enactment was, the security of the property.

How could the security of the property be endangered

by drawing the samples in the warehouses, where none but your own people, and the officers of the revenue, are admitted?—I should imagine, by the necessity of frequent access to particular warehouses, for drawing samples of particular sugars, and the necessity on some occasions, of removing the casks for that purpose; besides, by the mode in which the sugars are housed in the West India Dock warehouses, which is also complained of by the grocers; the present mode of drawing the sample (which I believe to be a very fair one), could not then be adopted.

You stated, in your answer to the grocers, that about seven pounds greater loss would take place in drainage to the planters, if their system was adopted, of suffering all the molasses to exude from the cask?—Give me leave to say, I quoted that from their petition which was presented to the House of Commons; they state, unequivocally, that if the sugar were housed as they recommend, the casks would upon the average lose seven pounds in weight, but that the sugar would be the better for it.

Does not that molasses, when the cask is rolled over, necessarily mix with, and deteriorate the great body of the sugar?—It is very possible the sugar might be better for losing seven pounds; but I think that if all the sugars at the port are submitted to a regulation which prevents their losing seven pounds, that is still a better thing.

Does not that depend upon the number of complaints to which this practice leads, and the allowances which are necessarily made in consequence of them?—Yes; it must depend upon the balance of conveniences and inconveniences, certainly; upon the result of such a comparison, my own opinion is, that the balance on making out such an account, would be very largely in favour of the present system.

However, no redress was ever given to the grocers on any of those complaints?—No alteration took place in the mode of drawing, or the mode of housing, because, though the grocers were referred to the proprietors and consignees upon the subject, no instructions upon that subject came from the consignees or proprietors; but on the contrary, a confirmation of their opinion, that the present plan was the best.

You have been asked some questions with respect to the sampling of sugars; have you had any complaint or remonstrance upon that subject, from any persons concerned in the trade; and if you have had, have these complaints been attended to?—In the year 1808, we received a memorial from the grocers, and other buyers of sugars, upon that subject, and within a very short time after receiving it, the court of directors transmitted their answer, which answer, if the Committee will permit me, I will deliver in, understanding the same complaint has been lately renewed, and conceiving that the answer, which I now deliver, will be deemed by the Committee to be very much to the purpose.

[*The Witness delivered in the same, which was read as follows:*]

"To the Committee of Wholesale Grocers.

"Gentlemen,

"I am commanded by the Court of Directors of the West India Dock Company, to acquaint you, that they have received and considered, with the utmost attention, your representation respecting the mode of drawing samples, and stowing sugars, in the warehouses at the West India Docks. As the protection of the revenue, the security, preservation and accommodation of the property, and the measures necessary to promote fair sales, and convenient and speedy delivery thereof, were the primary objects of the legislature in forming and giving effect to the establishment, it is, and invariably has been, the most anxious wish of the directors, so to discharge the duty imposed on them, as to give the most beneficial and extensive effect to those objects, with due regard both to the interests and the convenience of every description of persons concerned in the property committed to their care.

"The directors admit that the sample taken on landing, ought, as nearly as possible, to represent the commodity from which it is drawn; and that the bulk should be delivered from the warehouse uninjured by the mode of custody therein; they are thankful for the suggestion of any regulations that may contribute to perfect these objects; but they cannot agree with you, that they will be attained by the relinquishment of that system which they have adopted, or by the adoption of that you propose in its stead; it is, therefore, with regret that they must express their dissent from the generality of your statement, and from the inference you therein deduce.

"I am accordingly instructed to submit the following observations upon the matters contained in your representation:

"It must be premised, in the first place, that the merchant importers are the only persons with whom the Dock Company can have any intercourse, until the receipt of their orders for delivery of their goods; it was chiefly for their protection, and that of the revenue, and to reform or correct numberless abuses and frauds to which they were exposed, that this establishment was originally formed. To the importers, therefore, in the first instance, the directors look for advice, as to the regulation of their proceedings and conduct, and to the suggestions and recommendations of that body they feel it their duty to pay the greatest respect; like all other proprietors of goods, they are entitled to form their own arrangements respecting the mode of sale, as to which the buyers may object, but possess no right to control them.

"The period of drawing samples of sugar for sale, after previous consideration by the West India merchants, was submitted to and approved of by the legislature, and enacted into a law.

"The Dock Company have no power to alter it. The law provides, that persons to be appointed by the Company 'shall collect and take, or cause to be collected and taken, samples for sale of all goods, wines, and merchandize, which shall be landed on the said quays, before the same shall be removed therefrom.'

"The proprietors of sugars must (as you observe) be materially interested in the due execution of this part of the duty of the dock officers; and the Company feel equally so, and have uniformly enjoined and enforced, by every means in their power, the most pointed and scrupulous observance of the mode of drawing samples, prescribed to them by a resolution of the West India merchants, which was adopted at the suggestion and recommendation of a very considerable and respectable branch of the trade as buyers. With respect to samples being kept a long time previous to their being exposed to sale, that must be a fact, when it happens equally well known both to the vendors and buyers, or at least it is capable of being ascertained by the latter, if they choose to make the enquiry.

"Without entering into an examination how far the samples may have varied from their original state, or from the condition of the bulk from which they were taken, and without assenting to your proposition, that the bulk of the commodity becomes daily worse, while the sample improves, it is sufficient to say, that an ample remedy is already provided for this part of your complaint:—in all cases where the first samples, either from the distance of time or other causes, cannot be considered as fairly representing the quality of the bulk they were taken from, upon application of the proprietors, fresh samples are drawn; so that in no instance can there be a necessity for the buyers to purchase from a sample, which from the length of time it has been drawn is an unfair or inadequate representation of the bulk of the commodity. If, however, there is any thing erroneous in the system, it can only be varied by the authority which first established it; and the Dock Company will most readily submit to any variation which the West India merchants, under the sanction of the legislature, may deem it prudent and just to adopt.

"With regard to the other subject of your complaint, the mode of stowing sugars in the dock warehouses, it is right to observe, that the plan of stowage pursued by the Company, is that which is observed at the principal outports; consequently, from this cause, no comparison can be drawn injurious to the port of London, between the care and management of the commodity in that port, and at the outports. It cannot escape your observation, as men of business and experience, that in a great and extensive establishment, framed for general purposes, and calculated for public utility, such as that committed to the management of the directors of this Company, it is not practicable to vary and model their business in such way as to meet the views and wishes of individuals, or even particular branches of the trade with which they may be connected. The stowing of sugars in the dock warehouses must be uniform, and cannot be diversified upon the application of a part of the importers, much less at the request of one description of buyers, with whom the Dock Company do not come regularly into communication, until the orders for the delivery of goods are presented. It is scarce necessary to observe, that the business of the docks could not go on, if each importer had his option to direct the mode of stowing his goods. A very important body of the importers have publicly approved of, and positively refused their assent to any variation in the mode of stowage you complain of, from a conviction that neither the general quality of the sugar is injured, nor the quantity of feet thereby increased.

"We cannot assent to your proposition, that 'the port of London has sustained great injury, by having lost that preference, which, before the establishment of the docks, was universally given to it for the purchase of West India produce.' On the contrary, we are authorized, from experience, to state, that previous to the dock establishment, the expenses, pillage and other improper practices, that had obtained in the port of London, were so injurious to the planter, as to induce him, as far as possible, to give preference to the outports, to the great injury of the port of London. The principal object of the docks was to remove and remedy those abuses, which has been most satisfactorily accomplished, and the Company can confidently appeal to the increased importation of West India produce at the port, as the most decisive proof of the advantages derived from the dock establishment; and in their judgment, the West India planters and merchants are not interested in promoting the change of system you seem so anxious to obtain.

"I am directed to assure you, that upon all occasions, where the prescribed and regulated line of duty of the Company will admit of it, the directors will have much pleasure in doing every thing in their power to promote the interests, and to contribute to the convenience of the buyers of West India produce.

"I have the honour to be, Gentlemen,
"Your most obedient servant,
(Signed) "THOMAS MARSHAM, Secretary.

"West India Dock House, Sept. 1808.
"Henry Coape, Esq. &c. &c."

Does that contain the reasons you would adopt as your own?—I think I could hardly say more in answer to the petition presented to the House of Commons two days ago; I wish particularly to call the attention of the Committee to that answer.

In the answer of the dock directors to the memorial of the grocers on this subject, it is stated, that the mode of sampling the sugars was provided by law, and that the directors had no power to alter it; was their petition taken into consideration, as to the expediency of complying with their request, or making any alteration in the Act of Parliament, or was that thought quite conclusive upon the subject?—The opinion of the dock directors, who were parties to the Act of the 39th of the late King, was, that it was a regulation essential to the security of the property, that the sample should be taken on landing, that the sugar might remain more undisturbed in the warehouse; if the question refers to the manner in which the iron should be put into the cask, that was settled by the approbation of large bodies of planters and merchants, and also by personal inspection of the mode upon the quay of the West India Dock, with several of the principal buyers of sugars; I can mention Mr. Craven the sugar baker, being among the rest, I do not know of a more respectable man; that mode was deemed by the parties then present, to be the fairest which could be devised.

The directors were quite satisfied with their judgment upon that subject, and therefore left the grocers to seek that redress which they referred them to in their answer, the right of complaint when the sugars did not answer the sample?—The answer of the dock directors, now delivered in to the Committee as evidence; I wish that to be taken altogether.

Is it not the practice of the West India Dock Company, to have samples drawn of all the sugars, immediately on their being landed, before they are warehoused?—Yes.

If those sugars are not sold for a considerable length of time, are not the samples very liable to vary by the change of weather, from the quality of the sugar remaining in the hogshead?—In some cases it may happen; it would depend in a great measure on the manner of keeping the samples: the practice of my house is to keep them in tin boxes, and I have mentioned already in my evidence, that I do not think it occurs to us more than three times a year, that we have any occasion for a second sample.

Do not many houses think it necessary, when sugars have been kept a great length of time, in order to avoid disputes or complaints with the buyers, to have their sugars re-drawn?—I should think the practice is not so frequent, I do not know how to form an average of it, I can only mention my own practice, I do not think it is so very frequent.

You are aware that many houses have sugars re-drawn occasionally?—Yes.

Would those additional samples be necessary, if sugars were not drawn till the parties requested it, because they wished to bring them to market?—There would be less reason for drawing the second time; I do not think that even then the complaints of the grocers would be obviated; those complaints existed according to my recollection when the practice of drawing samples was quite different; and at all times, whenever there is a dull market, we are sure to have complaints of the sugars not answering sample.

How could a second sample be necessary to the importer, if the first was not drawn till the period when he wished to expose his sugars for sale?—I think there would be less pretext for the second sample.

Then is not this charge of the second sample on the importers, occasioned by the system of the West India Dock Company, of drawing the samples immediately on landing, whether the importers wished them to be drawn then or not?—That is a part of the system, but it is a part of the system enjoined by the Act of the legislature, and it must be considered as connected with the other views of the legislature in passing that Act.

Mr. Frederick Bowman.

Do the regulations of the West India Dock for sampling and housing sugars, appear to you to meet with the approbation of the sugar refiners in general?—I believe the regulations do; but the regulations are not always implicitly followed by the Dock Company's servants.

But the regulations which the Dock Company have in fact adopted, appear to you to be proper?—Very proper.

Is it your opinion that the sugars ought to be sampled on landing?—That I can give no idea of; we had as soon they were sampled on landing, if they were kept in proper places afterwards.

Then it is with the manner in which the samples are kept after they are taken, which does not rest with the

Company, that you understand the sugar refiners have been dissatisfied?—Yes; we attribute it to that.

And not to the sampling or housing?—No.

Alexander Glennie, Esq.

How would you say that the monopoly of the West India Dock Company has been disadvantageous to the West India trade?—Because it has increased the expense so much that it has drawn a great deal of the trade away from this port.

Do you not also say it has given you greater conveniences, and what you consider equal to those increased expenses?—No; I cannot say that.

And yet you do not prefer the old system to the present?—For a considerable time after the West India Dock Company were in existence we were seldom able to sell a board of sugars without being obliged to make an allowance for the false drawing of the samples.

Are you to be understood to say, that the faults in drawing of samples under the West India Dock Company were greater than those of drawing the samples under the old system?—I think greater.

You have spoken of improvements which might be made in the system of the West India Dock Company; you have said that you consider their mode of sampling to have given rise to complaint?—Yes.

Have you ever heard their mode of warehousing, in placing the cask on the bilge, found fault with?—Yes, the sugar bakers and grocers complain that it throws the syrup into the sugar more than when it is pitched on end, they can separate it more easily from the sugar when the hogshead is pitched on the end; and the rolling of the cask does not mix it so much as when it is on the bilge; common sense will tell us so.

Then, in your opinion, improvements might be made on the system of the Dock Company in both those respects?—Certainly, I always considered sugar being pitched on the head preferable to those lying on the bilge.

Francis Kemble, Esq.

How long have you been a grocer in the city?—Eighteen or nineteen years, perhaps rather more; twenty years from my first entering my father's counting-house.

At the time the establishment of the West India Docks was about to take place, were you led to expect that the allowance of extra cartage from the Isle of Dogs would be made to the buyers in the same manner as it had been made previously to that time upon sugars delivered from the up-town warehouses, where the distance was greater than from the legal quays?—I cannot answer that from my own knowledge; it was the general understanding in the trade, and I understood from those much older than myself, that they had had communication with some of the West India merchants, who had promised it; but I speak from general conversation, not from my own knowledge, for I was not then of an age to communicate upon the subject.

Did you hear the names mentioned of any individuals connected with the West India Docks by whom such assurance had been given?—It was understood in the trade it was Mr. Milligan on the part of the docks, and Mr. Saxon Barwis on the part of the grocers; but unfortunately both those gentlemen are dead.

What did you understand to have been understood distinctly between those parties?—That the extra cartage should be allowed from the docks, in the same manner as it had been from what are called the up-town warehouses, in contradistinction from the legal quays; the West India merchants were in the habit of warehousing their sugars then both at the legal quays and in the up-town warehouses; the cartage was greater from the up-town warehouses; the difference between that and the cartage paid from the legal quays was always allowed by the West India merchant to the buyer.

And the assurances given were that the same practice would be continued and the same allowance made?—I have always understood that such assurance was given, but not from my own knowledge.

The grocers have made complaints of the mode of housing sugars practised by the West India Dock Company; have the goodness to explain to the Committee in what the difference consists between that and the old mode?—Upon the old mode I can hardly speak from my own personal knowledge.

Were they warehoused on the head or the bilge?—The old mode was upon the head, and then we had comparatively few complaints; we hardly knew what it was to have one.

What is the new mode?—The new mode is on the bilge.

From your being in the habit of examining hogsheads of sugar, you are aware that there are holes left in the bottom head of each cask, into which a bit of sugar cane is generally put, and through which the molasses has an opportunity of exuding?—There are, and there are also gimblet holes into which no piece of wood is put, for the same purpose.

You also know that the staves in the bilge are perfectly tight and close together, so that it is impossible for any molasses to escape through them?—They are usually so, and I presume intended to be so, but the pressure of the ship will sometimes open them a little.

When the sugars are housed upon the bilge has the molasses the same opportunity of escaping that it has when they are housed on the bottom head?—It has not; nor any thing like it.

Then is not the consequence that a considerable quantity of molasses is left in each hogshead of sugar in question, in point of fact, to run out?—Unquestionably it is.

When the cask or hogshead of sugar is rolled over, is not the consequence of the molasses being left in, that it mixes with the good sugar, and deteriorates the quality of the whole cask?—The molasses has, during the time that it has run, impregnated a large quantity of what was previously good sugar, and that deteriorated sugar mixes with the other; it is not that the molasses run through it as a liquid.

Do you find this new practice disadvantageous to you as a wholesale dealer in sugar?—Excessively so, to a most enormous extent.

State how?—When the sugars are pitched upon the bottom head, the foot, which is the technical phrase for that sugar which has become saturated by molasses, and which is wet and moist, was found at the bottom; it was in smaller quantity, and could be easily removed without having injured the rest of the sugar at all.

You mean removed by opening the head and taking it out?—Yes, which it is the custom of every grocer to do; now by the present mode, the foot remains upon one side of the cask, and it increases in quantity, because the stratum immediately over the saturated stratum becomes also impregnated, and so it rises when the hogshead of sugar is not quite full, in the operation of rolling it over, which never takes place until after the sample is drawn; that quantity of deteriorated sugar becomes mixed with the good, and frequently so entirely alters the quality, that a common observer would not suppose the sample came out of the hogshead at all.

Have you now more frequent complaints or very frequent from the buyers, in consequence of the circumstance which you have just stated?—I think the books of our house will show we had not one complaint in twelve months under the old mode.

What proportion do the complaints you now have, bear to the number of sales you make?—They are not so numerous as they would be, in consequence of our never selling a hogshead of sugar by the dock sample without endeavouring to prepare the mind of the buyer for some inferiority; but they are still very numerous; indeed we have succeeded in establishing something like an understanding among the buyers, that a small difference shall be submitted to; and therefore our complaints now are only when the difference is very great indeed; but still they are very numerous.

Do you not in general have your sugars carted home to your own warehouses, and there have the foot taken out and have them examined, before you venture to send them to the buyers, in order to prevent complaints?—We invariably do; I am in the habit of offering to my country buyers to take off eighteen-pence a hundred weight, if they will take them from the docks; but I cannot get them to do it.

It has been stated to the Committee that the buyers of sugars are so desirous of having them directly from the docks, that there have been instances of carmen's certificates being forged, in order to induce the belief that they do come direct in that manner; how can you recon-tile this with the statement you have made?—That is only a part of the trickery of the retail trade, in the same way as you see "genuine importers of China teas" written up over a door, that perhaps never bought a single chest; it is the affectation of buying at the first hand, nothing more; it is very common, I am quite aware of the feeling, and to keep it up, I am in the habit frequently of delivering sugars by the town carts, instead of by my own waggons, because they like the appearance of receiving them direct; and they do not like to have their customers observe that they bought them of a wholesale grocer; but that has nothing to do with the subject.

Will you explain to the Committee the difference between the mode of drawing the samples of sugar by the West India Dock Company, and that which was formerly practised, and the effect you think it has upon the trade in general?—The Committee will be able to get much better information as to the mode of drawing the samples; for I was never but once there in my life.

Where is the sample drawn?—It is drawn apparently half way between the two heads, in the centre of the hogshead.

Where was the sample formerly drawn?—I have purchased the nearest thing I could to a sugar hogshead in my way up; the hogshead is pierced on the top, and the iron appears to slant through the upper side of it about mid-way, between the two ends; we are in the habit of taking out the top, and drawing it from top to bottom; we do not include the foot, or deteriorated part, in our sample.

The drawing iron is not of sufficient length to go from the top to the bottom, is it?—Yes; but the foot, when we have pitched it up, is on the side, and we do not feel ourselves bound to take that.

The samples were formerly drawn between the top of the cask and the chime hoops?—Yes.

To what cause do you attribute the sugars so frequently not answering the samples in the mode in which they are now taken by the West India Dock Company?—So far as I understand the mode in which samples are taken, it appears to me they never can take any but the best part of the sugar.

Is not another, and perhaps greater cause of complaint, the samples being taken the moment the sugars are landed, whether the importers mean to sell them or not; and the different character the samples assume in consequence of being kept a length of time before they are exhibited to the buyers?—That is a very great, I will not say a greater cause, because by the mode adopted they never can take any but the best part of the sugar; the other cannot be greater, but that is a very great evil, and it is that which most baffles the judgment of the buyer, because a very inferior sugar; that which appeared to be a very inferior sugar at the time of drawing, will not only be clearer by being kept some time in paper, but will appear to be a very good conditioned sugar by gaining colour some time afterwards; by gaining colour, I mean that it will appear fairer.

From your observations on hogsheads of sugar in your warehouse, do they appear to be drawn agreeably to the following regulations of the West India Dock Company: "Samples must be taken separately from each cask; casks of sugar are to be uniformly sampled in the mode following, viz. from the bouge in a direct line across, and half way down the cask between the chalk mark made in the ship at the top and the underside, the drawing iron to be passed as far through the sugar as it will admit"?—I should not think we can usually trace the course of the drawing iron in the hogshead when we examine them. I do not think that rule is observed.

In what respect?—In this respect, that I should take it the iron was to go across.

In your opinion, does this difficulty about the samples have the effect of injuring the trade of the port of London, as compared with the trade of the outports?—I am quite sure that it does; we used to have a decided preference in our favour over the outports, as grocers, and the preference is now against us; it is found, I believe, by experience, that the London sugars turn out worse; I do not know that the others turn out well; speaking from my own experience, I have no doubt I should sell at least one-fourth, and perhaps one-third more sugar, if I could depend upon the sample of sugars which is delivered to me.

Should you be disposed to pay a higher price for sugars, if they were drawn and warehoused in the mode formerly used?—I should certainly; it would save me some thousand pounds per annum in charges of trade; the whole of the heavy expense of taking the sugar from the docks to our own warehouse, endeavouring there to make it equal to sample, if it should not be found so, and then sending it back to wharfs, probably very near the docks, would be saved; and with regard to myself, a very great portion of my business is with Scotland; the Scotch wharfs are very near the docks, and therefore it is to me all loss of money, to the extent of 1*s.* 6*d.* a hundred weight certainly, for I offer to my customers to take off that if they will receive the sugar from the dock.

Then, according to your account, the disadvantage sustained by this system, of 1*s.* 6*d.* a hundred weight, is to the extent of 1*l.* 1*s.* a hogshead?—That is the disadvantage to be positively submitted to, whether the sugars turn out well or ill; but a much greater disadvantage is, the impossibility of carrying on our business comfortably, and the refusal of persons to deal with us, on account of a distrust of the sample, which would not take place otherwise.

If a retail grocer receives sugars from you, of a different quality from those which he purchased and expected, is not the disadvantage to him much greater than the real difference between the two sugars?—Yes, it is a much greater disadvantage to him; because the retailers can neither afford money, nor room in their shops, for a commodity which they do not want; added to which, the sellers of sugars usually refuse to go and examine a single hogshead, or two hogsheads of sugar, at a retail house, even if it should be inferior; and in such cases the wholesale grocer has usually to make an allowance out of his own pocket, or in many instances to take back the sugar as wholly unsuitable; which has happened to me, in many instances, within these few months.

Did not the wholesale grocers complain to the West India Dock Company, as a body, of the disadvantages they sustained under the present system?—They did, many years ago; but they received an exceedingly polite and respectful answer, but which said that the Dock Company did not know the grocers, and declined all further communication with them; from that period nothing has taken place.

You have stated that great injury is done to the quality of the sugar, from the practice of stowing the hogsheads on the bilge in the warehouses; is not this injury incurred in the hold of the ship in a voyage of two months?—To a certain extent; but if it is injurious, it would be more so, that the hogshead should be six instead of two months in that position.

If after the molasses has changed its position, by the hogshead having been stowed on the bilge during the voyage, you put the hogshead upon the head, will you not again produce another drainage in the molasses, which will injure another part of the sugar?—It would not, for this reason, that the molasses having been at the bottom when the hogshead is turned upon the head, it is not by any means propelled into that which was the upper or good part of the sugar, but falls by its own gravity downwards, and deteriorates only that proportion impregnated by it; and sugars which have drained very little during the time they have been in the docks on the bilge, when we come to pitch them up, drain a great deal, so that we have instances sometimes of hogsheads of sugar going out of our house a quarter of a hundred weight less than they came in, without the least imputation of pilferage; and part of the drainage, which we conceive should fall upon the importers, falls upon us by that means.

Would there be a larger proportion of foot if a hogshead was always kept upon the bilge than if it was always kept on the head?—Certainly; there being no draining holes in the bilge, the foot depends upon the retention or escape of the molasses.

In proportion as there is less of what you call foot, there would be a less weight of sugar in a hogshead; there would be greater drainage?—Yes, except that the sugars best cured in the West Indies have the best foot, and are subject to the least drainage.

It would be so far a greater reduction of the weight of the sugar?—Yes.

That would fall upon the merchants?—Yes.

The object of your application at present is to remove a loss from you to the merchant?—That is a very small part; the greatest thing is the inconvenience to us in the course of the trade; if I am asked, "If I buy these sugars, may I depend upon their being like the sample?" I am obliged to say, "I cannot hold out any such expectation." It should be borne in mind, a very small quantity of molasses will create a large quantity of foot; perhaps the escape of seven pounds of molasses would prevent a hogshead having a hundred weight of foot.

In what proportion when it comes into the market is the value of that which is touched by molasses reduced?—More or less, according to the value of the sugar, the loss of course being greatest upon the finer qualities; I have sold foot at *53s.* or *54s.* out of sugar costing 80*s.*; and I have sold foot at 48*s.* out of sugar costing 56*s.*; the loss being in one case 24*s.* per hundred weight, and in the other only 8*s.*

You state that you made representations on this subject to the Dock Directors?—Such a representation took place.

You were referred to the Act of Parliament; did you ever look to the Act of Parliament to see whether the Act has prescribed that the sugars should be kept in a particular way?—I have not looked to the Act of Parliament for many years, but I remember looking to it several years ago, in a meeting of the trade, with the intention of petitioning Parliament upon the subject, but we thought that the Act of Parliament gave the Dock Directors the power of drawing samples as they saw best; that it was discretionary.

Did you ever collectively make an application to the West India merchants?—That committee to which I have referred was appointed for the special purpose, and when that answer was taken into consideration I remember being present; and the answer was, the Act gives them a discretionary power, if they please to abuse it, we cannot help it; they will find out by-and-by how much they are mistaken.

You appear not to have made the application to those who could govern the decisions of the Dock Directors? —Not as a body.

What applications were made individually?—Repeatedly; I remember one merchant jocularly said to me, "Why should we interfere? if we get more than our due and give it up afterwards, we are only where we were."

In point of fact, the effect of this is to give a better price or a larger sum to the merchant at your expense?—That is the effect of it unquestionably, that is ultimately counteracted by the loss of trade through us; and I have no doubt that it does materially affect the price of sugar, for it has created such an utter disinclination to buying beforehand, or any thing like speculation, I have no doubt that sugar is frequently left on the importers; those that would, but for this distrust of the sample, be scattered among the middle or other buyers; if the difference in the sample were definite, if it were always one shilling, or always ten shillings, it would be allowed for in the purchase; but it is so indefinite, sometimes not exceeding a degree, which we can induce the second buyers to put up with, and sometimes extending to ten or even twelve shillings per hundred weight, it is impossible. I have received myself, within the last week, an allowance upon five hogsheads of sugar, of the very best sugar that came to this market; the broker tells me, "I give you the allowance on five, though you complain of only one or two, but the difference is so great on the one or two, that I have thought it best to give it you on the four or five; it will look better."

In what degree, do you conceive, by an alteration of the system, that uncertainty would be removed?—I consider that if the sugars were pitched up, for that is the wish, and drawn at the time of sale, there would not be a complaint from one year's end to another by respectable houses; the larger buyers are always willing to pass over small grievances, it is not worth their while to have any unfriendly discussion with houses with whom their transactions are very large, and usually on very liberal principles.

Do you think that a consequence of that additional degree of certainty would be an advantage to the West India merchants?—I have no doubt of it; there is one advantage they would even gain at our expense; all second rate buyers are now absolutely excluded from the market; none but a man who has large warehouses to take his sugars home to, and examine them there, can venture to buy in the market, otherwise the market would be more open.

What do you call the market?—The West India merchants sell their sugars in various houses, either their own, or those of the brokers and others; those houses are situate very nearly together, mostly in Mincing-lane and Tower-street, and the place in which those houses are situate is usually called the market; I mean to say that the smaller buyers, persons perfectly respectable, would either, through brokers or otherwise, find their way into the market, and there would be an increased competition, and ultimately a better price; but many have tried the market among them, some of my own country correspondents, they have tried the market, but they found that by the turning out of the market they lost more than the wholesale grocer's profit, and therefore they have declined coming again, and that has lessened the number of buyers.

Do you know whether, in consequence of representations made individually by you to the merchants, any representation was ever made on their part to the dock directors upon this subject ?—That I do not know ; I believe that such representations have been made, but I do not know it from my own knowledge, nor have I attended much to it ; I have heard a great many West India merchants and planters express their disapprobation of the mode adopted, and their wish that it might be altered.

William Frampton, Esq.

Do you find the new system introduced in the West India Docks, of warehousing the sugars on their bilge, instead of warehousing them on the lower head as formerly, very disadvantageous to you, as dealers in that commodity ?—Very much so ; I am sure, within the last three months, I have myself lost £300 from sugars I have purchased not answering the sample ; I am now a holder of 100 hogsheads of sugar, of which I should not have had one if they had answered the description for which I bought them.

Do you attribute that partly to the mode in which they are warehoused on the bilge, and the foot mixing with the good sugar, and partly to the mode in which the samples are drawn at the time of landing, instead of not being drawn till the time that the sugars are sold ?—Entirely to those two circumstances combined.

You think them both disadvantageous to you as dealers, and inconsistent with fair trade ?—I do.

Does the effect of that uncertainty, with respect to the manner in which hogsheads will turn out, induce you to give a less price than you would otherwise give to the planter for the sugar ?—We are obliged to give a market price ; the fact is, we make some allowance for it, and if we want sugar for a particular purpose we buy what by sample is a shade above what we want.

Is not the uncertainty to which you allude such as to depress, to a great degree, the market price ?—I think it has frequently prevented the buyers from entering into speculation, and being large holders, and in that way may have affected the market ; but I do not think a buyer can say he buys otherwise than he would have done if the sample were fairly drawn ; if all were alike, I have no hesitation in saying, if there was one set of merchants adopting one mode of drawing, and another adopting another, I myself would, and I think the trade generally would, give more for the samples taken in the one way than the other.

Then the necessary effect of limiting that speculation is to affect competition, and so, by affecting a competition, to lower the price of the article ?—I think it has frequently had that effect.

Would you not readily pay a higher price for sugars that were housed upon the bottom ends in the old mode, and the samples of which were not drawn till the time they were sold, than you would give for sugars housed upon the bilge, and the samples of which are drawn immediately on their being landed, in the manner now practised in the West India Docks ?—Certainly.

Are you not aware that a very small quantity of molasses being left in a hogshead, and that hogshead being warehoused on the bilge, and mixing with the good sugar afterwards, when the hogshead is rolled over, very much deteriorates the quality of the sugar in that cask ?—Yes.

Do you not think it would be more for the interest of the proprietor of the sugar to have the molasses completely drained out before the sugars were sold, than to sell them in the mode he now does?—I think it would.

Would not that mode prevent complaint being made of sugars, and do you not think the great quantity of foot is created by the molasses being now left in, which leads to complaints and large allowances?—Yes.

In your opinion, does not the system adopted in the port of London occasion a considerable quantity of trade, which would otherwise be brought there, to be transferred to the outports?—Yes, I am of that opinion.

Does not that have a tendency to lower the market price of sugar in London, compared with the prices at the outports?—Yes, in my opinion it does.

Is it not a fact that sugar drains more within the first month after it is made than it does within three months afterwards?—Within the first month after it is made it is in the West Indies, and I am not competent to speak to that.

If it is a fact that sugar drains more within a month after it is made, and if it be stowed in the ship on the bilge, do you not consider that it is better to stow that same sugar in the warehouse also on the bilge?—No, certainly not.

Are you to be understood to say, that from the way in which sugar is stowed in the warehouses of the West India Docks, when a hogshead is rolled over, the molasses deposited in the bilge gets into the rest of the sugar?—Yes.

Can you give any reason why, if the sugar be stowed on the end in the warehouse, the molasses deposited in the bilge during the voyage, should not get into the rest of the sugar?—Because it falls down and forms one foot at the bottom, and it only rolls over and over at the bottom and does not mix with the rest of the sugar; I speak from experience, I have been in the trade thirty years, and consequently before the West India Docks were erected, and at the early period of my life, for I succeeded my father in the house, and went through all the gradations of the business; and I took an active part in that part of the business attending to raw sugars, because I was myself to become the buyer of them, and I find a very great difference in the state in which sugars now come, and in which they formerly came, and solely arising from that circumstance, that a hogshead of sugar on the roll holds the molasses like a ball, and it is spread all along the whole bilge, consequently the first time the hogshead is moved the whole of the sugar goes in, and deteriorates it very materially, more than a person not acquainted with it would think; now if there is half a hundred weight too much foot in the hogshead, we can take it out, and we know our loss, 10s. or whatever it may be, but if it mixes with the sugar it is not 2*l.* or 3*l.* that will answer to the loss.

Do you know any thing of the mode in which sugars are stowed, or sampled, at the outports?—No, I have no personal knowledge.

Is not the injury to the whole of sugar in proportion to the time that it remains with the molasses settled in the bilge?—I think that the sugar will collect molasses by lying there a long time, and consequently that the injury will be greater if it is a long time.

That a much greater quantity of sugar would be deteriorated from its being in that position twelve than six months?—Yes.

And two years more than one?—Yes.

The only security against that is putting it into a situation in which the molasses will drain off?—Yes.

Were you a party to the application made to the West India Dock Directors?—I was.

Do you recollect the answer?—I recollect the answer perfectly well.

Do you recollect a part of that answer being, "that what they did was with the concurrence or at the desire of the West India merchants and planters?"—No, I do not; it was the committee of West India merchants that we met.

What do you conceive to be the interest of the merchants and planters in having given those directions, or expressed those wishes to the West India Dock Company, if they did do so?—Part of the merchants submitted to the thing as an experiment; another party, the Barbadoes merchants, tried to have it altered; but the Jamaica merchants, having the principal control of the West India Docks, would not listen to it.

Have the West India merchants any apparent interest in continuing a mode of stowage inconvenient to the buyers?—Inasmuch as any system that represents an article better than it is in fact, must be in their favour.

You conceive the effect of it to be, to give a better appearance to the article than properly belongs to it?—That is the effect of it, certainly.

No. XII.

WEIGHING COFFEE AFTER BEING WAREHOUSED.

John Tilstone, Esq.

Is coffee landed in the West India Docks, weighed before it goes into their warehouses?—Coffee is now under the management of the Excise; but I can answer the question in saying, that it goes into the warehouse previously to being weighed.

Is not the weighing coffees, before they go into the warehouses of any dock company, a great security to the proprietor, by enabling him to know what the casks actually weighed, when they were originally landed, and making the Company responsible for any future deficiency?—I have always been of opinion, that it would be better to weigh those articles on landing, before they were deposited in the warehouse; it certainly would enable the consignee to detect any thing that might happen between the shipment and the landing, which otherwise might be supposed to have taken place after the goods were deposited in the warehouse; though at the same time, I must observe, I think the goods are as secure in the warehouse before weighing in the docks, as any other goods, the weights of which are ascertained at the time of landing.

Was it not the practice, before the establishment of the West India Dock Company, uniformly to weigh the casks of coffee, or the bags, before they were warehoused?—Certainly; and it was necessary, at that time, when coffee was landed at the legal quays, because they carted it to very distant warehouses all over London, even as far as Hoxton; consequently, it was necessary to ascertain the weight before the goods were removed from the quay.

Mr. Thomas Burne.

What is the distance of the warehouses in the London Docks, from the dock itself?—I suppose about five and twenty yards.

Is it not double what it is in the West India Docks?—Yes, I think it is about double.

Thomas Groves, Esq.

Does not the cooperage of sugar, when first landed, require considerable room?—It certainly does.

Is not then the additional space between the London

Docks and their warehouses, an accommodation in that respect?—I should think it must be.

Is coffee landed in the West India Docks, weighed before it is warehoused?—No, certainly not.

Was not that the usage prior to the establishment of the West India Docks?—Yes, it was.

Did not that usage afford a great security to the proprietors against plunder?—I do not know whether it did or not; but this I know, that it created such confusion in the books and accounts of the revenue, that neither the Excise nor Customs could be said to have any account that could be relied upon at all; and therefore in order to obviate that, the present system has been adopted. I will state why it is necessarily adopted in packing coffee; in the West Indies, they have some apparatus, some sort of press, that they can pack coffee in less space than we can do it here. Suppose for instance a tierce of coffee is landed here, and you want to tare the cask, you pour the coffee out on the floor, and you want to get the same quantity of coffee back again, you cannot do it; there is, perhaps, in some instances, half a hundred weight; then, as the duty attaches on the quantity landed, you take this to be the quantity imported; you throw it upon the floor, then the cask is tared, and it is returned, and you charge the duty upon the quantity repacked in the cask; but if you were to attempt to get the same quantity into it as when landed, you could not do it, and therefore you do this from necessity.

What objection does that form to weighing the casks, when they are first landed, and before they are warehoused?—Perhaps it may be convenient between the ship owners and the merchant, and if the Dock Company choose to do it, it is very well; but I do not know any reason for the revenue doing it, for it would not be of any use to the revenue.

If it was of no use to the revenue, would it not be of use to the merchant, by his ascertaining the whole quantity landed, in the first instance?—I do not know that it would be; if it could be supposed that the cargo is subject to depredation, then it might; but as it is only rolling or carrying the cask over a wharf of sixty feet, I do not think the weighing on landing would be the least check for the revenue; in my opinion it is absolutely impossible.

Is not the regulation of tareing the coffee, at the request of the Excise itself?—Certainly; till this practice was adopted, neither Excise nor Customs knew the quantity of coffee they had in the warehouse; there was nothing but confusion.

The Dock Company offered to weigh the coffee in the warehouse?—Yes, it was a thing which occurred to myself, in the time of the late Mr. Milligan; it was like other new plans; it was at first very much opposed; it has been tried, and found to answer.

Thomas Tanner, Esq.

Are you aware that by the Act of Parliament it is ordered that the goods should be weighed upon landing?—It could not be done at the West India Dock.

You do not know that the Act of 42 Geo. III, relating to those docks, directs that those goods should be weighed on landing?—Yes; I know there is an Act of Parliament which directs that they should be weighed on landing; and it is done as soon afterwards as it can be possibly done.

They are not weighed until they are put into the warehouses?—No.

Then the Act is disregarded in that respect?—So far it is, certainly.

Can you state for what purpose it was enacted that they should be weighed?—As a security to the revenue, I suppose.

And a security to the merchant also?—Probably so.

(Committee.)—What is the reason the cask is not weighed before the coffee is taken out?—The coffee must be turned out and the cask weighed; that could not be done upon the quays; it is therefore done as soon after it is received into the warehouses as possible; the officer accounting for the cask.

Is not it taken by the crane from the ship into the warehouse?—No; it is taken by the crane, and then conveyed to the warehouse, if on the ground floor, by means of a truck, or by a crane if to be lodged in an upper floor.

(Mr. Ricketts.)—When weighed upon the landing it is possible for the owner to detect any deficiency between the shipment and the landing?—The owner might, certainly, if he had an account of the original weight.

In consequence of removing it into the warehouses, now the means of detecting the deficiency are taken away?—Yes.

Are you to be understood to say, that it gives greater security to the revenue to weigh the coffee when it is in the warehouse than when it is upon the quay?—I do not see that it could be weighed upon the quay at the West India Dock at all; there is not room for it.

Then, in your judgment, it is weighed as soon as it may be?—Yes.

At what distance is the warehouse from the ship?—It is about the distance from where I am to that farther wall.

Does this coffee, when taken into the warehouse, remain one day, or one hour, before it is weighed, or is it weighed instantaneously?—It lies there sometimes two or three days; and then it is weighed.

If it were more convenient to weigh and to tare the cask on the quays, would the breadth of the quays at the West India Docks be sufficient for it?—No, I do not think it would; it would impede other business; I do not know that it could be done.

Then the quays would be an impediment to it, if it were more convenient in other respects?—I think it would stop other business.

Did you ever hear of any coffee being tared in the open air?—No.

Is there any objection to the cask being weighed in the open air?—I do not see any; it might be weighed in the gross.

Why should not the gross weight of the coffee and cask be taken in the whole, and the tare of the cask taken afterwards in the warehouse?—It could be done certainly, but then there must be another weight ascertained; inasmuch as the same coffee is not returned into it.

If the quay at the West India Docks were not to be made as it is at the London Docks, an open market, what necessity is there for its being wider?—The question referred to the weighing of coffee. It would occupy more room to weigh coffee, than it does at present.

How would it occupy more room to weigh coffee than to weigh sugar?—If the coffee and sugar were both weighed, there would not be time to go on with the two operations at the same time; or it would prolong the time of landing from out of the ships; because many casks of sugar are remaining on the quays at a time, for coopering and sampling.

Would it diminish the time, if there were more labour and length of quay to cross over?—It would admit of more scales being fixed; and the business could then be conducted quicker.

William Mitchell, Esq.

Is it not the general practice to weigh all commodities at the king's beam immediately on their being landed?—At the West India Docks, I believe, every article of produce is weighed (with the exception of coffee) upon the quay, at landing.

It not that practice necessary to enable the importers, by comparing the landing weights with the invoice weights, in case of any deficiency, to ascertain whether the plunder took place on the passage while on board the vessel, or while in the custody of the warehouse keeper?—As a West India merchant, I can state I have been so frequently deceived between the actual invoice weight, as mentioned upon the bill of lading, and the actual weight of the package, I could never place much reliance upon it; but if it is asked me, as a merchant, whether it would be convenient for me, in many respects, I should say it would, that coffee should be weighed upon the quay at landing.

You may be very unfortunate in having incorrect correspondents; but does not the system adopted by the West India Dock Company of not weighing coffee when landed, deprive the consignee of his remedy against the Dock Company, or the ship owner, by rendering it impossible for him to ascertain where the plunder took place?—I beg to say, it is not the system of the Dock Company, but a regulation of the board of excise, which the Company have endeavoured to get altered, but without success.

Have not the importers of coffee complained of being deprived of that remedy which the importers of other commodities have in this case?—About twelve months ago an application was made on the part of the West India merchants to the West India Dock Company, to alter the practice in that respect; the answer of the West India Dock Company was, that they would have it carried into effect, as soon as ever they could obtain the permission of the board of excise for it: the secretary of the Company was directed to make immediate application to the commissioners, and frequent applications have been made, on the part of the Company, to that board for the permission, but as yet, up to this period, they have not been able to obtain that permission.

Then the complaints of the parties remain unredressed at the present moment?—They do, for the cause mentioned.

One of the surveyors-general in your docks stated, as the reason why coffee was not weighed on being landed, that there was not sufficient space between the dock and the warehouses for that operation, as well as the coopering of sugars?—If he has stated that, he must have done it under a misapprehension.

Are there sufficient means at the West India Docks for weighing the coffee upon the quays, if that should be thought expedient?—If it should be considered necessary to weigh the coffee, at landing from the ship, upon the quay, before it was carried into the warehouse, there is no doubt it could be easily managed.

There is no difficulty then arising from the construction of the docks, or the machinery that they have there, in carrying that into execution, if it should be thought expedient?—None whatever; an application was made some time ago by the West India merchants to the court of directors, for the purpose of having that carried into effect, and the answer of the court immediately was, that it should be done, but it was necessary previously to have the sanction of the board of excise; the court communicated the application of the West India merchants to the commissioners of excise, requesting their permission to carry it into execution; and from that time no answer has been received from the board of excise, although repeated applications, on the part of the Company to that board, have been made.

Are you to be understood, that the weighing of coffee in the warehouse, rather than weighing upon the quays, originates, not with the West India Dock Company, but with the board of excise?—It does, entirely.

There is no objection on the part of the West India Dock Company to do it; and there are the means of doing it, if it is thought expedient?—Certainly.

No. XIII.

MAKING COTTON MERCHANTABLE.

George Hibbert, Esq.

Do you recollect a complaint being made by the importers of cotton wool?—I do; in 1805.

And an assurance given, that as soon as the surplus funds of the Company enabled them, agreeably to the Act of Parliament, to take into consideration the reduction of rates, the rates on cotton should be one of the first objects of their consideration?—Something has made it necessary for me to go back to that time; and I believe there was such an assurance given.

Was that assurance ever fulfilled, and when?—I doubt myself whether it has been accurately fulfilled. I think there has been perhaps some inattention to that subject.

I do not mean to assert, that there has not been some relief granted to the importers of cotton, I think there has, but my memory does not exactly inform me to what extent.

Has there been any reduction of rates previous to the year 1817?—Yes, there was a very material reduction in respect to rum.

The question refers to cotton?—No, I doubt whether there was.

Have not considerable quantities of cotton been taken away from the West India Docks almost as soon as landed there, and warehoused in other places, for the advantage of buyers having access to them, for the convenience of sale, and of being made merchantable in a more advantageous manner, according to the opinion of the importers?—I have some recollection that such things may have happened, I think they may.

Then were not the dock rates paid to the West India Dock Company an extra charge upon those importers of cotton?—I am quite sure that they were framed with every attention to make those equivalent to the general charges of the port, but the circumstance of excluding the buyers of goods from the docks may have been inconvenient to the importers of cotton.

Alexander Glennie, Esq.

Do you consider the monopoly of the West India Dock Company as disadvantageous to the general commerce of the metropolis?—Yes, I certainly have considered it so; and have felt it so, very severely.

In what way have you so felt it?—By an increase of the charges on all goods sent into the West India Dock Company's premises, beyond what we ever paid before, and other inconveniences; and especially in the cotton trade, where the cotton from the West Indies was sent into that dock, and we were under the necessity, for a very considerable time, so long, indeed, as I had any consignments of cotton, of taking it away from their warehouses, and having it up to warehouses in London, where it could be made merchantable; none of the buyers would purchase it until it was made merchantable in other warehouses; that was one of the inconveniences we felt most severely and very extensively.

No. XIV.

WAREHOUSING RUM.

William Mitchell, Esq.

You have given an account of the difference between the landing-gauges and the delivery-gauges of rum in the year 1821; have you any corresponding accounts of the year previous to the building of the present rum vaults? —I have not.

Was not the deficiency there more considerable, and the subject of frequent complaints among the merchants? —I have not in my possession any statement of the fact at present, but I have seen a statement, whereby it appeared that the loss was considerably greater before the vaults were made.

Were not the rums then kept in cellars, under warehouses having a wooden floor, which of course led to considerable evaporation?—That alludes to a period of time when I was not a Director of the Company, and I am totally unacquainted with the circumstances of that time.

You are aware that when rums are warehoused, not in vaults, but in cellars having wooden floors over them, considerable evaporation of course must take place?—

Certainly; I should suppose considerably more evaporation must take place than where they are in cellars vaulted.

It has been stated, in the evidence of Mr. Longlands, that the new rum vaults were built in order to prevent evaporation, at the expense of £102,871, in the year 1817 and 1819; can you give any reason why that evil, which had continued since the year 1802, when the docks were first opened, was not sooner remedied?—I believe long before that time there were vaults belonging to the Company, but those vaults were not found sufficient for the quantity of rum which afterwards came to the port of London, and therefore the Company, when they found that they had the money to devote to that particular object, immediately executed the work, and gave a greater accommodation to that particular article.

But they did not make a discovery of the evaporation taking place in such cellars as they kept the rums in till the year 1817?—I must state again, that they had the same description of cellars before, but they were found insufficient for the amount of rum sent to this port, and therefore, in addition, they built the vaults which are more particularly alluded to.

Was that deficiency never discovered till the year 1817?—Perhaps the amount of rum imported before was not so considerable, but even if it was, I apprehend the attention of the Directors was bestowed immediately they had the funds to appropriate to that particular purpose.

Mr. Charles Stuart.

What is the nature of the accommodation provided at the West India Docks to receive the rums?—They are housed in warehouses, and likewise in the vaults, and are brought up to the warehouse for accommodation, when they are about being exported.

What is the Committee to understand by the term warehouses?—Warehouses over the vaults.

In those warehouses is there any thing besides the roof, interposed between the weather or the sun and the spirits? —Nothing between.

Do you consider that to be quite adequate to the preservation and protection from waste or evaporation of the spirits so deposited?—I think less advantageous than the vaults.

Can you inform the Committee what proportion the evaporation or wastage on the spirits deposited in the vaults, bears to that on the spirits deposited in the warehouses you have described?—I suppose it might make one-third difference.

Supposing the wastage in the vaults was a half per cent., what do you suppose would be the annual wastage in the warehouses above the vaults?—I suppose it might be nearly double that.

Then to that extent you consider the warehouses are less adequate to the deposit of spirits than the vaults?—Perfectly so; but they are not kept any longer in the warehouses than they can be let down into the vaults at the West India Dock.

Have the goodness to inform the Committee what the comparative extent of accommodation is in the vaults and in the number of warehouses, what proportion of the 30,000 you have stated can be received into the vaults?—I should suppose nothing like a sixth part could be above.

Is that within your knowledge, or is it merely conjecture?—Merely conjecture.

There is one very large vault at the West India Docks, do you know the quantity it contains?—I cannot tell.

Have you ever heard that the vaults contain about 20,000, and that therefore, if the quantity is 30,000, there must be 10,000 in the warehouses?—I should have thought the vaults held more.

In the deposit of wines or spirits at the London Docks, is any part of them deposited in warehouses similar to the warehouse at the West India Docks?—No, they are not.

Where are they deposited while in the docks?—They are deposited in vaults as soon as an opportunity can be afforded for it.

Then does it not follow, that to that extent the accommodation is superior at the London to that at the West India Docks?—I should think not.

If the whole were accommodated in the vaults, the excess of evaporation would be saved; as at the London Docks the whole is accommodated in vaults, must not the advantage be in that proportion?—Certainly, it would be.

No. XV.

MODERATION OF CHARGES.

Henry Longlands, Esq.

Did not you understand, that the dock rates could not be lowered till all the money borrowed was paid off?—Most assuredly; it is so provided in this Act.

That the dock rates should not be lowered till all the monies borrowed were paid off?—Yes.

Then was not that money withheld for ten years, in order that all the money borrowed should not be paid off, and so the dock rates not be lowered?—I do not apprehend that that was the reason; not having been secretary of the Company at the time, and not at that time being present at the deliberations of the directors, I would say that, one of the directors for the time being, would be one of the most proper persons to speak to that.

But you know, that in fact, some reduction was made

as soon as that £30,000 was paid?—Most assuredly; it was in contemplation of that reduction that the money was repaid; because, until it had been repaid, that reduction could not take place.

But the Company had funds to have repaid that £30,000 at any time during the ten preceding years, or thereabouts?—They had previously the means of paying it, certainly.

For how many years before?—I am not prepared to state for how many years before; I see that in 1812, they had only a balance of £55,000, and they certainly could not have repaid out of that £30,000 with interest thereon.

How much had they in 1811?—I see there are certainly balances that would have admitted of the re-payment of that sum of £30,000, but whether they would have admitted of the re-payment of it, consistently with the other claims upon the Company, I cannot say, it is only the directors who can speak to that circumstance.

(*Committee.*)—In what year was it paid?—In 1817.

What was the balance at that period?—The balance appears by these accounts to have been £482,980, that appears in the account No. 15.

The Company have divided a clear profit of ten per cent. from the beginning, have they not?—They divided five per cent. until their docks opened for business.

That was in September in the year 1802?—Yes; and for the first half year they divided seven and a half per cent., subsequently to that they have regularly divided ten per cent.

Have those been made up ten per cent. by any subsequent payments for the early part of the time?—No.

They also to the year 1810, paid that ten per cent. clear of property tax?—For a short period they did.

And until it was objected to in a Committee of the

House of Commons?—For how long a period I cannot state from recollection; they certainly did pay the property tax on their dividends, till the exception was taken in that Committee.

They did not pay it themselves, but they had their dividend clear of the property tax?—The proprietors had the dividend clear of the property tax.

That being paid out of the funds of the Company?—Yes.

And substantially out of the rates and duties?—Certainly.

From your knowledge of the transactions of the Company and the accounts, instead of £1,200,000, have not the Company sunk as much as £2,000,000 in works and land? —I think a great deal would depend, as I before stated, upon what is to be considered works; I do not believe that in the accounts, as heretofore kept, the distinction between works and repairs has been so accurately preserved as it might have been, nor do I think, in my own opinion, that the title "works" is a proper one to have used at all; I think the proper title for those things which now come under the head of works, would have been "extensions and improvements."

Suppose the whole of this great establishment was upon sale, is there not that to sell, land, buildings and works, that has cost at least two millions of money, instead of £1,200,000?—Taking the substitution of new works for old, and every thing which has been expended upon that establishment, I have no question that it may be nearly two millions.

That there is now in land, docks and buildings, a capital of at least two millions?—If it is put up for sale, I think the value must be a matter of very speculative opinion.

In your judgment there has been expended in the purchase of land, and in the construction and extension of the works, at least two millions of money?—If it is meant to be limited to those things, I cannot go so far; if repairs and alterations are taken in, then I believe it is nearly correct.

In works and repairs together, a great deal more than two millions?—As much, I should think.

Has not each proprietor, always meaning one who has continued such for the whole term, received his full principal and interest at five per cent. in the course of twenty years?—He has received ten per cent. continuously for twenty years.

Does not that repay him the whole of his principal with interest at five per cent.?—That is, taking it at compound interest, receiving interest of ten per cent. for twenty years, he certainly will double his capital.

Then he has received his capital back with interest?—He has certainly doubled his capital; but I think it is going too far, to take it at compound interest.

That capital, according to the selling price, has been doubled, or nearly so, in the proportion that £185 bears to £100?—Exactly so.

If instead of £185 it were £200, that would be his capital three times told?—Yes, if it was £200, certainly.

Have those additional rates, and the whole of the first rates, at any time been charged together by the Company, upon the West India trade?—Certainly; from the passing of the Act of the 42d of the late King, those additional rates which were for special and additional services, were charged together with the original rates.

Those special services were surveying and examining the cargoes?—"In consideration of the great additional "expense and trouble which will be occasioned by such "survey, and examining and ascertaining the cause and "extent of any injury or damage, and the amount thereof, "and also by taking samples of the said goods," and so forth.

Then from the year 1802 to the year 1817, the whole of the original, and the whole of the additional rates, were charged upon the trade by the Company?—They were, up to 1817.

You say that those rates could not be regularly reduced without the approbation of a general meeting?—They could not.

So that it depends altogether upon the discretion of a general meeting of the proprietors, whether the planters and merchants shall or shall not have the benefit of a reduction in the rates?—The provision for lowering the rates requires that any reduction shall be approved at a general meeting of the proprietors.

So that the persons who are to judge of the fitness of reducing the rates, are the very persons most interested to keep them up?—Not to keep them up unnecessarily, I should think.

Does not the Act establishing the West India Dock Company, contain a clause providing for the reduction of rates whenever they exceed the dividend of ten per cent. upon the capital of the Company?—No.

Is there no clause making any provision for the reduction of rates?—There is; but not dependent upon that contingency.

Be pleased to state upon what contingency it does depend?—The clause is the 160th of the 39th George III.; the only contingency specially mentioned in that clause is, that "when by the means last mentioned, or "otherwise, the principal monies so to be borrowed by the "said Company shall be all repaid," then the rates are to be lowered.

Have not those borrowed monies been repaid?—No monies were borrowed within the meaning of this clause.

Then was there any real objection to the reduction of rates whenever the profits of the Company did more than enable them to divide ten per cent.?—Assuredly there was.

Are you aware that applications were made for a reduction of rates, long before any reduction was granted? —I am, twelve months before; I think only twelve months before.

Do you know of no application for a reduction of rates, made longer than twelve months before the reduction was granted, which was in the year 1817?—It will be recollected that I was not secretary of the Company prior to 1817, but I have a general knowledge, having access to all the minutes of the Company, and upon this subject I have particularly referred to the applications made; I recollect a special application of the ship-owners, prior to that in consequence of which the reductions of 1817 took place; I recollect that that application was refused; I recollect the grounds upon which the application was made, that it was made upon the ground of the low rate of freight; I recollect the answer given, that the directors could acknowledge no connection between the rate of freight and the amount of their charges; the application was again renewed at the end of the year 1816, and in March 1817 the reduction took place.

Did you never read, in the letter book of the West India Dock Company, the copy of a letter written by Mr. Marsham, the secretary, and dated 31st of August 1805, being an answer to an application from the importers of cotton wool, requesting a reduction in the port charges, and stating how much heavier they were in

London than in Liverpool; and this particular passage, being the concluding paragraph of the letter: "The "court, however, beg leave to assure you, that whenever "the situation of the surplus funds of the Company will "enable them, agreeably to Act, to take into considera-"tion the subject of a general reduction of port charges, "the article cotton will certainly be one of the first sub-"jects of their attention." This letter being addressed to the committee of importers of cotton wool, and directed to Joseph Marryat, Esquire?—I have no distinct recollection of the letter, but when the date was mentioned, I thought the honourable member was about to refer to the application of the ship-owners, and that would be about twelve months before the application that was alluded to; I mentioned also, in my first answer, that it was a general application that I alluded to; I knew that there had been, from time to time, various applications of particular trades, relating to the charge upon a particular article, to that I did not mean to speak.

If the rates continue to be applied to increased accommodation, and the business of the West India Dock Company continues to increase, is it not likely that the reduction of rates, contemplated by that clause in the Act of Parliament, will be defeated?—I do not think it at all likely that it will be defeated by those circumstances, because, I think, if that extended accommodation be prudently provided, it may be the means of increasing revenue, and thereby accelerating a reduction of rates.

If the rates collected are applied to the purpose of extending and improving works, instead of being applied to the reduction of rates, how can such a reduction of rates take place?—As I stated, if the money be prudently expended, I think it will assist in the ultimate object of that clause; one of the extensions and improvements that have been made now operates in that way, I allude to the mahogany shed, a work of very great superiority: I myself have minutely investigated what the effect of establishing that shed has been, and I find that from the great saving of labour, the weekly pay lists of the Company of that department have been most materially reduced; I think that that mahogany shed will more than pay itself in a very short time.

Is not the effect of the appropriation of the rates to the extension and improvements of works, that of transferring the benefit of a reduction of rates from the present generation to posterity?—I think the present generation, if the trade absolutely requires the accommodation, have the immediate benefit of the expenditure.

Wm. Mitchell, Esq.

You were in the direction in 1817, were you not?—I was.

At that period, it is understood, a reduction of the rates took place?—A reduction of prime rates took place in March 1817.

From what considerations did that reduction take place in March 1817?—After the termination of the war, and when the directors could have any view that could be relied upon, of what their situation was likely to be during a period of peace; they then came to the determination of lowering the rates.

You have stated, that in 1817, a reduction was made in the rates; and it has also been given in evidence, that a further reduction has lately taken place; it of course has been part of your duty, as chairman of the dock directors, to consider the nature and amount of the last reductions that have been made, and their effect?—It has.

Do the last reductions place the rates as low as in your judgment they can be put, with reference to the interests which you are bound to protect?—My answer to that question would be, that viewing the present income and expenditure of the Company, taken upon an average of the three last years, which are the three years that the reduction of the rates in 1817 have had their proper effect, the last reduction of rates would be considerably more than would allow of giving ten per cent. dividend to the proprietors of stock.

Whatever security the West India Docks give to the property of West India planters, it is given at a very great expense, is it not?—There is no doubt that the system pursued at the West India Docks is an expensive system.

A very very expensive system?—I cannot proceed quite so far as that, but it is an expensive system, greater expense is incurred by the additional precautions taken.

So that with respect to the convenience of the docks, in respect to sampling and so forth, that is given to the planter and merchant at a great expense also, for which he pays?—I am not aware that that is done at a great expense, but certainly every duty the Company have to perform, and all their different descriptions of business, create expense.

You have stated that the system of the West India Docks was expensive; in what way do you consider the system to be expensive?—I was then alluding to the regulations and precautions of the Company rendering it to them expensive; but I did not mean to state that the system of the Company created a greater charge to the persons paying the rates.

Then your meaning was, that your course of proceeding required an expensive establishment to carry it into execution, paid by yourselves, but that did not impose by that means an expensive charge on others?—I meant to state, that a very considerable permanent establishment was provided by the Company, in order that they might have individuals experienced in each department of the docks; that they should keep up an effective police; and in various other matters, that they were put to an expense which certainly made it to be considered as a more expensive establishment and system than one which did not require such precautions as were used at the West India Docks.

You have been asked whether the business might not be conducted as well upon the same system by other dock companies elsewhere; could that be effected without a considerable time at other places?—Undoubtedly some time would be requisite to obtain that experience which is necessary to perfect a system; besides that, I may also state, that if the system was pursued at other docks, I consider that a good deal of inconvenience would result to the merchant by having to perform his business in different places.

Do you consider that any attempt at economy, by a change of system, would be beneficial to the merchant, or planter, or ship-owner?—Entertaining the opinion that I do, that this system is necessary for the due protection of the planter, and the convenience of the merchant, I should certainly say, that any expense saved by an alteration in that system would not prove a beneficial economy.

You were asked a question, whether in proportion to the facility and dispatch with which the business was done, it ought not to be done cheaper; is that consistent with your opinion?—I think not; for this reason, that the Company are obliged to have a permanent establishment of experienced men; and that whether a ship is discharged in two days or two months, it is the same to them; if they had ships to discharge from other parts of the world, immediately after the discharge of a West India ship, or when the West India ships were not occupying their docks, that would then bring in a great revenue, and they could afford to do the business cheaper; but, situated as the West India docks are, confined to the West India trade, I do not see that that could be of any advantage to them, they being obliged to keep up a permanent establishment of persons experienced in, and the machinery and every thing else adapted to that peculiar trade.

Do you mean, that it would be more advantageous both to West India planters and the public, to have the advantage of receiving and unloading ships belonging to different trades?—No; I gave no opinion upon that.

That they would be able to unload cheaper if they had the opportunity of unloading ships in other trades?—I meant to state this, that the Company are obliged to have a permanent establishment of experienced persons for the purpose of discharging the West India ships; that those persons are sometimes not fully occupied; that if they had business to perform at that time that they were not so occupied, it might bring in a greater income to the Company, which might make a little alteration as to the charge for that particular work.

The Committee apprehend you to mean, that while the docks continue upon their present establishment, for the accommodation of the West India trade, as the trade is particularly full at one period of the year, and slack at another, there are times when the officers whom you are obliged to keep are not fully employed?—I mean to state this, that the more business the West India Dock Company have to do, the more property they could make of it; but I could not state this, that if the trade was thrown open to all the docks, we should have more business than we have at the present moment.

Do you mean to state that the indiscriminate resort to this dock, of all other vessels, would be beneficial to the docks, or would it not interfere with their system?—I do not mean to state it would be so.

You do not mean to state that you would consider it advantageous, with reference to the objects with which they were connected, that there should be a general resort to them to give employment to your people at times when they were not fully occupied?—No.

Samuel Turner, Esq.

Do not you think the continuance of the monopoly of the West India trade would render the interests of the Dock Company, in their capital, a great deal more permanent and secure, than if there was no monopoly at all?—That would depend very much upon circumstances; I consider that there is a monopoly, if I may call it so, on two parts; the West India Dock Company have the monopoly of the business of the West India merchants, if it should be so called; but the West India merchants have the monopoly of those docks; it is confined to them; the West India trade confine the docks to that particular kind of business: and it is very questionable with me, whether the West India Dock Company, having very considerable warehouses, and great accommodation for trade, might not get quite as large a portion of trade if it was open to all manner of business; but, as a West India merchant, I should deprecate opening that very strongly; because I think it would be very injurious to the West India trade, if the Dock Company were enabled to devote that which was built expressly for the West India trade, to any other objects.

As far as your observation has gone, the West India Dock Company have confined their business to the West India trade?—I believe they have; they are bound to do so by the Act; such has been the general understanding of the trade.

In your opinion, would it be as profitable to the Company that the monopoly should be discontinued?—It is very difficult indeed to answer a question of that kind.

If you were a large proprietor of stock, would you rather have the monopoly or lose it?—I am rather inclined to think, that if I was a proprietor of stock, I should be very much inclined to lose it; but as a West India merchant, I should hold that we should not (if we could prevent it) suffer them to lose it.

How do you suppose it could be more profitable to the Dock Company to lose the monopoly?—I look upon it, of course, that if they lose their monopoly, their docks are to be open to all trades whatever, that they may take their general share of the trade of London.

But still, if by law they can divide only ten per cent., what advantage would that be to them?—I do not know any particular advantage, if they could only insure their ten per cent.; it might enable them to continue the ten per cent.; whereas I look upon it, at the present moment, we have, on the part of the West India body, to make a new bargain with the West India Dock Company, and I think we ought to induce them to take a less rate; a considerable part of the accommodation having been founded upon, and the warehouses built by means of a rate levied on the West India body, giving the West India body, *pro tanto*, an equitable claim to the extent of the money of the West India planters and merchants so expended.

So that you think if the Company have already laid out in new works £700,000, and have got £500,000 more in hand, the planters and merchants have some equitable claim to the benefit of that?—Most decidedly, a very strong equitable claim.

Considering the prosperity of the concern, and the great security of its emoluments, what would be a fair dividend for them to have, and a reasonable one in future for the renewal of the monopoly?—Upon my word it is hard to say; what one person may esteem fair, another may conceive drawing the string excessively close; the only way in which I could say what would be a fair dividend would be this; supposing we were beginning *de novo*, and we could get respectable parties to come forward and establish new docks, at what rate they would be content, at the present time, to fix the maximum of rates; what that extent may be it is hardly fair perhaps for any one to determine; it would depend upon those parties coming forward to establish new docks, with a monopoly of course, at what rate, (supposing that monopoly to be granted) they would undertake to perform the business.

Suppose you were one of a new company beginning a new undertaking of the same kind, and to have the exclusive monopoly of the West India trade, what do you think would be a satisfactory compensation, in the shape of dividend, to allow any such new company?—I should think certainly considerably lower than ten per cent.; the same hazard that attended the original establishment, when the system of docks was quite new to the port of London, would not attend any new undertaking, where the extent of the value of that monopoly can be pretty clearly ascertained, from the return averages of twenty-one years. That being the case, I certainly, myself, should think that a great number of persons would be willing to come forward for the establishment of new docks, provided they could obtain a monopoly of twenty-one years, at a much lower rate than that charged by the West India Dock Company, for the business performed by them, during the last twenty years, for the planters.

Would you be so good as to state, as a man experienced in the West India trade, and with a full knowledge of all the circumstances of the case, what you would judge to be a satisfactory compensation for yourself, if you were a subscriber to such new dock, to which a monopoly was to be annexed; would not seven per cent. be very ample?—I certainly think we could get people in the city of London to come forward, to do the present duties of the West India Dock Company, if they were secured in the monopoly for twenty-one years, at a maximum of seven per cent., especially at the present time, when the interest of money is considerably lower than it has been.

In your judgment, is it not fit that the Company should, forthwith, reduce their surplus, by a further reduction of the rates?—I certainly think the Company ought to do so; the Company have already lowered their rates to a considerable degree.

Do you consider it at all necessary, for the interests of the planters, that the Company should retain in their hands 4 or £500,000 as a surplus?—Certainly not to that extent.

Of course, if the Company have received, for twenty years, ten per cent., you understand that they have received back their capital, with five per cent. upon it for the whole time?—They have received back considerably more than that; in fourteen years and a quarter they had received that.

Having received all those advantages, and got so large a surplus in hand, with this magnificent establishment, do you not think it fair, they should do the business of the planters on more reasonable terms in future ?—Most decidedly so.

Then it is to be taken as your opinion, that though the granting of this charter to the Dock Company is of much more consequence to the merchants than to the Company, you consider that the permanent dividend of the Company ought to be cut down ?—I certainly conceive that the interest of the West India trade at large is greater than the interest of the West India Dock proprietors ; but I think the maximum dividend of the dock proprietors ought to be reduced in equity, because at the expiration of the term, it has appeared that they have enjoyed a most profitable trade for the twenty-one years ; and at the present period, if the same monopoly were granted to another body, they would do the work at a cheaper rate than the West India body have done ; for instance, I believe that the London Dock Company, if Parliament would grant them the monopoly for twenty-one years, might afford to do the business of the West India body at large at a cheaper rate than the West India Dock Company have ever up to this period done it.

Mr. Charles Stuart.

You have said that the charges at the West India Docks are fair and reasonable ?—They are so.

Are not those at the London Docks fair and reasonable ?—No ; because they are sixpence a puncheon for a week, and at the West India Docks but half the sum.

Then it is their warehousing charges that are not so reasonable ?—If they are suffered to remain, they are still more reasonable at the West India Docks than at the London Docks.

Do not you consider that the West India Dock Company can well afford to be more reasonable, for having a monopoly of the West India trade ?—That is a business

I never investigated sufficiently to know; they are the best judges of their own case.

But they have brought you here to judge about them? —No, they have brought me to speak to the truth of what I know.

They have brought you here to speak to your opinion of the reasonableness of their charges?—Then I think they are very reasonable indeed, because the rent upon a puncheon of rum is only three pence per week, and at the London Docks, upon a puncheon of brandy, or any other spirits of the same size, they would be six pence.

Perhaps you can favour the Committee with an answer to the question just put; do not you think that the West India Dock Company can well afford to be more reasonable for having a monopoly of the West India trade?—I do not know how I can answer that question.

You are a spirit broker; if you could have a monopoly granted you of the whole business of spirit brokers in the city of London, could not you afford to do the business for smaller profits than you can at present?—That is most certain.

Then you consider a monopoly as an advantage, and one that enables a man to do business on more moderate terms?—In the manner in which the question is put, most assuredly the business might be done cheaper.

Then if there was no monopoly at all?—I do not know the drift of that question exactly.

Never mind the drift of the question; but do not you think that any business might be carried on on easier terms with a monopoly than without one?—If I had the whole business in the manner in which the question was put just now, if I had the whole business of the West India concerns, I should think it might be done on less terms.

You are understood to have said that a puncheon of rum would be charged for warehouse room at the West India Docks, three pence a week; do not you know that till very lately it was six pence?—Certainly I do.

How long since has the alteration been made?—Upon my word I cannot say directly.

Within these few weeks?—No.

A few months, was it not?—I think it must be.

Was it not in 1817?—I am afraid to give the date.

It is not five years ago, is it, since the alteration was made?—I should think not.

N. Pallmer, Esq.

Are you able to form any judgment whether the dock charges are high, or too high, upon the West India trade? —I consider them, unquestionably, too high.

Is the West India trade, from the present value of the produce, so well able to bear those high charges as it has been hitherto?—Certainly not.

R. H. Marten, Esq.

Should you not be disposed to accept any business which would give you seven per cent. upon your capital, instead of three and a half?—Certainly.

You would rather have ten per cent. than seven, of course?—If the temptation were placed in my way, I think it probable I should.

You would not require that the dividend should be ten per cent.?—I should not refuse it if it were offered, but I should not require it.

If you had a reasonable chance of getting five per cent., would you compound for your maximum being seven?—I should have no hesitation in saying that I should, speaking individually.

Have you referred to the West India Dock rates?—I have; and there are many that I am satisfied we could do the business under, and be glad of it too.

Alexander Glennie, Esq.

Could you afford at your dock, to do all that is done for West India produce at the other docks, at lower rates?—Yes; I think we certainly could, excepting rum.

Every other species of West India produce, you could receive under precisely the same circumstances, and perform the same operations at lower rates?—Yes.

In your judgment are those rates made too high?—Does the question allude to those they have charged, or what they are about to charge?

What they have charged?—What they have charged; I do not allude to what they have charged upon rums; but by the reduced rates which I have seen lately, all articles have been, in my opinion, too high.

In your judgment, could they have continued so high for such a length of time, without a monopoly?—I should think not; before I leave the article of cotton, I will mention one circumstance that happened in a mark of only twenty bales of cotton; the West India Dock officers charged me with more cloth for mending six bags, than would have made bags for the whole twenty; it is but justice I should mention also, that on giving them proof of that, the charge was reduced considerably.

How long ago is that?—I do not recollect; it is some years ago.

Thomas Tooke, Esq.

Are you to be understood, when you speak of the expenses of the port of London being high, that you exclude the charges at the two docks you have particularly mentioned, namely, the London and the Commercial Docks?—I exclude those; but I include particularly some charges of which my house has had recent experience; having a quantity of pepper in the East India Docks, we found that the charges there were extravagantly high; that is the only experience I have recently had of any of the docks in possession of monopoly.

Is that the only charge at those docks, the three you have mentioned, the Commercial, the London, and the East India Docks, that appears to you to be unreasonably high?—I have not spoken of the London or Commercial Docks as being unreasonably high.

Is the charge on pepper, at the East India Docks, the only one that appears to you unreasonably high at either of those docks?—I mention that as the only one I have a recent experience of; I have spoken of the general impression of the charges being high for other articles that I am not acquainted with.

You do not think that the charges at the London or the Commercial Docks are unreasonably high?—No, I do not.

What circumstances would have the effect of restoring the trade to its highest pitch?—I am not sufficiently acquainted with the details in the port of London, and in other ports, but such a reduction of charges as would place us, in point of expense, on a level with other ports.

Have you formed an estimate of the difference of expense?—I have not; but the present charges are apparently high enough to drive away a considerable portion of the trade from the port of London.

F. Wilson, Esq.

Have you ever imported spirits into the London Docks? —Not of late years, very largely during the war.

Were the regulations established at the London Docks sufficient to give protection in respect of your spirits?—I think quite.

Were the spirits on your own account?—On commission.

With respect to the charges, is the comparison unfavourable to either?—I had intended to have brought a comparison with me, but the notice being delivered at eight o'clock last night, and having been since in the country, has prevented me; the West India Dock Company have lately reduced their charges very much.

Previously to that reduction, was not the comparison in favour of the London Docks; were their charges lower than those of the West India Docks?—I think generally they were.

Have you any account of charges you have actually paid on any merchandize in the London Docks?—We have very voluminous charges in our counting-house, but I have not any with me.

Could you supply the Committee with any if it should be thought desirable?—Certainly.

Do you think that under the reduction which has taken place, the charges at the West India Docks are now lower than those at the London Docks?—On some articles, certainly; on spirits, I believe the West India Dock Company have reduced the rent on rum, from seven pence to three pence a week.

What are they at the London Docks?—On brandy, for the first twelve months, sixpence, and afterwards seven pence.

William Frampton, Esq.

You are a partner in a very old established house, as wholesale grocers, in the city?—I am.

Do you recollect, at the period of the establishment of the West India Docks, any promises being made to the wholesale grocers that they would be indemnified for the additional expense of cartage from those docks, if they were established at the Isle of Dogs, in the manner that they had been indemnified for the additional expense of sugar being placed in the up-town warehouses, when the difference between the cartage from thence and the legal quays was allowed to the buyers?—Certainly I do; but I cannot expressly say whether it was an official communication or not; I was one of the Committee that attended the Committee of West India merchants in Bishopsgate-street, and Mr. Milligan either met Mr. Barwis and myself in Tower-street, or communicated to us; at that time he told us to be quiet upon that subject; that we need say nothing; that it would be allowed to us as heretofore; that if we would keep ourselves quiet, the things would be collected by little; and the West India merchants had no other desire but to do what was right by such a respectable set of individuals.

When you say that you were cautioned to be quiet as to your objections to what was going on, do you mean to the establishment of the West India Docks at the Isle of Dogs?—It is a long time ago now; but there were several meetings on the subject, and I believe the particular objections we made were to the manner in which it was pointed out that the sugars were to be stowed and drawn, and to the manner in which the samples were to be kept; these things, Mr. Milligan said would be remedied, if it was found that the system adopted was not a proper one.

And some assurances were given that you would be indemnified for the extra cartage from docks established at the Isle of Dogs?—We were certainly promised it by Mr. Milligan; but I do not think it was an official communication; he met Mr. Barwis in the market; I do not exactly recollect whether I was with Mr. Barwis or saw him immediately after; and he told me what had passed between Mr. Milligan and him; I think I was with him, but I am not quite certain, it is so long ago.

Were the assurances given such that the wholesale grocers were satisfied with them, and were quiet, to use your phrase?—Yes; I think that was one of the things that prevented the trade making any opposition.

Was that assurance ever acted upon?—Not at all; immediately on the Bill being passed, we were told we were all on a footing; and that it was the same thing to us, and we must consider it upon our sales.

Then it was an assurance given to keep you quiet at the moment, and the instant the Bill was passed the substance and spirit of it were completely violated?—Certainly; just so.

Did Mr. Milligan tell you in what way the allowance was to be made?—As it had always been before; I live in a situation that I had my sugars, prior to the erection of the docks, home for 2*s*. 3*d*. a load, that is a load of two hogsheads; if I had them from any other situation, for at that time, owing to a great increase of business, sugars were housed in many parts of London, whatever I paid more than 2*s*. 3*d*. the merchant allowed me in settling the account.

Then Mr. Milligan stated, that when a parcel of sugar was sent to any particular merchant, there was to be an allowance upon the cartage of his sugar from the West India Docks, as compared with the legal quays?—Certainly; and we made a point of it in our communications with the merchants; and not getting it allowed in this way, we endeavoured to get it when other persons were seeking compensation for the erection of the docks.

No. XVI.

REPAIRS AND IMPROVEMENTS,

AND

No. XVII.

ACCUMULATION FUND.

Wm. Mitchell, Esq.

Upon the face of the accounts, it appears that a considerable balance now exists; a surplus to the amount of about £448,000, which has been increasing within the last year or two, and originated some few years back; will you state to the Committee the motives which led the directors to keep that balance going on from year to year?—Part of that balance originated before I had any connection with the docks; but, I presume the directors, at that period, had the same motives which guided the directors subsequently; that there were various improvements and additions to be made to the works of the Company, to give effectual accommodation to the trade, and that for that purpose, a very considerable sum of money would be required.

In your judgment then, did the surplus fund, which accumulated from year to year after a certain period, arise, in a large proportion, from the trade which was accommodated in consequence of those increased extensions and improvements?—I should suppose that it must, for if my recollection is correct, in 1813, the first considerable balance arose, and that must have occurred from the stagnation of commerce in West India produce; in the years 1810, 1811, and 1812, there was a previous balance of the surplus fund, but not to any considerable amount.

If the West India Dock Company, instead of applying the funds in hand to the extension and improvement of the works, which the West India trade required, had applied for and obtained an allowance to increase their capital, would it have been more or less beneficial, in your judgment, to the planters and merchants, than to lay out the fund which they had in hand?—Had the directors of the Company in 1808 or 1809, when it was necessary to afford this great accommodation, applied to Parliament for the addition of £400,000 to their capital, the payment of a dividend of ten per cent. upon *it*, would, I apprehend, have absorbed the whole, or nearly so, of the present surplus capital of the Company, as well as the money laid out upon additional works; and from that circumstance I should presume it must have been a very beneficial measure to the ship owners, the planters and merchants, the laying out this sum from the surplus profits of the Company. I was not at that period a director of the Company, but I have no hesitation in saying, that it appears to me, the directors at that time seem to have been more guided, in the measures they took, by their desire for the advantage of the ship owners and the planters, than for their own individual benefit; for had they added the £400,000 at that time to their capital, the proprietors of stock would not only have been getting ten per cent. upon it ever since; but at this moment, their additional £100 would have been worth to them £185.

Was the state of the West India trade, at the time those extensions and improvements were made, such as imperiously to require that some accommodation should be afforded somewhere to that trade?—I can only answer that in the way I have already done; that it appears to me that from the progressive increase of the West India trade, additional accommodation was required, beyond what was originally contemplated.

Do you know of any remonstrance or objection being made on the part of the West India trade, or of any other persons, to the works which were made for the purpose of affording increased accommodation at that time?—On the contrary, I have stated in my previous evidence, that in respect to the export dock, complaints were urged against the Company, that they did not provide sufficient accommodation.

Are you to be understood, that neither from the knowledge which you had acquired as a West India merchant, previously to your becoming a director, nor from the knowledge you have had of the concerns of the West India Dock since you have become a director, do you know of any objections or remonstrance having been made to the improvements and extensions during the time of their going on?—I have never heard of any.

You never heard of any, till this time?—Never, till the present moment.

Is the election of directors generally in favour of those directors whose interest as West India merchants and planters is paramount to that of dock proprietors?—It appears that the proprietors of stock have been in the habit of electing persons as directors of the Company, who are themselves merchants, ship owners, and I may say, planters.

Are those the class of dock proprietors who are preferred by the proprietors of dock stock?—They are.

Do you apprehend that at the time when eleven per

cent. was paid upon the dock shares, the interest of the West India planters and merchants was predominant in the directory at that time?—I was not myself in the direction at that time; but it appears from what was then stated, that they divided one per cent. more than they ought to have done.

Did that show a great regard and attention to the interests of the West India body, in preference to the interests of the dock proprietors?—If they were only entitled, which it was stated they were, to ten per cent., the division of eleven per cent. was a misapprehension on their part.

A misapprehension in favour of the holder of dock stock?—Certainly.

There may be instances, in which the directory have so managed this business, that it has been rather for the benefit of the proprietors of stock than for the benefit of the West India merchants and planters?—I am not aware of that, for had I been a director at that time, and thought that under the law I was entitled to eleven per cent., I should not have conceived I was doing an injustice to the planters and merchants if I took that eleven per cent.; if I had done it in error, certainly I was wrong.

Upon the whole, with regard to the management of the directors, do you think that management has given greater satisfaction to the proprietors of dock stock, or to the West India trade?—I have never heard the proprietors of dock stock complain of the management of the directors, therefore I presume it has given them entire satisfaction; nor did I ever hear that the West India planter or merchant was dissatisfied, until lately.

There have been applications for the reduction of rates?—On the part of the ship-owners.

You have heard complaints about the exorbitancy of the rates, have you not?—I have frequently heard complaints with respect to the amount of rates.

That was not on the part of the dock proprietors?—No; I am alluding now to casual conversations, not to any direct application on the subject to the court; but in casual conversation I have heard persons state that the charges of the West India Dock Company are higher than the charges of similar establishments; but I have never yet been able to find any person who could distinctly make that out.

But you know the fact, that the West India traders and merchants have complained of the exorbitancy of the rates?—Not as a general complaint.

Have they been satisfied, that they are as low as they ought to be?—I have already mentioned, that I have heard complaints upon the subject, but those complaints have always appeared to me to have arisen from a want of information, in the person who complained.

Still they complained; they conceived that the directors did not take sufficient care of the interests of the West India traders, by keeping up the rates to that amount?—I am speaking of former times, not of the present time, of course; I never knew a general application on the part of the merchants and planters; I have heard some individuals, not a great many, state that the charges ought to be lower, on one pretence or another, but I never knew those persons that could make it distinctly appear, that the charges of the West India Dock Company were higher than the charges of other establishments for the same description of business, for similar services performed.

Have the proprietors of dock stock complained of the accumulation of this surplus?—Never.

Have the proprietors of West India property, deposited in the warehouses of the West India Dock Company, complained of the exorbitancy of warehouse rent?—I recollect a complaint that was made by the late Mr. Beeston Long, that the rent of sugar in the Company's warehouses ought to be lowered; the directors immediately took the same into consideration, and begged the favour of seeing Mr. Long and Mr. Manning upon the subject. At an interview which the directors were favoured with by those gentlemen, it appeared that the complaint of Mr. Long was, that he had kept sugars a very considerable time beyond the usual period, in consequence of a slack demand for the article, and on that account he thought there should be a reduction of rent; the result of that interview was, I believe, to satisfy both gentlemen that the Company had acted perfectly proper in that respect.

That is the only instance of a complaint on that point that you recollect?—I do not recollect any other formal complaint at the present moment.

Do you recollect any other complaint?—I have already stated that in casual conversation, and being in the habit of mixing among merchants and planters, one would say you must lower your rates, and so on, without the complainant knowing at the moment exactly how the thing stood.

But still he complained?—Yes, so far.

And they complained against the charges of the dock and the warehouse rent?—I am not aware that the warehouse rent was mentioned specifically, but the charges generally were mentioned.

The proprietors of dock stock have not been dissatisfied with the accumulation of this surplus of £440,000? —I never heard that they were.

Do you think the West India merchants and traders are satisfied ?—I should rather think not.

They may think that the directors have paid too much attention to the interest of the dock proprietors, in accumulating that sum ?—I do not know what they may conceive; they have certainly made an application to the Company, to apply that surplus fund to the reduction of rates.

The accumulation of that surplus has, in fact, had the effect of enhancing the value of dock stock ?—It is very likely that it might.

Do you not think it has ?—I should think that it had.

And that at the expense of those who had, in fact, paid the monies with which this accumulated surplus has been formed ?—I am not aware of that, because this surplus was formed for the purpose of being laid out for the accommodation of the trade.

But still, if the Company were not in possession of that surplus at this moment, the price of dock stock would not be so high as it is ?—I have already stated that it might at the present moment so operate in some degree, but at the time that that fund was accumulated, it was for the purpose of being laid out in works and in improvements of the dock for the accommodation of the trade; and therefore the whole of that surplus, instead of being as a reserved fund for the eventual benefit of the stock holder, might have all been expended for the accommodation of the trade, as was originally proposed.

As you became a director in 1815, how can you say that that surplus was not accumulated for the purpose of increasing the value and the security of dock stock ?—I did not become a director till 1815, but from what I have seen of the Court of Directors, since the stock-holders did me the honour of making me a director, I am quite sure that fund was originated for the purpose of being laid out for the accommodation of the West India trade.

But you cannot take upon yourself to say it was not formed for the purpose alluded to?—I can only conceive what the motives of the directors at that time were.

Do you not know that it was the prevalent opinion among the proprietors of dock stock, that at the termination of the twenty-one years, they might divide that surplus among them?—Upon the contrary; I am of opinion no such opinion prevailed.

Have you never heard it?—If I have heard of it, I believe that was not the prevalent opinion.

Have you not heard it mentioned?—I have heard an inquiry made, but perhaps not by a stock-holder; but among the directors the opinion was never entertained for a moment.

Has not the question been submitted to counsel, what interest the stock-holders had in that fund, and whether it was divisible or not?—A question to that effect may have been submitted, because the general interest of the stock-holders and planters and merchants, in the whole of the affairs of the Company, have been so submitted.

The amount of the rates to be levied, although fixed by the directors, is entirely under the control of the proprietors at large; they are settled at a general meeting of the proprietors of dock stock?—They are.

How much of that surplus do you calculate will be expended annually in aid of the rates and duties?—From as near a calculation as can be made, it appeared that the rates were now lowered to that amount which would require a call upon the surplus fund annually to the extent of £30,000; and I should state, that as the dividend upon the surplus fund is applied now to the income of the Company, so in proportion to the sum which is laid out in further extensions and improvements, and also in repairs, and the sum which is annually taken from this surplus in this reduction of rates, to which I have been alluding, that source of income will annually diminish.

Applying £30,000, part of that surplus, together with the income of the Company arising from the rates and duties, the Company will still share ten per cent. dividend upon their respective shares?—At the present moment they will.

Taking £30,000 from the surplus fund?—Yes.

How long do they mean to go on reducing the surplus fund by £30,000?—I am not aware that they have any present intention of making an alteration.

If the exclusive privilege should not be renewed, do you think they will stop that application of the surplus?—It is quite impossible for me to hazard an opinion on so improbable a case.

If the charter of the West India Dock Company was not to be renewed, might not a great part of the West India trade go to other docks, and other trades go to the West India Docks?—I see no reason why it should not be so.

In that case, how could the accumulated fund be returned in the reduction of rates to the owners of West India produce by whom it had been paid?—It certainly would be returned to those who would frequent their docks, either in point of further accommodation, or in any other mode in which it might be applied.

But those who had contributed to that fund, and who might send their vessels to other docks, would not receive back their shares of it?—Certainly the produce upon which the rates had been paid, and the shipping which had entered the docks, upon which rates had been paid, would not derive the benefit of any accommodation granted after the produce had gone away, or the shipping no longer frequented the docks.

Could those parties, whose vessels did not continue to frequent the docks, receive back this accumulated fund of rates they had paid?—They certainly would receive no benefit from any further accommodation, or application of the surplus fund, after they had left the docks.

Ought not then, in point of justice, this accumulated fund to have been appropriated to the reduction of the rates, before the expiration of the present charter?—It certainly was the intention of the directors, that that should have been the case, and I mention it to my own knowledge, as far back as 1815, that it was the intention of the directors so to apply it, though circumstances have arisen from time to time preventing it, but the directors still wish that it should be applied for the benefit of the West India trade.

As their charter expires in the next year, and under the reduction of the rates lately made, they calculate to apply only 35,000*l.* out of this accumulated fund per annum, how is it possible they can divide 448,000*l.* before the expiration of the charter?—I think it has been stated in evidence, that to put the works of the Company in that order in which they ought to be placed, it would take the sum of 168,000*l.*; and if we add to that the sum of 50,000*l.* as a reserved fund, making a sum of 218,000*l.*, a very few years at 35,000*l.* per annum, with a diminution of the dividend upon the surplus fund, would extinguish that balance.

But can this possibly take place before the expiration of the present charter?—Certainly not.

Might it not have taken place, had the £30,000 ber-rowed been repaid at an earlier period?—I am not aware that it could.

Not if the rates had been reduced in 1811?—Certainly, if the rates had also been reduced.

Could the rates be reduced till that sum was repaid, which was repaid only in 1817?—The rates could not be reduced, until the repayment to the treasury of £20,000 loan had taken place; but I am not aware that if that repayment had taken place at an earlier period, the consequence would have been a reduction of the rates; because, as I have already stated, so far as my own knowledge extends, and so far as I have been informed by others, that certain works were imperiously called for, for the accommodation of the West India trade, and therefore, in the exercise of that discretion which the legislature entrusted to the directors, the West India Dock Company would not have been warranted, even if they had repaid the loan to the consolidated fund, in reducing the rates, until all those further improvements and extensions had taken place.

Were not such works as were imperiously called for immediately executed by the Company?—They were not all immediately executed, for various reasons; in the first place, it was not until the end of 1812 that they had any fund that they could apply, and then they could not execute all the works at one time.

The Committee see that in the year ending the 1st of January 1811, the Company had a balance remaining in their hands of £66,215; that in the year 1812, all the expenditure for works was £35,790, still leaving a balance in their hands of £30,400; do you not consider that all the works considered necessary were executed?—On the first of February 1811, there appears by the account a balance in the hands of the Company amounting to £66,215 6s. 7d.; but I should apprehend, that out of that fund there were a great number of unsatisfied demands to be paid; I merely suppose that, because I know from my own experience, that, at the end of every year there are accounts to a great extent, which call upon the Company for a very considerable sum of money, and that sum was estimated in February last to amount to somewhere about £50,000; if, therefore, that was the case on the 1st of February 1811, there would have been actually a balance of only £16,000 applicable to any demands on the Company for further accommodation.

In the year ending the 1st of February 1813, the Committee see the balance in hand applicable to outstanding demands was £207,429?—That was so.

And in the whole year preceding, their expenditure on works was £3,334; with such a sum of money in their hands, were not the directors inexcusable in not making new works, if new works were then thought necessary?—They certainly would have been; but I apprehend, that when that balance had accumulated, their attention was immediately drawn to the fact of this further accommodation being required, and that they immediately commenced affording that additional accommodation; because I observe in the course of the same year they expended in new works no less a sum than £73,733.

You mean in the ensuing year, ending the 1st of February 1814?—I do.

Had they not then a balance of £291,516?—They had.

And if further works were thought necessary, was not that an ample sum for their being erected?—It might be so; I was not in the direction at that time, but from what took place upon my entering into the direction, I should conceive that the attention of the directors had been drawn to the further accommodation that was required: and, in my opinion, (I am stating it from my knowledge of the West India Docks at that time), it could not have been drawn to a more important subject than to the additional accommodation at the export dock.

In the following year, ending the 1st of February 1815, the Company had a balance in hand of £398,462, and in that year the whole sum expended in works is described in their account as being £5,449?—It is so: and the only reason I can give for that is, that as I presume the attention of the directors had been called to the circumstance of the inadequate accommodation afforded by the export dock, they had in contemplation the making of another; and I am confirmed in that opinion by the fact, that when I entered into the direction of the Company, I found the attention of the directors applied to that subject.

Was not the balance then in hand much larger than the estimate for making the additional export dock?—Not a great deal larger; because the estimate delivered in by the late Mr. Rennie, was little short of £300,000, and if I deduct, as I before stated, those unsatisfied demands against the Company which appear at the end of every year, and say that they amounted, as they did in last February, to £50,000, the actual surplus would have been very small after those objects had been accomplished.

In the year 1816 the balance in hand was £417,651, and the sum expended in works £2,757; in the year 1817 the balance was £482,980, and the sum expended in works only £280 12*s.* 1*d.*; with such an immense balance in hand, if those works were thought necessary, what excuse had the directors for not erecting them?—I can state, from my own knowledge, that as to the export dock, the treaty with Government, if I may so denominate it, for adding the canal to the export dock, was still going on, and the Company had hopes to accomplish it; and it was not until they had lost all thoughts of being able to obtain the canal, that they then directed the late Mr. Rennie to make out an estimate of what would be the cost of a perfect new dock; the balance, on the 1st of February 1817, was £482,000; that balance was certainly more than sufficient for the construction of the new dock, on that account the attention of the Court was directed to those further improvements which the accommodation of the trade required, and in the course of that very year, 1817, an expenditure took place of near £70,000.

£70,000 bears a very small proportion to £482,000; and the Committee would ask, whether it is by making estimates of new works, or the attention of the directors being turned to them, or by their being actually executed, that accommodation to the trade is to be afforded?—If we deduct from the £482,000, the balance on the 1st of February 1817, the sum that was necessary to carry into effect the wish of the directors in regard to the export dock, and we also deduct the same sum I have allotted for the unsatisfied debts of the Company, of £50,000, from £350,000, the sum of £68,000 will be found to be as much as the directors could, that year, with prudence and safety apply to the further accommodation of the trade, because the total of that would be little short of £420,000, leaving about £60,000 surplus for any casualties that might arise.

You have stated that the directors have now abandoned the plan of making a new export dock, therefore has not the sole effect of keeping back this large sum in hand, been that of postponing the reduction of the rates, which the West India trade had a right to expect?—Certainly, if the directors had not had the objects in view which I have been mentioning, but had reserved, without such an object, so large a sum, it might have been supposed that they were reserving more than those casualties and accidents which all docks are liable to warranted.

George Hibbert, Esq.

If instead of laying out the accumulation in making those additional improvements, an application had been made to Parliament for an increase of the capital of the Company for that purpose, would it in your judgment have been more or less advantageous to the planters and merchants ?—I conceive it would not, but it is a question we never put to ourselves; we did what we did, conceiving the spirit of the Act rendered it our duty.

Do you believe, that if power had been obtained from Parliament, to increase the capital of the Company to the extent of the sum laid out in additions and improvements, it would have been more beneficial to the planter and merchant than employing the accumulation as it has been employed ?—I do not think it would.

There would then have been a dividend of ten per cent. to have been paid upon a larger capital ?—There would.

There was a sum of £30,000 borrowed by authority of Parliament for a particular object ?—There was; for the purpose of building the offices appropriated for excise and customs, and the building a wall round the export dock.

Some questions have been asked with respect to the repayment of that sum; was the repayment of that sum withheld for any period of time, with a view to prevent the reduction of rates ?—I can safely say that it was not; I can say more, that I never heard from any director, or any proprietor of stock, such a thing suggested even in a whisper. I beg leave to mention, that Mr. Milligan and myself, who were always looked up to in the direction of that Company, had some difference of opinion, whether it would or would not be right to charge Government with the expense of erecting the offices for the purposes of the revenue; he rather leaned to the opinion, that we ought to make such a claim; I did not, I was of opinion it would be better to simplify the whole matter, by taking that expense upon ourselves; unquestionably, the little discussions which took place upon that point occasionally did delay a decision upon the subject; and it was not necessary that we should pay it, until we had made up our minds to the reduction of rates; when it became necessary, it was done.

Was there any reason why it was not paid sooner?—I mention what I have mentioned as a circumstance which might delay it, but I do not give that as a reason; it was not necessary to pay it until it was intended to reduce the rates.

Do you recollect a note sent to the Dock Company on the 15th March in the last year, of which that handed to you is a copy?—Yes; I recollect that perfectly well.

[*It was delivered in and read as follows.*]

"To the Directors of the West India Dock Company.

"We, the undersigned West India Planters, and Merchants and Agents for the West India Colonies, having been apprised that the West India Dock Company have accumulated and are possessed of a surplus fund, to the amount of £334,000 and upwards, do hereby require of you, as the Directors of the said Company, forthwith to apply the said surplus fund (or so much thereof as the said Company are bound by the Acts of Parliament relating to them, to apply) to the reduction or discontinuance of all or some of the rates and duties, now payable to the said Company, by virtue of the said Acts, in such manner and to such extent as the said rates and duties ought to be reduced or discontinued, under the terms and according to the intent of the said Acts.—Dated the 15th day of March 1821.

(Signed)

Charles R. Ellis.
Simon H. Clarke.
C. N. Bayly.
G. Carrington.
J. Colquhoun, agent for St. Vincent, Nevis, Dominica, and the Virgin Islands.
C. N. Pallmer.
F. S. Bayley.
David Hall.
William Holmes, agent for Demerara.
William Murray.
John Daniel.
Charles Grant.
N. Winter.
William King.
John Ellis.
Augustus Elliott Fuller.
A. Browne, agent for Antigua and Montserrat.
J. Montgomerie.
R. Gordon.
R. Bernal.
G. H. D. Pennant.
James B. Wildman.
Emanuel Lousada.
G. Watson Taylor.
W. Dickinson.
Edward Cust.
Vassall Holland.
William Manning.
Henry Swann.
William Mitchell.
Thomas Naghten.
Charles Armstrong.
Joseph Marryat.
John Mitchell.
Alexander Grant.
J. Blagrove.
A. C. Grant.
J. Higgin.
George Chalmers, agent for the Bahamas.
James Blair.
George Blackman.
Rose Fuller.
C. A. Francklyn, agent for Tobago.
Robert Home Gordon.
Samuel Turner.

Benjamin Adam.
G. W. Lawrence.
D. H. Rucker.
J. A. Rucker.
John Bulfour.
J. F. Barham.
John Fuller.
J. H. Massy Dawson.
Frederick R. Coore.
G. W. Jordan, agent for Barbadoes.
George Whitely.
Joseph Wartnaby.
Samuel Boddington.
Richard Sharpe.
William Vaughan.
William Peatt Litt.
Romney.
H. W. Martin.
Neill Malcolm.
William Linwood.
John Wood Nelson.

Was the request contained in that notice complied with, or any measure taken for the purpose, prior to the present application to Parliament on behalf of the Company?—There was; a considerable reduction was made before the present application to Parliament, particularly in respect of that wherein it was most demanded, the article of rum.

Is the Committee to understand, that that reduction took place between the 21st of March in the last year and the present year?—I am not very certain, that between March 1821, and the reductions which lately took place, that any general reductions took place.

Are you aware of any reduction taking place, between the service of that notice and the preferring the petition of the Dock Company, for the renewal of the Act?—In confidence of the statement made to me by Mr. Mitchell, who is chairman at present, I should say, that the reduction I have alluded to, did take place after that notice.

Samuel Turner, Esq.

Does it strike you that the expenditure which is incurred in the management is quite necessary?—I should look upon it, that the expenditure which has hitherto taken place has been quite just and necessary; the rates which have been levied have been, I think, a great deal higher than was necessary for the purposes, inasmuch as the Company have accumulated a larger fund than was called for; as far as the money has been laid out, whether the West India interest receives an equitable reduction of rate, *pro tanto*, to the extent of the warehouses which have been raised, and the additional accommodation afforded by means of the rates levied, or whether money had been borrowed for those purposes, it comes eventually to the same thing, supposing the West India Dock Company are still confined to the exclusive work of the West India planters and merchants; for instance, the original capital of the Dock Company was only £1,200,000; the sum expended in buildings has been about £1,700,000; the West India trade at large, at the present moment, have only to pay a dividend on £1,200,000; the £500,000 laid out having been created by means of the rate, the buildings ought to be held, as I conceive, free, for the benefit of the West India trade, and not for the benefit of the West India Dock Company.

And ought, in your judgment, to continue to be so held in trust for the West India trade?—Decidedly so, in trust for the West India trade.

And the surplus also?—Yes, excepting such part as may be necessary for the contingent expenses; all above that, I consider as held for the benefit of the West India trade, not for the benefit of the persons who have raised it at their expense, as I conceive, contrary to the principles of the Act.

Andrew Colville, Esq.

You heard it stated, that there was an equitable interest,

in some persons, in the warehouses which had been built out of this fund, and in the surplus which had accumulated, and was now standing as a balance; are you enabled to ascertain in whom that equitable interest could be found to exist?—I cannot conceive any other interest to exist, either in the extensions or improvements made in the works of the docks, or in any balance in hand, than what is stated in the Act of Parliament.

If any body could have an equitable interest, should you not conceive that the equitable interest would be in favour of those who had paid the money?—If any such equitable interest could exist at all, it would exist with those who had contributed to that fund.

Do you agree in the position, that that fund has arisen from rates contributed by the planters of England, interested in West India property?—If the accounts were taken anew, I think it could be made out that the existing surplus, and the money which supplied the means of making those extensions and improvements, has arisen, in a great degree, from the produce of the foreign colonies, and in a great degree, from rents which accrued to the Company, in consequence of the stagnation of the markets, those rents arising principally upon produce, after such produce had been sold by the planters, and therefore coming, in fact, out of the pockets of the speculators.

It would, in your opinion, be very difficult to make out that any part of this came out of the pockets of the English planters, properly so called?—I certainly think that a very small proportion of it could be so made out; and I cannot conceive any mode by which this equitable interest could be distributed among the parties who are supposed to possess this interest.

The purpose for which this fund was accumulated was

with a view, principally, to make a new export dock?—The fund was not accumulated for any particular purpose; but the delay, in reducing the rates, arose from the uncertainty of the extent of the demands which might come upon the Company for additional extensions and improvements, among others, for an additional export dock.

And during that delay it was thought fit rather to increase the fund, than to diminish it, by reducing the rates in contemplation of those intended works?—Of course the Company continued to receive the old rates till a new scale of rates was settled.

But it was not thought prudent to stop the increase of the reserved fund, as long as it was in contemplation to make those new works?—I have stated that, in effect, in my answer.

If those new works had not been intended, the Company would not have thought it right to accumulate this fund, but would rather have decreased the rates and duties? —I conceive, if the directors had not contemplated those extensions, they would rather have reduced the rates, so as to prevent an increase of the fund in hand.

They would not have thought it right to raise the surplus fund to that amount, except for the purpose of making those new works?—I do not say so.

Is there any other purpose for which it would have been right to accumulate a surplus fund to that amount?—In my answer, I gave as a reason for the delay in making any alteration of the rates of the Company, that they contemplated heavy claims upon them for various extensions and improvements of the works; what might have been the determination of the directors, under other circumstances, it is impossible for me to say.

Were you a director at that time?—I was.

Would you have thought it right to accumulate that

surplus fund for any other purpose but those intended works?—Unless under the contemplation of those demands upon the Company, I should not have considered it necessary to accumulate so large a fund.

Would you have considered it right?—That is implied in my answer, I think.

The question is asked as to your opinion of the propriety of it?—If I had not considered it necessary, I should not have considered it right.

Is it not better for the interests of the planters and merchants, that the Company should be restrained from accumulating a surplus fund, with a view to build the works which are in contemplation, and which, by possibility, they may never build, and that for the purpose of enabling them to make those works, they should, whenever it is decided upon, borrow the money upon the credit of the rates and duties?—I do not see much difference if that money so borrowed is to be paid off by rates and duties.

The works may be unnecessary, and the accumulation, therefore, unnecessary, may they not; and rates and duties may be levied upon persons who never may have the benefit of those works?—All these circumstances may be so, or they may not be so.

There is a clause which empowers the directors to discontinue all the rates and duties, if they think fit; by the 146th section of 39 Geo. III. it is provided, that it shall be lawful for the directors to reduce or discontinue all or any of the rates and duties thereby granted and made payable to the said West India Dock Company; you might, under the authority given you under that section, discontinue all the rates and duties which you are authorized by that Act to levy, and apply the whole of your surplus to the defraying the expenditure of the Company?

—I have no doubt we have that power; but I should not consider it a discreet exercise of the power.

Still it would not be a very indiscreet act to reduce it more than £30,000 a year, would it?—As to that, different men may form different opinions; I can only say, that the question was deliberately considered, and that I am still of opinion that the determination to which the Court of Directors came, was a proper and discreet determination.

What were the grounds on which the Court of Directors acted, in saying that £30,000 a year was the utmost limit to which the Court could go in reducing the rates?—The determination which they came to, was from a view of the whole circumstances of the case; I should not think it a discreet conduct, on the part of the directors, to do the business of the West India Docks for nothing for one or for two years, thereby expending £240,000 of their balance all at once; on the contrary, I think it more judicious to distribute the reduction over a series of years.

Why?—I can give no other reason than that it is the result of my judgment upon the case; that was the determination of the Court, after a full consideration of the circumstances of the case; they came to that decision in the exercise of the discretion left to them by the Act of Parliament.

C. N. Pallmer, Esq.

Do you consider the West India Dock establishment to be beneficial to your interests as a West India planter?—Yes, I do, in some respects.

In what respects?—I consider the West India Docks to have been beneficial to the interests of the West India planters in respect to security of property, its classification, and its being deposited in a place known to the owners, and exclusively applied to its reception.

Has the establishment been in any respect injurious to your interests as a planter?—I think it has been very injurious to the interests of the planters in respect of the very high charges which the Dock Company have kept up when they might, and in my humble opinion, ought to have reduced those charges; I think the charges were unnecessarily kept up by reason of the Dock Company retaining in their hands a large fund, which they might and ought to have applied to the purposes of the Acts of Parliament relating to the docks; and by reason of their introducing into their contingent account various items which, in my humble opinion, were not legal or proper. I allude particularly to a sum of (I think) £12,314 for a volunteer regiment; £1,000 for a free school at Poplar; £500 to the Waterloo subscription; £210 to a girl's charity school at Limehouse; one hundred guineas to the Caledonian asylum: I mention these as a few of the items to which I object; there is also a very heavy charge for the support of a naval school. I consider that, if the fund (amounting to between 4 and £500,000) had been applied to the reduction of rates, and such charges as those which I have described (amounting as I believe in the aggregate to many thousand pounds) had not been made, the charges to the West India planter would have been much reduced at a time when he was labouring under great pressure, and in want of every relief he could procure.

You have stated that you consider certain appropriations as illegal appropriations of the planter's money; do you consider the fund out of which those appropriations have been made as arising solely from the rates paid by the British planters?—I consider it as a fund constituted by the Act for the purposes of the Act, and that those appropriations are not any of those purposes.

The question is, whether those appropriations are made out of a fund constituted solely by the British planter, in your opinion?—I do not know in what way that fund was collected; but it appears to me, from the accounts of the Dock Company, that it is a fund in their hands under the Act of Parliament; and seeing it a fund in their hands, retained by them under the Act of Parliament, I consider that it is applicable to the purposes which the Act of Parliament points out.

The question is applied to your observation of its being an appropriation of the planter's money, whether you consider the British planter as having formed that fund?—I consider the British planter as entitled to that fund the moment it appears upon the accounts of the dock directors as in their hands. The British planter is entitled to it under the Report of the Committee of the House of Commons which I have mentioned, and the Acts of Parliament, to be applied according to the purposes of those Acts; and the appropriations made by the Dock Company being, in my humble judgment, none of the purposes of the Acts, I raise the inference that these appropriations are illegal; but I have no knowledge of the particular quarter from whence the fund arises.

Are you aware that from the year 1810 to 1813, a very considerable accumulation of foreign produce took place in the West India Docks, the detention of which tended very considerably to the increase of that fund?—I have heard so, and I dare say it may be the fact, but that was always my opinion as to the applicability of the fund.

No. XVIII.

JUST REGARD TO PRIVATE INTERESTS.

John Inglis, Esq.

You have stated, that the capital invested in the London Docks was £3,250,000; was not that capital subscribed with a view to a participation in the general trade of the port of London?—No doubt of it.

Has not that expectation been much disappointed by the monopoly of the West India trade given to the West India Docks?—To a certain extent, no doubt it has; but that privilege had taken place, I should state, before certain parts of this capital was raised; we raised the capital as we found our business extend.

Was not that capital raised in expectation of enjoying a portion of the general trade of the port of London, when the period for which the exclusive privilege was given should have expired?—Certainly, it has always been in contemplation, that the period would arrive, when those works, which will last far beyond the period contemplated, would, in the efflux of time, be made to pay part of the expenses of improvements.

Has not the effect of that exclusive privilege been to make the capital of £1,200,000 of the West India Company equal in value to the £3,250,000 of the London Dock Company?—It has no doubt made it of greater value from their dividends.

Do you not consider the continuance of this exclusive privilege to be such an interference in the value of private property, as would entitle you to claim an indemnity, if such a measure should be resorted to?—I cannot very well judge of the question.

If the continuance of this exclusive privilege should be granted, would you not consider it as such an interference with the property of the London Dock proprietors, as would entitle them to apply to Parliament for an indemnity, on the same principle as an indemnity was formerly granted to the wharfingers and warehouse-keepers of the port of London, whose trade was affected by the establishment of those docks?—I could hardly give an opinion upon the subject of the propriety of that, for the West India Dock Act passed previously to the London Dock Act; but I should consider the continuance of the monopoly of the West India Dock Company as not for the interest of West India proprietors, provided the same rates and charges were to exist as now, and we can never remove the produce near town; one strong objection to the West India Docks is, their distance from the usual places of business; the export dock I consider to be particularly inconvenient, because it requires the cartage of goods there, and an attendance of clerks that obstructs the current business of a merchant's counting house.

R. H. Marten, Esq.

Did you not, in subscribing to the Commercial Docks, look forward to the period when these monopolies should expire, in the hopes of obtaining a general participation in the trade of the port?—I should reply, that in the outset we had the promise of a monopoly, and we went to very great expense, that the revenue might be made secure, for which security the preference was promised us, and that put us to the expense of raising such a large capital; but when this promise was not made good to us, and the privilege was extended to others of less capital, we next looked to the opening of the other docks from monopoly as the only means of remuneration; for we went to the expense on the promise of preference in wood goods, as the means of saving the duties on the wood trade to government, in which trade, before the dock, there was much smuggling.

No. XIX.

DISCONTINUANCE OF COMPULSORY CLAUSE.

W. Mitchell, Esq.

Are not the West India Docks very short of being full, during a considerable part of the year ?—They are.

Is it not necessary to indemnify the West India Dock Company for this disadvantage, by giving them higher rates than might otherwise be demanded ?—I am not aware that that is so to any extent; that it may be so in some measure is certainly true, because they keep up a certain establishment at each warehouse; but in the daily dispatch of the business, if there is more doing at one warehouse than the establishment of that warehouse is sufficient to perform, then an additional strength is sent from the warehouse which is less employed.

The Committee see that the quantity of sugar now in the West India Dock warehouses, from the return presented on Saturday last, is only 6,400 casks ?—I was not aware that it was so low; I have not seen the return.

Of course the Company are making a very small proportion of warehouse rent to what the warehouses are capable of giving them at the present moment ?—It appears by this statement that there were only 6,400 casks in the dock warehouses on the 18th of May, last Saturday.

For how many hogsheads of sugar have you room in your warehouses ?—I think there have been warehoused there at one period from 120 to 140,000 casks ; I believe I should say that this return does not include the foreign produce, only the British plantation sugar.

What amount of foreign sugars have you at present?—There was a very considerable importation from the Havannah; I cannot speak from any information I possess of the stock on hand.

Does it amount to 5,000 chests?—I should think upwards; but that is loose conjecture.

Which would be equal to 2,000 hogsheads?—Not more.

Then a very considerable portion of the warehouses is at present quite empty?—I should state that the reason of that is owing to the state of the wind; for the last three or four weeks we have had a continuance of easterly winds, and a great number of ships in the Channel have been lying out, which could not get up.

Is not it a general circumstance at this time of the year that the stock of sugars is small?—It is generally larger than this, but small.

Last year was not it reduced to 8 or 9,000?—Between 10 and 11,000 British plantation sugar, besides foreign.

If the other description of commodities were admitted into the West India Docks, so that the warehouses were more generally full, would not the Directors be able to transact their business at a lower rate of charge?—I do not know how to answer that question, except in this way, that viewing the capital of the Company, and the accommodation they afford, and their situation generally, they could certainly afford to do the business upon more reasonable terms than many other dock establishments; and if they had more full warehouses they must be deriving a greater income than at present, when for a part of the year their warehouses are empty.

This is a disadvantage that naturally follows their being confined to the West India business only?—I am not aware of that; it would depend upon the general proportion of the trade of the country that would frequent those docks, which is a matter of speculation, in some measure.

Are not raw sugars generally used for home consumption?—They are, for home consumption; and to be refined for exportation.

Is not the general average import of sugars into the West India Docks from 180 to 190,000?—That is about the average.

Would it not be a great saving of expense to the consumer to have the cartage of those sugars to pay only from the London rather than from the West India Docks?—That will entirely depend upon where the premises of the party purchasing are situated.

Are not the West India Docks at a much greater distance from the sugar refiners in general than the London Docks?—I should think the greater number of them.

Are not many articles now obliged by law to be landed in the London Docks that are sold for exportation, for instance, the produce of the Brazils?—The produce of the Brazils must be exported again.

Foreign wines of a particular quality imported for exportation only?—I am not aware as to any wines of that sort.

If no compulsory clauses existed, do you not think that all commodities would find their proper places; that those intended for exportation would be warehoused in docks as low down the river as possible, and those intended for home consumption be brought up the river as high as possible, to the docks nearest to the metropolis?—I think a great number of considerations must be taken before it can succeed exactly to that, because I apprehend, in a very many instances, it depends upon the ship-owner as well as the consignee of the produce;

perhaps, when I am giving an opinion upon the question last put to me, I am going a little out of my depth; I am confined to the regular British West India trade, and I know the fact, that many ships are solely under the control of the owner of the ship.

Would not the consignees naturally, when their interest required it, make their bargain with the shipowner, as well as to the dock where she is to be discharged as to the rate and freight?—I do not see how the consignees can do so, but a man who charters a ship for a particular voyage can make what conditions he pleases; but where there are a number of consignees, who do not know whether their produce can come in one ship or another, how it is possible for them to settle that point, I cannot tell.

George Hibbert, Esq.

Suppose, at the expiration of the twenty-one years, the West India trade should withdraw from those docks, and repair to the Commercial Docks; in your judgment would the West India Dock Company be still enabled to divide ten per cent. upon their capital?—It would depend, in a great measure, upon the circumstances in which the present investigation may leave them.

In your judgment, as having great experience in the West India trade, and an intimate knowledge of the docks, is it your opinion, that if the monopoly were not continued, but the trade was at liberty to go to the Commercial Docks, the West India Dock Company would be able to continue to divide ten per cent. upon their capital?—I must again revert to what I have before said, that it would depend very much upon the circumstances under which the present examination, and the consequences of it, that is, any legislative measure affecting them, might leave the Company.

Supposing no legislative measure whatever to take place, but the monopoly simply to expire by lapse of time; what, in your opinion, would be the consequence?—My opinion is, that with due attention to the management of their concerns, being left in possession of all their resources, and allowed to make the most of their docks, for the advantage of the proprietors, it is very likely they might continue to divide ten per cent.

With the assistance of the surplus of nearly half a million you mean?—I do not exactly mean that, for that surplus might or might not be applicable to other things, in order to put their docks into a state that would accommodate the general trade of the port.

Supposing, at the expiration of the twenty-one years, the West India trade should resort chiefly to the Commercial Docks, and the Company were not enabled to divide ten per cent. by the profits of each particular year, the surplus would be applicable to that purpose as it has hitherto been?—No doubt; whatever surplus was left under their own control and management.

So that, if the monopoly is not renewed, the Company will have the surplus in hand in aid of future dividends?—I have explained myself upon that subject, I think.

Is it not your opinion, that if the West India trade did resort to the Commercial Docks, there would be as great a security from plunder, as at the present West India Docks?—I am so far from believing that, that I do most firmly believe the direct contrary.

If they adopted the West India Dock system?—I do

not see how they could adopt the West India Dock system, unless they had a monopoly of the trade.

A monopoly of the trade is essential to the prosperity of the West India Docks, in your opinion?—In my own opinion, it is essential to the system which at present protects both the planter and revenue.

Is it not, in your judgment, essential to the prosperity of the dock proprietors?—No.

It is not essential to their dividing ten per cent. yearly? —No.

In your judgment, they will still be able to divide ten per cent., without the aid of the surplus?—I did not say so; my answers are taken down, and I do not think I could explain them further than they explain themselves.

Are the Committee to understand, that it is your opinion, the West India Dock Company would be able to divide ten per cent., though the monopoly was not renewed?—I have said, I think it is possible they might, if left in possession of all their resources. I have been asked, whether I consider that compulsory clause as essential to the prosperity of the Dock Company; to the first question, I have said I think it possible they might divide ten per cent., without giving a precise opinion that they would; to the second, I have answered simply no; that I do not look upon it as essential to the prosperity of the proprietors of dock stock.

In your judgment, is it essential to their obtaining ten per cent. dividend, for many years to come; of course, while the surplus lasts, that will afford it?—I have said, that I do not think it essential to that.

Do you think, that if the monopoly was not renewed, and there was no surplus, the Company have still the prospect of dividing ten per cent. every year as hitherto?—

I am by no means certain they might not, by the means of all their resources, even deprived of the surplus; it is a speculation; it is impossible for me to give an opinion worth the Committee's taking; but I do not consider it essential to the proprietors of dock stock, that they should have a continuance of the compulsory clause.

Do you think they would have as reasonable an expectation of dividing ten per cent. for the next twenty years, as they have had for the last twenty?—Further than can be gathered from the answers I have given, I cannot undertake to answer that question.

Andrew Colville, Esq.

In the event of Parliament withdrawing their assent to the continuance of the restrictive clause in the present Dock Act, taking a view of all the advantages which attach to the remaining privileges, and the other circumstances of benefit which belong to the docks, would you, as a director, have any doubt of dividing ten per cent. from the remaining trade, which the Company can bring within its compass?—Any opinion upon that subject must be formed upon an estimate of the future general trade of the port of London; but supposing that the general trade of the port shall not decrease, and taking for granted (which I cannot for a moment doubt) that Parliament will take no measure in contravention of those Acts, upon the faith of which the docks have been established, and the money for their erection subscribed, I have a very confident opinion, that the business of the Dock Company could easily be so managed, as to give the proprietors ten per cent. dividend.

Would you, therefore, as a director, consider yourself justified in recommending to the proprietory, to accept of seven in the place of ten per cent. for the continuation of the compulsory clause?—Certainly not; I should feel it my duty to state my candid opinion upon the affairs of the Company; and that opinion certainly would be, that they should stand upon their Act, rather than accept of any renewal of the compulsory clause, upon a less dividend than that at present allowed them by Act of Parliament.

Do you take into your consideration, in that answer, the power of combination on the part of the dock companies against the public?—No; I have taken into my view the situation of the Dock Company generally, and the probability of their obtaining such a portion of the West India trade, and the general trade of the port of London, as would certainly give them ten per cent. dividend upon their 1,200,000*l.*; I certainly do not contemplate what may be called any improper combination.

Would you not, as a director, advise your proprietors, in all instances, against any improper combinations?—Certainly so.

Is it in your knowledge that any combination was ever contemplated?—Never; such a thing was never thought of.

Mr. John Drinkald.

It is still so obviously for the advantage of the West India trade to frequent the West India Docks, there is no reason to apprehend that the trade will forsake them?—If I had any thing to do with it, I should not be afraid of throwing it open; if I had it as a legal quay wharfinger, I should not be afraid of doing much better with the West India Dock Warehouse, with the present system, than by having the monopoly of the West India trade, and being excluded from other trades, as they are at present.

You understand them to be excluded from other trades?—So I understand.

Who excludes them?—I understand the House of Commons.

Your understanding of the matter is, that the West India Dock Company are restricted by law from receiving any other trade than the West India trade?—That is my understanding of it; I do not put myself in competition with those better acquainted with the law.

Do not you think that the West India trade would continue to resort to the same docks as hitherto, though the monopoly were to expire?—I think so; they might in the first instance, till experience taught the owners of the cargoes better, go elsewhere, but afterwards, I have no doubt, they would get the whole trade back again, from the superior management and the system adopted at one dock, which the other could not give.

Which no other body could afford?—Not with the present establishments; in the port of London, neither one dock or the other.

Is there room in the West India Docks and warehouses beyond the exigencies of the West India trade now?—They have more room than they want at present, I believe.

So that they have been able of late to accommodate more than the West India trade?—Yes; when the ships came in fleets it was otherwise; but since the peace they have had more than sufficient accommodation for the whole of the West India trade.

Therefore if they are confined to the West India trade, their establishment is larger than necessary?—More than sufficient, in my opinion.

They have spent more upon that than you think quite prudent, perhaps?—I am not quite aware what they have spent upon it.

The extent of an establishment demonstrates the expenditure?—I think they have not.

You think it is not too large for the accommodation of the West India trade?—Certainly not; for times may come again, such as we had when we had not too much room; for instance, in the export dock there is sufficient room, but certainly not too much.

You are not a proprietor, are you?—Yes, I am.

To what amount are you a proprietor?—I think my present share is about £1,200; I was an original proprietor.

C. N. Pallmer, Esq.

Do you consider it for the advantage of the West India trade that the exclusive privilege, as it is called, of the West India Dock Company should be continued?—I consider that, with the combined view of interest and convenience, and under certain restrictions and regulations as to charges, it would be desirable for the West India body that the exclusive privilege should be continued; but not without those restrictions and regulations as to charges; and I believe that is the opinion of the West India body at large: I found that belief upon a document which I beg to be permitted to tender, and which is a proposition made by the West India body to the West India Dock Company, containing the terms upon which, and which alone, they wished the restrictive clause to be continued.

[*The Witness delivered in the same, which was read as follows:*]

" 26th April, 1822.

" 1. That the term of renewal of the compulsory clause in the dock charter shall not exceed seven years.

" 2. That the rates now proposed by the dock committee shall be considered as maximum rates.

" 3. That the maximum of the dividend be lowered, but that the amount of such reduction shall be left to the discretion of Parliament.

" 4. That the capital of the surplus fund shall be annually reduced at the rate of £50,000, by lowering the rates.

" 5. That the expense of all repairs or additional works shall also be defrayed out of the surplus fund; but,

" 6. That such reduction of the surplus fund shall discontinue when it shall amount to only £50,000.

" 7. That any additional works or buildings, the estimates of which shall exceed £10,000, shall be stated in the annual accounts rendered to Parliament, and not executed until after the session of Parliament.

" 8. That provision be made for giving to the West India body a simple and an effectual remedy for the purpose of redress, both at law and in equity, in the event of any misapplication of the funds of the Company, or upon any grounds of complaint where such remedy is not provided under the existing Act."

(*Mr. Pallmer.*)—I should mention, that I speak of the opinion of the West India body, because this subject was considered by the fullest meeting of the West India body which I ever recollect to have seen, and I never recollect more unanimity of sentiment in a public meeting than appeared to prevail upon that occasion, with the exception of those gentlemen present who were connected with the dock establishment.

Will you have the goodness to explain to the Committee what description of persons the West India body is composed of?—The West India body is composed of planters, merchants, and ship-owners, and persons connected with the ramifications of those principal constituent parts of the West India trade. At the meeting to which I have referred, a very full committee was appointed for the purpose of settling with the Dock Company the terms upon which the West India body should consent to a renewal of the restrictive clause in the Act of Parliament; and the terms contained in the paper that I have produced were, after much consideration, determined upon as the only terms upon which it would be advantageous for the West India body that the restrictive clause should be renewed. I beg to state, by way of explanation, that in these terms the question of the maximum of interest to be allowed to the Dock Company in any new Act, is left to the decision of Parliament, because it was found that the parties negociating could not agree upon that point: When the West India body pressed upon the dock directors a specific reduction of maximum, they did it, not upon the principle of requiring persons who could get ten per cent. for their money to be bound to take less; but because they thought that, when they were called upon to consent to a restriction upon themselves, they were at liberty to state upon what terms they would consent to that restriction; they considered, having the power of making such a proposal, that the Dock Company having enjoyed ten per cent. for twenty-one years, and their shares selling at an advance of 85 or 86 per cent., might be very reasonably required to be content, in future, with a smaller rate of interest; they also considered that a material difference prevailed between the Dock Company and other similar public establishments; they considered the West India Dock establishment to be more rigidly restrictive upon those who deal with it than any other public establishment: I know of no public establishment but the West India Docks, with respect to which the public has no alternative; and, under the regulations of the present Act, it appears to me that the affairs of that Company must be badly managed by the directors, if (as experience has proved) what the law constitutes a maximum is not made a minimum also; therefore, when I say that I think it would be desirable that the restrictive clause should be renewed, I always mean to give that opinion subject to the conditions contained in the paper which I have produced; should, however, the restrictive clause be not continued, I confess I, for one, see no reason to fear that a competition among the wet dock companies should not produce the usual and natural effect of competition in a reduction of charges; I have heard of combination among water companies, but I do not think so ill of the directors of the dock establishments as to suppose that they would enter into any such combinations; and, if they did, I have no doubt such combinations would be defeated by the interference of Parliament, or the employment of new capital in the erection of new works; I cannot for a moment think so ill of the directors of the Dock Companies as to suppose that a competition would be a competition of improper indulgences; I therefore, as I said before, see no reason why competition should not produce its usual and natural effect in a reduction of charges.

Suppose the undertaking was now to be begun, do you think it would be practicable to borrow money upon the future rates and duties of such an establishment, so as to pay off the money borrowed within the course of the next twenty years?—I do not think myself competent to form an opinion upon that point.

Within the last twenty years that has happened; do you think, from your knowledge of what has passed, and of the general course of the West India trade, that supposing the rates to be continued as they have been for the next twenty years, there is a reasonable prospect of their producing as much as they have done for the last twenty? —I cannot speak to that precisely; because, unless the circumstances of the next twenty years are the same, the result probably will not be similar.

Is there any other objection you have to make either to the rates or to the general management of the establishment? —I feel it but justice to the directors of the establishment to say that I believe that, except in regard to the particulars which I have mentioned, the establishment is extremely well conducted.

You say you have not personally made any complaint to the Company; but you were understood to say the West India body had made complaints of the amount of the rates?—The West India body have required a reduction of the rates, founded upon the fund in hand, which they thought applicable to that purpose.

Have the West India body at any time made any application to the West India Dock Company for a reduction of the rates, but without success, and have they endeavoured, in consequence of their refusal, to seek for legal redress for their complaint?—In consequence of their refusal, and of the investigation which the West India body has found it lately necessary to make into the transactions of the

Dock Company, it has been necessary for the West India body to resort frequently to the Acts of Parliament which relate to the Dock Company; having, myself, read those Acts of Parliament very attentively, I venture to give my opinion that they require considerable alteration for the protection of the rights of the West India planters according to the spirit and intent of those Acts, and without infringement of the rights of those persons who claim benefit under them; for I apprehend that the West India Dock proprietor (whatever vested interest he may have under those Acts) can have no interest in preserving their doubts and obscurities: and I think that without infringing the rights of the dock proprietor, it will be found necessary for the protection of the West India planters, to make considerable alterations in the Acts; but I should certainly have not ventured to offer this opinion if it had not happened that in the course of the investigation to which I have alluded, the doubts which the West India body entertained impelled them to resort to professional advice.

You say you applied without success to the directors of the West India Dock for redress; why did you not apply to the courts of law?—In consequence of the doubts which we entertained ourselves, of our having redress in the courts of law, we applied to counsel for their opinion upon that point; and we found so many doubts, difficulties, and contrarieties in the opinions of the counsel to whom we referred, as to lead us to conclude, as I was stating before, that we have no redress in case of grievances, unless considerable explanations and alterations are made in the Acts of Parliament.

If the exclusive privilege should be continued, do you think it is consistent with the interests of the planter that it should be left wholly to the discretion of the dock directors, at what amounts the rates and duties should be assessed?—I think it is not.

Do you think it is for the interest of the planters that the Dock Company should retain a large surplus in hand for undefined extensions and improvements?—Certainly not.

In your judgment, what would be a sufficient surplus for the Dock Company to retain for all the legitimate purposes of the establishment?—My own judgment upon that subject has been formed upon the collective judgment of the Committee appointed to negociate with the West India Dock Company; and I think the sum mentioned in the paper which contains the propositions of that Committee to be a sufficient sum.

Have you not entertained an opinion that the system which is adopted at the West India Dock is peculiarly beneficial to the trade?—Certainly, because I knew that that system was a good one, and I was not disposed to change that system unless the circumstances were such as to make it advisable for me to do it.

Have you not thought it was worth while for the West India merchant even to pay more than he now does, rather than suffer that system to be destroyed?—I once thought and expressed an opinion, that, for one individual planter, it would be desirable to pay more rather than that the system should be destroyed, but that planter was myself; when the proposition was first made for a renewal of the restrictive clause, I stated that I would personally make a considerable sacrifice, rather than there should be any difficulty in the way of an accommodation between the West India body and the West India Dock Company; but I beg to state that that sentiment of mine was founded upon combined considerations. I certainly felt satisfied with the security which I enjoyed under the

Dock Company; I felt that a contest between parties who had been so long connected together would be so uncomfortable, that some sacrifice ought to be made for such a purpose; but I ought at the same time to say, that when I used that expression I had not looked so minutely into the state of the accounts of the Dock Company, or the management of the directors, in the respects to which I alluded in a former part of my evidence, as I have now done.

You have stated that you have no knowledge yourself of the Company's affairs; what means have you had of forming an opinion as to the sum necessary to be retained by the Dock Company to meet contingencies?—I have stated, I think, before, that I have formed my opinion upon the collective opinion of the West India Committee appointed to negotiate with the dock directors; and that I had no other mode of forming my opinion than the collective opinion of that body, after they had deliberated upon the subject.

What greater means of forming an opinion had the persons you refer to?—It is a large Committee, consisting of planters and merchants who have very large transactions with the West India Dock Company, and who have looked more minutely, I believe, than I have, into the accounts; and I therefore am disposed to form my judgment upon theirs, in that respect.

If in your judgment it was necessary to reserve £50,000 to meet contingencies, why do you think it right to restrict the Company from laying out more than £10,000 without the consent of Parliament, however extensive the mischief from accident might be, or imperious the necessity of immediately laying it out?—Having found from experience that the Company have exceeded by 4 or £500,000, the capital limited by Parliament for their buildings; having found that the Company have omitted to comply with the 162d clause of the Act of Parliament, requiring them to lay before Parliament from time to time their progress in their buildings, I certainly readily concurred in the proposal which went to require that, before they laid out any larger sums of money in future, they should give notice of it to Parliament, and thus afford the West India body an opportunity of interposing.

Are you not aware that an accident might occur requiring the laying out of a much larger sum than £10,000 immediately?—Certainly; when that proposition was made it never was intended that a provision should not be made for such extraordinary emergencies.

But such a proposal was not made?—No; it was a proposal made subject to such modifications as might be necessary.

Then the proposal was in that respect imperfect?—It did not make provision for such an emergency.

Which in your opinion is necessary?—I should think it very fair and reasonable that such an extraordinary emergency should be provided for.

John Inglis, Esq.

In your opinion would the proprietors of the London Dock consent to resign their exclusive privileges, if the renewal of the exclusive privilege of the West India Dock Company should not be granted?—I cannot answer for what a General Court of Proprietors might do, but as an individual I should feel no hesitation in proposing it to them.

Have you any reason to believe, from any communications you have had with the individuals among the proprietors, that that is a general sentiment?—I believe it is a sentiment that prevails with the directors.

Alexander Glennie, Esq.

The Committee are to understand, that in your judgment, it will be advantageous to the commerce of the City of London, that the monopoly should no longer continue?—I certainly think so.

Has it in your judgment, had the effect of driving away any of the commerce of the metropolis?—It has generally been believed to be so.

Mr. John Manning.

You have stated that wood destined for the West Indies is frequently sent from the Commercial Docks to the West India Docks, to be shipped from thence; how do you account for that additional expense being incurred?—From the necessity of sending it to the exporting vessel, which lies in the West India Dock.

Are not the vessels bound to the West Indies obliged, by the compulsory clause of the West India Dock Act, to load out in their dock, or to load below Blackwall?—I believe those are the conditions.

Does not that obligation make it necessary to incur the expense of sending wood in lighters from the Commercial Docks, instead of shipping it direct from those docks taking it in there?—It is rendered necessary in consequence of the compulsory clause, of course.

No. XX.

COMPETITION OF DOCK COMPANIES.

William Mitchell, Esq.

You say that if the compulsory clause was taken away, the West India Dock Company could not maintain their present system for the protection of property?—I am decidedly of that opinion.

If the West India Dock Company were to so far relax as to establish a new system that admitted of plunder, would not the consequence of that be, that ships would give a preference to other docks that continued to act on a better system?—The Company certainly would have a system which would be the means of drawing ships to their docks, and therefore, I do not apprehend that that system, whatever it was, would be such as to induce the owners of ships not to come into the docks.

Would not the consignees take care, for the protection of their own property, that ships should go into docks where such an arrangement and such a system was adopted, as would keep them perfectly safe?—If one dock was worse than another dock, and a consignee had the power of directing the movements of the ship, I certainly think the consignee would prefer that where his property was best protected.

Would not the opening of the trade of the port of London lead to competition between the different Dock Companies, and induce them to vie with each other in establishing such a system as would give the most effectual security to property, and the greatest accommodation to trade, at the most reasonable rate? —I should rather fear it would be the reverse, as it relates to the West India trade.

George Hibbert, Esq.

A monopoly of the trade is essential to the prosperity of the West India Docks, in your opinion?—In my own opinion, it is essential to the system which at present protects both the planter and revenue.

Was not the original plan for the improvement of the port of London a plan for establishing wet docks at Wapping?—The original plan for improving the port of London was for establishing wet docks; and in a very short time resolutions were adopted for fixing upon Wapping in the first instance.

Was not the establishment of docks for the West India trade in the Isle of Dogs, an after-thought?—It certainly was an after-thought; but the thought followed immediately (the execution did not), upon the adoption of the resolutions.

Was not the original plan for improving the port of London a plan of open competition, without any monopoly, compulsion, or restriction whatever?—I separated so soon from the Committee that were conducting the general plan, that I cannot exactly answer as to what the spirit of their plan was; if I was to go to the practice, the Wapping Dock very soon had monopolies.

Did you never read or hear the resolutions of the Committee of Subscribers to the wet docks at Wapping, after the plan for establishing the docks at the Isle of Dogs had commenced, which was transmitted to the Select Committee of the House of Commons, and which contains these words, "that they have given no opposition to any plan, and desire no other sanction or patronage, than a liberty to make docks in Wapping, under equal advantages with any other plan, wishing for no monopoly, compulsion, or restriction, leaving their plan to its own merits, for public encouragement?"—It is very possible; I cannot answer that; I remember those words, and I have no doubt that they did form a part of some memorial from that body; but they very soon departed from those principles, for they took a monopoly in the first instance, or very soon after.

Was not the first monopoly given, a monopoly to the West India Docks, in the Isle of Dogs, of the

West India trade?—I believe it was; except you call that a monopoly, which existed for many years, in which all the goods of the port were obliged to go to the legal quays, between the Tower and London-bridge.

Did not the West India Dock Company, by obtaining that monopoly, suspend, for a considerable time, the plan of the originally intended docks at Wapping?—I remember that a certain feeling of discontent did arise, when the West India body thought fit to ask for a separate accommodation for their trade; but I also recollect, that before we determined to do that, we did ask the question, whether the General Committee would undertake to give to the West India trade a dock fitted for the purpose of receiving their ships lower down the river; and the answer to that was, that they could not undertake to do it.

Did they not state to the Select Committee of the House of Commons, "this Committee have ever considered the West India trade so important, and so necessary to the support of any docks, that they cannot take upon themselves to decide what encouragement could be given to the merchants, to proceed in a great and hazardous undertaking, if the West India trade should be totally excluded from Wapping; they further beg to state, that with the ability to accommodate the whole of that trade, or any part of it, that every accommodation could be given as to room, and to the allotment of a dock for its peculiar reception, in a short space of time; and that the revenue, as to its security and economy, would be as much under the control of the revenue officers in Wapping, as in any other situation?"—I have no doubt that is part of the memorial referred to; at the same time, I beg leave to state, upon perfect recollection, that Mr. Milligan and myself had a conference with the gentlemen who conducted that plan, and that they did not undertake to give us a dock lower down the river, so as to obviate the danger of plunderage in the passage up the river, and so as to receive the ships, as quickly as possible, from sea.

In fact, after the monopoly of the West India trade had been given to the West India Docks at the Isle of Dogs, was not a monopoly of other branches of trade given to what are now called the London Docks at Wapping, in order to induce them to proceed with their undertaking?—I only know the fact, I do not know the reason why those monopolies were given to it, very possibly that is the reason.

In point of fact, instead of having an establishment founded upon open competition, we now have an establishment of different monopolies, as the means of carrying on the commerce of the port of London; is not that the fact?—There is a monopoly of the West India trade at the West India Docks, and some other monopolies at the London Docks; and in regard to that with which I am most conversant, I am perfectly satisfied that it has been granted upon the most valid grounds.

Samuel Turner, Esq.

Are you acquainted with the system adopted at the West India Docks?—I believe I am.

Do you consider that any advantage would result to the planters and merchants from permitting the West India vessels to discharge where they pleased?—Certainly not.

Do you consider that it would be disadvantageous?—Highly so.

Have the goodness to state your reasons for that opinion?—I conceive it would be destroying, in a great measure, the system on which the docks were first established; that it is of the utmost importance both for the West India trade at large, and for the security of the revenue generally, that the trade should be concentrated as much as possible.

Would any advantage in your opinion be derived to the planter and merchant by a competition between dock and dock?—Certainly, a competition as between dock and dock might, in the first instance, get the business done at a cheaper rate; and, inasmuch as it did so, would tend to the benefit of the planter; but I look upon a monopoly, if I may use such a term, to be almost essential to the system, and that the business being concentrated in one place, does enable the party, if they choose, to do it at a cheaper rate than it possibly could be done if the business were laid open.

Can you state at more length the reason for the opinion you give, that the parties may do the business at a cheaper rate by its being concentrated?—I will state the grounds of my opinion: I consider that originally there existed an arrangement and understanding between the West India body, and those who were engaged in the first formation of the Dock Company, that by concentrating the business, and throwing it into the hands of one large establishment, the business might be done, so that a certain number of labourers would be equal to the performance of the whole business, which number of labourers could not effectuate the same business, if it was dispersed generally abroad; and that this would be the case may be clearly understood, if I should say that any one man having one warehouse, the moment he got that warehouse full, all the persons he employed in the discharge of a ship would be useless, until that warehouse was empty; whereas the business being concentrated, though one merchant may feel it his interest to keep for a considerable time, another will not do so; and therefore, all the hands can be constantly employed; some one warehouse will get empty; whereas if the business were dispersed, as heretofore, the moment a warehouse was filled, no fresh business could be done by the owner of such warehouse, until it was again discharged; and, consequently, the persons he must necessarily employ to conduct the whole of his trade, would not get employment during such time; and he therefore could not afford to do the work at so low a rate as a public company, when the business was not dispersed.

It is your opinion then, that this trade can only be conducted securely, and in fact, that it can be conducted most cheaply by way of such an arrangement as that which now exists?—I cannot say it could be only so done; but I think it could be done decidedly best and cheapest by such an arrangement; I consider that as the very foundation of the original establishment.

And that the effect of a competition between the docks, though it might at first diminish the prices, would be ultimately to raise them?—I am quite satisfied that any competition between the docks would be something like the competition between the water companies; that though for a short time the competition might induce persons to do the business at a cheaper rate, that still the business being concentrated in one spot, enabling the party to do it really at a cheaper rate, it ought, at all events, to lead to a reduction of rate below that at which the business could be done where it was more dispersed. Whether it will do so is a different question.

In suggesting the probability that individuals might be found who would create a dock, and form an establishment at the present time, satisfied with a lower maximum than that under which the West India Dock was established, do you take into consideration the various contingencies to which their trade is exposed, and the great deterioration to which their works are exposed, and the period that might arrive when the dock walls and dock gates and entrances might be to be restored at perhaps a very great and considerable expense?—Certainly, in giving the opinion that a company of new speculators, if I may make use of the word, might be induced to come forward and establish new docks, I took into my consideration all the circumstances which are referred to; but I was induced to come to the conclusion, in consequence of a clear statement that the rates which have been levied during the last twenty-one years have been equal to pay a dividend of ten per cent. during that time; and also to raise, very nearly, if not more than a million of money; besides, with that clear evidence, I do not think it is saying too much to say, that men of sense and capital and consideration in the City of London, would undertake a new dock, secure of the same business that the West India Dock Company are to receive, supposing they get a renewal of their charter; that, secure of that monopoly, persons of the consideration I have mentioned, would be induced to come forward to establish new docks, though they should not divide among the proprietors so large an amount as ten per cent.; and I believe, people might come forward who would be content with seven per cent. in the present times.

Would you propose, in fixing the rates at a maximum of seven per cent., that those rates should be such as would afford, in addition to the means of paying that dividend, a sufficient resource to maintain and to restore those docks from all the consequences of deterioration which must attend them from time to time, and to meet the possible contingencies and fluctuations of trade that might lead to a reduction of their receipts for certain periods?—I should say, that in all equity, I should conceive, that if the West India Dock Company had their charter renewed, they would be entitled to such rates as would ensure a certain dividend, supposing the maximum to be fixed at seven per cent.; I do not give seven per cent. as that which ought to be the rate; I do not give any opinion upon the amount; but that supposing the maximum fixed, the West India Dock Company would be entitled to receive such rates as, after paying that maximum, would support all the necessary charges for the repairs which must take place in such an establishment as docks and warehouses, and that it is essential the dividend should be fixed, not varying one year at five, and another at four, and another at three per cent. The general prosperity of such a concern does depend upon its character in the mercantile world, which character cannot be well supported if its proprietory have not that just confidence in the directors, without which, no directors of any public establishment can properly act and do their duty to the public.

Do you know what dividends are made by the other wet dock companies established on the river Thames?—I know nothing of any but the London Dock Company, which I believe makes a dividend of four per cent.

Do you know the dividend made by the Commercial Dock Company?—I do not.

Do you not think that the London Dock Company, who now divide four per cent. upon their capital, would be extremely happy to take the West India business upon such terms as would give them seven per cent. upon their capital?—There can be no question that the London

Dock Company would be glad to take the West India Dock business, and to do it, if they could get seven per cent. upon their capital for so doing; but I very much doubt whether the London Dock Company could, without fresh warehouses and great expenditure, perform the business which is now performed by the West India Dock Company.

Are you aware that they have a large extent of premises not built upon?—I am aware that they have a part of the ground given to them by the Act of Parliament, still unbuilt upon, and subject to such purposes as may be carried into effect hereafter.

You mean the land originally intended as an export dock, and that might still be converted to that purpose?—I believe so.

Andrew Colville, Esq.

Do you consider the concentration of the trade at one point, that is, at one establishment, as of importance to the planters and merchants?—I consider, to use the term, the West India Dock system, that that system is founded entirely upon the whole of the West India trade coming to the port of London, being conducted at one place, as upon that alone could the various regulations, which tend so much to the security of property, be adopted.

Do you consider that concentration of it at one place to be of essential benefit to the interest of the planter and the merchant?—Certainly.

According to your judgment, could it be carried on separately by different docks, in competition with each other, with equal advantage to the planter or the merchant?—I conceive not; because if the West India produce were dispersed over two or three docks, it would be impossible, in my mind, to adopt the same restrictions and regulations in those docks, that are now adopted in the West India Docks; many of those regulations which are necessary for the security of the property in the West India trade, would be extremely burdensome, in my mind, and oppressive to many other trades: I allude particularly to the exclusion of all persons from the docks, except those employed by the Dock Company and the revenue.

You consider that exclusion, which is one part of the system of the West India Dock Company, as essential to the security both of the revenue and the planter and merchant?—I think that most essential.

And that no dock which could not adopt that system, and exclude all persons but those employed by the dock, could carry on the business with equal advantage to the planter and the merchant?—Certainly so.

Do you think the effect of the competition would be to lead to cheaper rates in the docks?—I think the effect might be cheaper rates, perhaps, in some respects, and dearer in others.

Do you think that likely to be prevented by combination?—Undoubtedly; if the effect of competition was to reduce the rates below that which gave an adequate profit on the business, the evil would be corrected by a combination on the part of the dock companies.

Have not the merchants and planters rather opposite interests in this question?—I think not.

Are not the docks of very great convenience to the merchants?—I should have a very contemptible idea of a merchant who sacrificed the interest of the planter to his own convenience.

Is it not a fact that the docks are a very great convenience to the merchants?—Unquestionably; I think the existence of the docks of very great convenience to the merchant, and also of very great benefit to the planter.

Still the charges fall upon the planter, not upon the merchant?—Of course they fall upon the planter.

You have stated, that if competition led to reducing the rates so low as not to give a sufficient profit to the companies, that might be corrected by combination; did you form that idea from what has appeared in respect of the water companies?—No doubt what occurred in the violent competition among the water companies, led me in part to give that answer; but I think it is the necessary effect of competition being carried too far.

Do you think there would be much facility to that combination?—I think there may be, because there are fewer docks than water companies.

Do you think it would be likely to lead to the creation of a variety of other docks?—I do not think any new dock would be created, merely for the chance of business.

Mr. John Drinkald.

Supposing the trade to be opened, and that there was a competition with the legal quays or other docks, do you not think that competition would lead the West India Dock Company, in order to retain a great part of the trade, to lower their charges?—That is a matter of calculation, compared with the expense of the establishment.

Do you not think that the legal quays or London Docks would be induced to lower their charges to obtain the business?—I do not think the legal quays could reduce their charges; and they could not afford to do the business at the rate for which it is done by the West India Dock Company.

Do you not think the Commercial Dock would lower their charges with a view to attract the business?—I do not think any merchant or planter would allow his goods to go to those docks.

Do you not believe that they would put their charges below those of the West India Dock Company?—I do not think they would, or that they could afford it.

John Inglis, Esq.

The London Dock Company have a monopoly of some parts of the trade?—They have.

Have the goodness to state of what trade?—They have a monopoly of wine, spirits, tobacco and rice; I should state that that monopoly was not solicited by the London Dock Company, it was given to them by the Lords of the Treasury; they were offered it for the protection of the revenue; the London Dock was established on the principle of freedom, for the purpose of receiving such trade as should prefer the use of their docks from their own free will, the monopoly was made part of our first Bill.

In your opinion the freedom of trade is a proper principle for docks to be established upon?—Individually I certainly have no objection to answering the question in the affirmative.

As a merchant you would prefer a system of open competition to that of monopoly among wet docks?—No doubt of it.

You have stated that you could give considerable accommodation to the West India trade; you have the greatest part of the land that was originally intended to be applied to the export dock?—We have part of it.

If the trade of the port of London was opened, and an additional portion of it came to the London Docks, have you still the means of making that export dock?—Yes, we have.

Is it not probable that that measure would then be adopted?—I think it is very possible, and that an Act of

Parliament would be applied for, to enable the London Dock Company to carry it into execution.

You say you have warehouses already built that could be raised upon, and that you have the means of adding more ?—Yes.

With the additional export dock and the alterations in the warehouses, could not every accommodation that is given in the West India Docks be given in the London Docks to the West India trade ?—I believe so.

You say that you consider the West India proprietors would be injured by the continuance of the present rate of charges; are you of opinion, in case of competition, that your charges at the London Docks would be lower than those at the West India Docks ?—I conceive that a new scale of charges would be made in case there was a competition, and consequently they would be lower; the dividends which have been paid, and the sum remaining in the hands of the West India Dock Company, prove that it can be done for less.

Have you the means at the London Docks of transacting the same business that they have at the West India Docks ?—I will not take upon myself to say that, but I think there is a person competent to give evidence upon that subject, and in his judgment, I believe he would say, that the London Dock Company could do the same business as is done by the West India Dock Company.

The advantage you suppose would arise, the Committee are to understand, is not positively founded upon any present rate ?—Not having been tried, I cannot give an opinion as to the positive fact.

How much are the present rates at the London Dock lower, in your opinion, than they are at the West India Dock ?—We have no rate for the same business; the tonnage upon the shipping is lower considerably.

Is the tonnage upon the shipping lower when contrasted with the services performed?—I cannot answer that question.

Was it ever in your contemplation, that the West India Dock Company might be inclined to give up their monopoly upon sugar, in case you gave up yours upon tobacco?—That would depend upon the revenue; it would make no difference to us if we got sugar instead of tobacco, and from circumstances which have taken place, it appears as though it would be more profitable.

Mr. Dennis Chapman.

In case the monopoly of the West India Dock should expire, could a considerable portion of the West India trade be well accommodated at the London Dock?—Perfectly so; I have not the least doubt of it.

As cheaply?—If it was not so cheap, the merchants would not resort to it.

As securely?—I think fully as securely.

And as conveniently in all respects?—I think more so; because the cartage to the different sugar bakers and grocers would be cheaper.

If any extravagant charges are made at either of the docks, would not the best way of preventing them be to take away the compulsory clauses in both the Dock Acts, and to open them to competition?—Certainly, I consider that best for the merchants and the docks also.

R. H. Marten, Esq.

Is not, in your opinion, fair and open competition the best means of obtaining accommodation at the cheapest possible rate?—I think it is so; I am satisfied of this, that unless something of that kind shall be thought of, the port of London will lose its trade.

In your opinion, it will be for the benefit of trade that the exclusive privileges of the different dock companies should be done away with?—That is my opinion.

What reason have you to suppose that if there were an open competition, you could induce West India ships to come to your docks?—By the offer probably of greater accommodation, we should strive to give more accommodation, and striving to have the consignments of those with whom we should be friendly.

Could you give greater accommodation than is now afforded at the West India Docks?—We would try for it.

Do you think there is a reasonable chance of your affording greater accommodation?—I think we could.

In what way?—From our concern not being so large, and from the natural competition rousing up our own powers to endeavour to get all we could.

Could you unload the ships more expeditiously?—I do not know that we could do better than they could, if we were both put to a trial, for they have every accommodation.

Do you think you could afford as great a security of the property from plunderage?—That I have not a doubt of.

Could you adopt the same strict regulations before the ships came into your docks?—I see no reason why we should not.

Should you be disposed to seek a preference, in which of these two ways, by affording greater security to the property, or by affording greater indulgences to the ship-owner and the other people concerned in the trade, who might be disposed to plunder?—I should hope we should give no indulgence to any body who might be disposed to plunder, but we should be disposed to do all we could to invite trade to this dock.

Do you mean you should not be disposed to enter into a competition of indulgences, if the trade were thrown open?—Of lawful and proper indulgences.

You are quite sure you would not try to get business in that way?—I think, if I know myself, I would not.

Have you never professed that you would be driven to do so?—I do not understand the question.

Have you ever professed that if the trade were thrown open, you would be driven into a competition of indulgences which would lead to plunder?—I never have.

Have you ever heard of any dock company that has made that offer?—I never heard of it.

It appears in your mind very preposterous that any dock company should hold out that they would grant indulgences to plunder?—I think they must have lost their senses before they could say that.

If all the West India business was opened to you, which gives at present to another Company profit which enables them to divide ten per cent., would not you make a race of that business by doing it on lower terms?—Most assuredly; but without any indulgence whatever to smuggling.

Are you sure it would not be more to your interest to pay court to the captains of the ships and the crews of the ships, and to relax the restrictions against plunder, than to enforce strict regulations for the purpose of securing the property?—Indeed I think, according to the old proverb, honesty is the best policy; and so morality would be;—and I think nobody would suspect I would countenance such a thing.

The question is not on your disposition, but on your interest?—Certainly not, for in the long run it would be our ruin.

You would consider it your interest to secure the

property placed in your warehouses?—I should look upon our first interest to be to secure the revenue and the merchant, and let all other things take their course.

Have you referred to the West India Dock rates?—I have; and there are many that I am satisfied we could do the business under, and be glad of it too.

Alex. Glennie, Esq.

You are one of the directors of the Commercial Docks?—I am.

How long have you been in that office?—About six or seven years.

Have you considered whether your docks and warehouses are capable of accommodating any portion of the West India trade?—Yes, I think they are; we have had sugar in the warehouses since I have been a director.

Within the last six years?—No; I have been a director longer than that.

Are you aware of any difficulty in giving perfect security to the property of the merchants, and to the King's duties?—None at all.

Supposing the monopoly of the West India trade to be removed altogether to your docks, would your Company receive that branch of trade, do you think, on more reasonable terms than the West India Dock Company do at present?—Yes, I think we could; I am confident we could.

Would you be satisfied to be limited to a lower dividend than ten per cent. if you had all the advantages of that trade?—That is a question I can scarcely answer, except individually.

Would you be content to accept the monopoly of that trade, upon lower terms than ten per cent. dividend?—

Yes, I suppose the Company would; I can only answer for myself individually, I should.

Would it be advantageous to the Company to undertake that entire branch of the commerce of the river on less terms than a dividend of ten per cent.?—Yes, I certainly think it would.

Would it, in your judgment, be advantageous to the proprietors of your docks to undertake the whole at a dividend of seven per cent.?—Certainly it would be more advantageous than the trade that the dock is employed in at present.

In your judgment, would the Dock Company be glad to undertake, upon those terms, the monopoly of the West India trade?—I can scarcely answer that question.

In your judgment, would it be advantageous to the general commerce of the river, that there should be an open trade altogether?—I most decidedly think so.

Do you think a competition amongst all the various dock proprietors, for the general commerce of the river, would be advantageous?—Yes, I think it would be highly advantageous to the trade of the port of London.

You stated that all the rates, excepting those on rum, you could reduce?—Yes.

At what rate would you take sugars?—I think, on looking over the reduced schedule I have seen, as proposed by the West India Dock Company, that the Commercial Dock Company could do it at about ten per cent. less, and I think they would be very well satisfied to do it at that rate.

Every thing else in the same proportion?—All the reduced charges I have seen, excepting rum.

Not more than ten per cent.?—I will not say not more; but I think we should be very well satisfied with the trade at ten per cent. reduction of the rates.

You are calculating upon an expenditure of a considerable capital to put you into the same situation to perform those services?—Yes.

You would perform the whole of the services?—Yes.

And adopt the same system of police and watching?—I do not think we should adopt the same system; I should hope we may improve upon the system.

Do you intend to build a wall?—We should do every thing to satisfy the revenue officers.

In what way should you improve upon the system to satisfy the revenue officers?—I do not know; we should have to consider of that; but though the system of the West India Docks is a very good one, I think it admits of some improvement.

Has it occurred to you in what instance?—I think it is not quite fair for the directors of the West India Dock Company to ask me to put them in possession of that which we might do hereafter.

What capital do you calculate must be laid out to provide for those accommodations?—I have not made any calculation of the capital; unless I saw there was a probability of our getting it, it would be a waste of time.

What time would you require to enable you to receive this produce?—I should think, a less time than the West India Dock Company took to get ready to receive the produce.

What time was that?—I think, upwards of three years; but I do not recollect exactly; but I am confident we could be ready in as little time, perhaps less; we are, in a measure, prepared.

You say, that in your opinion, some of the trade of London has been sent to the outports, by their charges being lower than in the port of London; do you know any thing about the Havannah trade having been driven to the Continent, from the same cause?—Yes, I certainly do; I had at one time a considerable deal to do in the Havannah trade, and we found the charges of the port were such that we were obliged to give it up.

In fact, it has been the subject of complaint among parties who shipped from the Havannah to London, that the charges were so much higher here than on the Continent, that a great deal of business has been prevented coming to London, and goes now to the Continent?—Just so.

Can you state the charge for rent for Havannah sugars, by the West India Dock Company, and that made at any free port on the Continent?—No, I cannot state that with any degree of accuracy.

You only know that it is so much lower as to produce the effect you have spoken of?—Yes; it had such an effect at the time of the opening of the ports on the Continent; I kept a ship, solely loaded with Havannah sugar, out of the port of London, until the ports of Holland were opened, and then sent her there, which saved me at least twenty-five per cent. upon her cargo, taking into consideration the price and the charges.

Then, in your opinion, the same facility as is given in the West India Docks might be given in other docks in the port of London, and at a lower rate of charge, if the compulsory clause were at an end?—Decidedly.

Will it not in your opinion tend very much to the accommodation of the trade, that this monopoly and exclusive privilege should terminate?—Yes, I think it would; I would not support any application on behalf of the Company for an exclusive privilege; I think it is a disadvantage to the traders of the kingdom that such monopolies should exist.

Thomas Tooke, Esq.

In your judgment, can the commerce of the port of London be better accommodated by an exclusive monopoly, such as you probably understand the West India Dock Company to have, or by an open trade?—I have no hesitation in giving a preference to an open trade, on all occasions.

Do you think the commerce of the port would, all circumstances considered, be likely to be better accommodated?—I think it would.

And at less expense?—And at less expense.

In your judgment, would it be advantageous to the commerce of the port of London, that the present monopoly of the West India Dock Company should continue or expire?—I should have no hesitation in considering that the commerce of the port of London would be very much benefited by a cessation of the monopoly at the West India Docks.

Do you think it would tend to a reduction of rates?—It would tend to a reduction of the rates, and remove that which is the great obstacle the port of London has to contend with in its competition, not only with the ports of foreign states, but with the ports of Liverpool and Bristol; namely, the exorbitant charges to which the trade of the port of London has been hitherto subject.

Are the Committee to understand that the port of London has the reputation of exorbitant charges?—So I have always understood; and I do at present understand it to be higher, taking all the trade collectively, than any other port, probably, in Europe; certainly higher than any other port with which I am acquainted.

In your judgment, it would tend mainly to promote the prosperity of the port of London, to reduce the port charges?—Very much so indeed.

Do you know that vessels destined to London have frequently gone to adjacent ports on the Continent, in order to avoid the high charges of some of the Dock Companies that enjoy exclusive privileges?—I have, in general terms, heard of such circumstances.

You have spoken of the high charges on pepper at the East India Docks; is it within your knowledge that a ship from India called the Amity (Gray), belonging to James Hunter and Company, of this city, gave, only on Saturday, an additional premium of 7*s.* 6*d.* per cent. to the underwriters, and an additional freight to the owners, that she might carry over her cargo to Rotterdam instead of coming up the river Thames?—I was not aware of that particular circumstance before, but from the experience I have recently had of very heavy expense upon pepper in the port of London, I should myself prefer sending a cargo I might have the disposal of to Amsterdam or Rotterdam, having heard of the comparative moderation of the charges at those ports.

You were not underwriter upon that ship at the Royal Exchange Assurance Office?—I believe not; but I have not been there within this day or two.

Do you know that vessels, with cargoes of sugar from the Havannah, frequently have orders to stop, in order to determine whether they shall discharge in the port of London, their original destination, or proceed to a different port on the Continent to warehouse their cargoes there?—I have occasion to know it, certainly, for I purchased a cargo, within the last fortnight, that was in the

Channel, destined for a market, and sent her on to the north of Europe.

The name of your house is one attached to the petition to the House of Commons against the renewal of the privileges of the West India Dock Company?—It is; I believe I signed it; and I did so, considering myself interested as a merchant who desires the prosperity of the port of London; and as a consumer, likewise, interested against any monopoly.

Then it was not from any knowledge or experience of your own of any of the inconveniences which were represented in that petition against which you felt it your duty to petition?—It certainly was not from any direct experience of them.

Then you felt it to be your duty to petition, not because of any knowledge which you possessed, either of the good or evil which belonged to that institution, but upon general principles?—On the principle that if the monopoly were found to be unconnected with any charges beyond what would have existed without that monopoly, it would be nugatory, and therefore not the subject of controversy one way or the other; but, in fact, it was upon general information, which was uncontradicted within my circle of acquaintance, some of whom were West India merchants, and acquainted with the details of that description of business; that the charges were really very considerably higher than they should be; and that there was very great inconvenience and expense attending the greater distance; which must be felt ultimately in the price of the article.

Then the same interest which you felt, and which induced you to sign that petition, would belong, upon the principles which you have stated, to any other merchant or trader in the City of London?—Precisely so.

Francis Kemble, Esq.

In your opinion, if the West India trade was extended to the different docks in the river Thames, would there not be a greater disposition to give every accommodation to the trade than has been shown under the monopoly enjoyed by the West India Dock Company?—I should say if there was any, there would be greater, so far as my own experience goes; but I am decidedly of opinion, that there would be greater, because a great many merchants have expressed their wish to stow and sample their sugars in a way that would be satisfactory to the buyers; and if one fairer mode than the other were adopted at any one dock, I presume, ultimately, it would be adopted at all, not excepting the West India.

Then you take for granted, that sugars lying in that dock which adopted the mode considered most fair and equitable, would obtain a higher price than sugars in another dock that continued the mode now used by the West India Dock Company?—They certainly would; because the knowledge that we should receive the article that we purchased, would in itself be worth paying for, independently of the charges of trade that we should avoid.

Are you to be understood as attributing the mode in which sugars are sampled and stowed, to the exclusive monopoly of the West India Dock Company?—I have no means of answering that question; it exists under their monopoly, and in my opinion would not exist, if the monopoly did not exist.

Do you believe that if any dock was opened which was capable of receiving the West India produce, in which another system was practised, it would be an inducement to many of the merchants, as far as they can, to send their sugars to that dock ?—I have no doubt of it; I cannot impute to West India merchants any deliberate intention of adopting an unfair mode; I believe that the mode was adopted in ignorance, and persevered in a little, perhaps, from a different feeling of the circumstance that I have alluded to, that the West India merchants are under no necessity (it does not come before them in the course of their trade), to see their sugars at all; a great many see nothing more of their sugars than the little sample sent to them in blue paper represents.

Do they not feel it as comparing the present value of the sugar with that which it might have produced ?—They only feel it in general impression; I have sometimes had West India merchants in my own house, and taken them to show them their own sugars, without lodging any complaint, or claiming any deduction in price, and they would not believe it was their own sugar; they have got candles to examine the marks, and they would not believe it was the sugar they sent.

Have you any doubt that if there was a means of competition, those other evils would be remedied ?—I have no doubt, that if there were competition, that would be remedied; I take for granted, that if merchants found that sugars stowed and sampled in a particular way, obtained a preference in the market, they would either remove their sugars to the docks in which such plan was adopted, or they would use their influence with any docks they did house their sugar in, to obtain the necessary alterations; either would answer the purpose of the buyers, perfectly.

William Frampton, Esq.

If the West India trade were open to competition among all the different dock companies, would not, in your opinion, that mode of housing and sampling sugar be adopted which was considered most advantageous by the importers and the buyers?—I think it would.

REPORT

FROM

THE SELECT COMMITTEE

OF

THE HOUSE OF COMMONS,

APPOINTED TO CONSIDER OF THE MEANS OF IMPROVING AND MAINTAINING

The Foreign Trade

OF THE COUNTRY.

WEST INDIA DOCKS.

REPORT.

THE SELECT COMMITTEE appointed to consider of the Means of maintaining and improving the FOREIGN TRADE of the Country, and to report their opinion and observations thereupon to The House; and to whom the several Petitions, which were presented to the House in the last Session of Parliament on the subject of the extension of the exclusive Privileges of the WEST INDIA DOCK COMPANY, were referred;—HAVE agreed to the following REPORT:

YOUR Committee having taken into consideration the Petitions referred to them, and continued their investigation to the close of the last Session, have thought it their duty on their re-appointment to apply themselves immediately to the further prosecution of the Inquiry which had been interrupted by the Prorogation. In the course of their proceedings they have called for various Documents which were calculated to throw light upon the subject of their investigation, and have examined a great variety of Witnesses, as well in support of the allegations contained in the Petition of the West India Dock Company, as of those in the other Petitions that have been referred to them; the respective Prayers of which involved the expediency of further continuing the exclusive privileges granted to the West India Dock Company by the 39 Geo. 3. Under this Act the Dock in question was constructed; and the Subscribers were constituted a Joint Stock Company, by the name of "The West India Dock Company." Certain conditions were at the same time imposed upon them, in respect to the amount of the Sum to be raised as a Capital or Joint Stock; the period within which the Works were to be completed; the amount of the Dividend to which they were to be entitled, and the application of the surplus Receipts, if any should exist. In addition to these, was a Clause compelling all West India Ships to land their Cargoes in this Dock for the term of 21 years; and the privilege of warehousing all West India produce brought to this Port was subsequently added by the Warehousing Act of the 43 Geo. 3.

In referring to the Evidence adduced before

Your Committee, it will be observed that a considerable part of it tends to show the advantages derived from the establishment of closed Docks, both to the revenue and trade of the country, as compared to the system that previously prevailed. The value of these institutions, whether in giving facility to commerce, in securing the collection of the revenue, or in protecting the interests of the merchant, is so unquestionable, that Your Committee feel it would be an unnecessary waste of time to enter into any detailed discussion on that branch of the subject; and the more so, as the question of a recurrence to the former imperfect system, does not appear to Your Committee to be at all involved in that of discontinuing or prolonging the exclusive privilege enjoyed at present by the West India Dock Company.

The maintenance and encouragement of the Dock establishments are objects of equal interest to all parties concerned in the commerce of the country; and the principal question for the consideration of Your Committee appeared to be, whether the advantages confessedly resulting from them, could be preserved to the Public most effectually, under a system of exclusive privilege, granted to each Dock respectively, by which the trade should be by law divided and apportioned; or one of competition, operating freely amongst them, in which the convenience of commerce, whether arising from local position, regulation or charges, should be alone the measure of employment or advantages enjoyed by each several establishment.

The points into which the subject may be divided, and to which the evidence in the Appendix applies, are very numerous. The material ones however, and those on which the decision appeared to Your Committee to rest, were those only which are connected with the security and facility of collection of the revenue, and protection of the property of the merchant, inseparable from it; and how far these advantages are dependent either generally, or in the case of the West India Trade in particular, upon the continuance of the system of exclusive privilege.

The advantage to the Public of open competition, wherever applicable, will not as a general principle be questioned. It is not, however, to be adopted without limitation, or to be presumed that various cases may not present themselves, in which a departure from that principle may not be of such importance to the public interests, as to be fully warranted by every consideration of prudence and expediency. This was the case in the original establishment of the

Docks, when it was necessary to hold out liberal compensation to those who invested their capital in a speculation which, whatever advantages it might eventually promise to the Adventurers and the Public, was, in its commencement, of doubtful success. It appears, however, to Your Committee, that admitting the existence of cases to which this exception applies, it belongs to the parties soliciting exclusive privileges, to show that so strong an especial case exists in the particular instance, as to offer advantages sufficient to preponderate against the generally recognized beneficial principle of competition.

In the present case, all the claims that arise from the hazard of doubtful experiment, which originally recommended the grant of exclusive privileges, have long vanished. The success of the experiment is decisively ascertained—the investment of capital has been fully compensated —and the advantages of Docks are universally acknowledged. To sustain the claim, therefore, it must be shown, that there is something in the nature of the trade received into the West India Docks, that indispensably requires a particular system of separate accommodation, protection and management, or that the advantage derived to the Public from the Dock system, is inseparably dependent upon a continuance of exclusive privileges to each of the various establishments.

In confining their Report and Opinion chiefly to these points, Your Committee feel that they shall best consult the intentions of the House, in the reference made to them; and they are the more inclined to this course, because, if the House should concur with them in their view on these questions, and adopt the conclusion to which they have come, the various subordinate points will be, as it appears to Your Committee, sufficiently provided for in the practical measures that must obviously result from it.

Much evidence has been adduced to show the perfection of the system, and the value of the regulations introduced and practised in the management of the West India Docks; and the effect produced by them in affording security to the collection of the Revenue, protection to the property of the Merchant, and facility in the conduct of his business. With some slight exceptions in the latter point, Your Committee are disposed to give a ready concurrence to all the claims preferred by the Directors of the Dock Company on this head. Both from the evidence they have received, and from their personal observation, they can venture to state, that no Establishment of the kind can, in their opinion, surpass, in these particulars, the Establishment of the West India Docks: but it is not the positive excellence alone which it is their duty to consider—it is the comparative, or rather exclusive, excellence belonging to them that must be regarded, and by which the grounds of their decision are to be furnished. And here, Your Committee cannot but observe, that whatever degree of perfection, in regard to dispatch and regularity, may distinguish the West India Docks, great facility towards these objects is incident to the warehousing in that Dock being confined to the cargoes of peculiar ships, and the articles of merchandize to a comparatively confined number; and to this circumstance of strict limitation, in respect to goods and ships, it must be ascribed, if exactly the same degree of perfection in the conduct of business, and in the classification of merchandize, is not to be found, nor is, indeed, attainable in a Dock of more extensive use, and more general resort.

Admitting the advantages arising from this circumstance, Your Committee has directed its attention to ascertain how far the very strict measures of precaution adopted in the West India Dock are necessary to the chief practical purposes of the Dock Establishment, and whether the effect of the system of exclusion and separation, which is said alone to admit of these precautions, so much exceeds in value to the public interest, the more open system prevailing in other Docks, as to call for its preservation, if involving the continuance of a general system of exclusive protection, as it appears to Your Committee must be the consequence of maintaining it in this instance. In proceeding to offer an opinion to the contrary, Your Committee are fully prepared to believe that the Directors of the West India Dock Company, in contending against alteration, are actuated by no feelings of pecuniary interest,—that their interests, in fact, as Planters or Merchants, are infinitely superior to any they can have as Dock Directors; and that they are influenced only by their impression of the utility and advantage of this Establishment, as affecting the public through the peculiar branch of commerce to which it is appropriated; increased, perhaps not unnaturally, by a solicitude for the preservation of that which they have, with great care and attention, fostered and brought nearly to perfection.

If, indeed, Your Committee could take the same view as that entertained by the Dock Directors of the particular regulations established in the West India Dock, and consider the security arising from them, as the effect of their exclusive privileges, or could they believe that there was any thing so peculiar in the West India Trade that, without the extreme perfection of their institution, the public purposes for which the Dock was intended could not be accomplished, they should not hesitate in the recommendation they should offer to the House; but believing that the perfection (however admirable) is carried, in some particulars, beyond what is necessary to the purposes either of security or accommodation, and that there is no peculiarity in the nature of the Trade in question which so distinguishes it from other Trades as to counterbalance their conviction that the public interests are best secured in all matters connected with Trade, by leaving it freely to act for itself, and to follow its own convenience, without compulsory restraint or direction, their inquiries have been directed to satisfy themselves, whether the practical utility of the Dock Establishment is not compatible with a system to which the advantages of competition can be safely afforded.

On the subject of security, which appears to Your Committee to involve the whole question of comparative preference, between an exclusive and an open system, there is a great variety of evidence from persons every way entitled to attention, consisting both of Merchants, Revenue Officers, and others.

On one side it is stated, that not only the regulations and conduct of the West India Docks are as perfect as such an Institution is capable of being made, (which Your Committee are disposed to admit); that they have answered every purpose that was expected from them; and that, from the circumstances of the Trade, if the exclusive privilege is not continued, the same security, either to the Revenue or the Trade, could not be attained.

On the other, it is stated, by authorities equally respectable, that the regulations and system of the London Dock Company, though, from the circumstance of its admitting more general Trade, they must be of a nature adapted to that difference, have yet been found practically sufficient, for the necessary protection both of the Revenue of the Crown, and the property consigned to them; and that arrangements could be made for depositing West India produce, both within them and the Commercial Docks, with perfect safety.

The Evidence adduced before your Committee may be divided into that of witnesses who speak exclusively to the West India Docks; who speak exclusively to each of the other Docks; and to those who, in some degree, speak with a knowledge of both. The officers and others connected with the West India Docks have confessedly spoken from little, or with very imperfect, knowledge of the practical effect of any other system than that with which they had been concerned; their evidence is positive as to the merits of the West India Docks as applicable to West India ships and produce; and in speaking of the defects of any other system with which they admit themselves to have no adequate means of comparison, they state merely their belief, founded on a difference from that system which they consider as essential to the due protection of the particular Trade.

Mr. Mitchell,
" Colville,
" Tilstone,
" Tanner,
&c.

On the other hand, the evidence of those who speak to the conduct of business in the London Docks is equally positive in denying that the defects attributed, conjecturally, to a more open system, are found practically to exist;—that although at one time, from the defect of the system, and the conduct of the Revenue Officers, Goods had been delivered without payment of duty, since the reform then introduced, no depredation on the property, or difficulty in the collection of the Revenue, is known to have occurred.

Mr. Inglis,
" Tooke,
" Chapman,
" Gibson,
" Sawtell,
" Cooper,
&c.

Of the witnesses who appear to have some knowledge of both Establishments, some seem to give a preference to the protection afforded by the West India Docks, in consequence of the exclusion of persons from the Quay, and the separation of the Import and Export Dock. Others rather incline to believe there *may* be some advantage from particular regulations (on which *however* there exists a difference of opinion), and some of the Officers of the Revenue speak confidently to equal or sufficient security being to be found in both Establishments; and (as stated by one) that to neither can a decisive preference be given. In reference to this point, Your Committee called for the establishments of the Excise and Customs maintained for the protection of the Revenue in each of the Docks respectively. In the London Docks the establishment of the Excise is nearly the same as in the West India Docks, the excess being rather in the latter; while that of the Customs in the West India Docks falls very far short of that employed in the London Docks. The Revenue collected too in the West India Docks is much more considerable, and collected at a less percentage than that in the London Docks. The difference however of the systems pursued in these two Docks, necessarily arising from the difference in the nature of the Trade received into the one and the other, makes it impossible to draw any conclusion from the circumstances adverted to, in regard to the comparative security belonging to each.

Mr. Groves, „ Drinkald, „ Domett, „ Stuart, &c.

It has already been stated, that the prospect of great and otherwise unattainable advantages to the public interests, incontestably shown by those who claimed exclusive privilege, could alone warrant a departure from the principle of open competition. The particular advantage in this case could only be shown in the inseparable connexion of those privileges with the security of the collection of the public Revenue, and the property of the Merchant. But such advantage is not to be found alone in the exclusive system of the West India Dock Company. The result of the testimony received by Your Committee, and to which they beg to refer, appears to them clearly to establish whatever merits may belong to the system of the West India Docks; in other respects (and Your Committee are ready to do it ample justice) they feel that they are insufficient to redeem this defect, or to warrant them in recommending a continuance of an unnecessary compulsion upon one branch of the Commerce of the Country, which might involve in it a similar compulsion upon others, and ultimately lead to a general system of restriction and monopoly.

Your Committee do not feel it necessary to enter into any detail upon the various subordinate points that have been introduced, connected with the question of comparative dispatch and accommodation, and the particular utility of the provisions made at one or other of the Docks; these will be found described in the evidence. All those provisions (independently of those which are applicable only to a Dock, confined to a limited description of merchandize) are capable of being extended, if thought expedient, to any other establishment.

There are two things, however, on which much stress has been laid on the part of the Dock Company, and to which Your Committee therefore deem it right to advert. One, the classification of the several articles of merchandize, as facilitating the operation of the Merchant, and the duties of the Revenue Officer. The other, the removal of the crews from the ships, (which is inapplicable to Docks of general resort), as the best security against depredation, and as conducing also to dispatch in unloading the cargoes.

With respect to the first, although the same perfection of classification is incompatible with the admission of the articles of general Trade, which is easily effected with respect to those of a single branch of it; it is to be collected, from the testimonies of those whom they have examined, that it may be and is effected in the London Docks, sufficiently for those purposes for which it is alone important, and is therefore applicable to any establishment of a similar nature.

With respect to the second, both of the particular merits attributed to it, are, from the evidence, subjects of question. Whether, the discharge of a ship is performed with greater promptitude and facility by hired men under the inspection of officers of the Dock Company, or by the seamen under the inspection of their own officers, Your Committee entertain considerable doubt; while, as far as it appears, there is no reason to believe that the continuance of the crews on board leads to habitual depredation. Some objection, indeed, has been stated to the removal of the younger part of the crews from their ships; but in order to provide against the danger that might be justly apprehended to the morals and good conduct of the apprentices in consequence of such removal from them, without employment, and freed from control and discipline, a vessel has been provided by the Admiralty, which the Directors of the West India Dock Company have prepared for the accommodation of 400 boys, who are received upon application, and during the time they remain, have the advantages of care and education. The largest number of boys that at any one time have taken the benefit of this establishment, Your Committee are informed, has not exceeded above half the number it is capable of admitting.

Your Committee, in recommending the adoption of an open system of competition in preference to one founded on exclusive privileges, cannot omit a reference to the testimonies, borne by gentlemen deeply interested in the question, to the advantages of the West India Docks, which accord with the strong feeling expressed by the Dock Directors, and are desirous not to be understood as intending to convey any objection to the continuance of as much of the regulations, to which such importance is attached, as, in the discretion of the West India Dock Directors, may be found compatible with the interests of the Company, and useful to the particular branch of trade they are desirous of receiving.

With respect to every point that relates to moderation of charges and the accommodation of the Merchant, the best security for these being attended to on the part of the Dock Companies, will be the interest of those who may be induced to lodge their Goods in the Docks; nor are we apprehensive that this can be carried to an improper length, or become, as has been thrown out, a competition of indulgences dangerous to the Revenue. Against this, the known respectability of those to whom the management of each establishment is intrusted, and the consideration, that the interests of the Docks are bound up with the interests of the Public, is a sufficient protection—whatever can affect the Revenue must equally affect the Merchant and Proprietors, who would readily find the means of discontinuing the use of any Dock in which the merchandize consigned to it was not sufficiently protected against fraud and depredation.

Another point to which the attention of Your Committee has been drawn in the course of their proceedings, and to which much of their consideration has been directed, is the fund that appears to have accumulated to a large amount in the hands of the West India Dock Company, from the excess of their Receipts above their Expenditure. The amount of this fund, by the last account rendered to Parliament, was £393,910 2*s.* 7*d.*, subject to all the outstanding demands against the Company. On this amount, however, a good deal of question has arisen. On the part of the Planters, it was urged, that the works were limited to a certain time in which they were to be completed, and a certain amount of money which was to be expended upon them; and that although the words "extensions and improvements" are used in the clause directing the application of the funds received by the

Company, that extension and improvement had reference only to the original works, and did not include new and distinct buildings for the accommodation of trade; that, therefore, the cost of all their works, and the purchase of ground connected with them, beyond those in the original plan, was in effect an increase of the Capital beyond the sum to which it is limited, and should be carried to the amount of the surplus. It was also contended, that in addition to this, the sum paid by the Company in discharge of the income tax on the dividends should be included as a part of the same surplus, as well as some smaller sums stated in the accounts. With reference to the application of the Capital of the Company to the discharge of the income tax arising on the dividends, it has already been the subject of consideration and animadversion to a former Committee which sat; in the sentiments of which Your Committee have only to express their concurrence. With respect to the works, whatever doubts Your Committee might have entertained as to the extent of the discretion intended to be given by the Act, under the words "extension and improvement," had it rested upon the original Act alone, they feel themselves relieved from them by the subsequent Acts of the 42d and 44th George 3, the preambles to which either recite the completion of, or contemplate the most material improvements made; and the application of surplus rates to defray them, are recognized and sanctioned. With this authority, Your Committee cannot deem those applications to be an expenditure unimportant to the purposes of the institution and the interests of the West India Trade, or that the sum ought to form an addition to the accumulated fund, for which the claim on the part of the public is preferred.

The accumulation of the surplus fund, and the mode in which it has taken place, the House will observe, has been the subject of much discussion before Your Committee: on the one hand, it has been adduced as a proof of the extravagance of the rates exacted by the Company; and, on the other, it is stated to have arisen from an accession of importation much beyond any calculation previously formed, and owing to particular political circumstances during the operation of which, those importations occurred and remained in the warehouses of the Company; and that so far from the rates being too high, had the rates been confined to the produce of our own Colonies, which could alone be calculated upon, the surplus would not have exceeded the sum of 36,000*l.*; a sum certainly less than necessary to provide for annual repairs and contingencies, to which works and buildings of such a description are liable.

Your Committee, however, must observe, that this calculation appears to be formed by including the payment of all those buildings which have been erected, and paid for out of the Rates, which, although subsequently sanctioned by Parliament, are in this view to be considered as surplus, and so considered, do not appear to Your Committee to bear out the expression that the Rates, although not unreasonable in themselves, have been as moderate as they might have been, had the Dock Company availed itself of the means the accession of trade above alluded to afforded them of relieving the Trade by reduction.

The manner of the accumulation, however, in the opinion of Your Committee, does not at all affect the right of the Public, under the law, to the full benefit of it.

39 Geo. 3, cap. 69, sect. 160.

The Act of 1799, which directs the appropriation of the Funds in the hands of the Company, enacts, "That the aforesaid sum of Five "hundred thousand Pounds, subscribed or in-"tended to be subscribed or contributed by the "said West India Dock Company for their

" Capital or Joint Stock, and all other Monies " which shall be hereafter subscribed by them " for increasing their Capital as aforesaid, toge- " ther with the several sums of Money to be " produced and received by and from, and raised " and borrowed upon the credit of, the Rates " and Duties granted or made payable to the " said Company by this Act, shall form and be- " come one aggregate consolidated Fund; and all " the Monies which shall be subscribed, collected, " received, levied, raised and borrowed by the said " Company, or by the said Directors, by virtue " or in pursuance of this Act, shall be applied " and disposed of, in the first place, in paying " the remaining equal half part or share of the " Charges and Expenses incident to and incurred " in obtaining and passing this Act, and after- " wards in paying and discharging the conside- " ration or purchase-money and the other costs " and charges incident to the purchasing and " obtaining conveyances of the messuages, lands, " tenements and hereditaments which by virtue " or in pursuance of this Act shall be purchased " for the use of, and conveyed or vested in trust " for, the said West India Dock Company as " aforesaid; and in the next place in paying the " interest of the Monies which shall be borrowed " by the said Company upon the credit of the " last-mentioned Rates and Duties, if any shall be

" so borrowed, and the interest or dividends upon
" the principal monies, which for the time being
" shall be so subscribed by the members of the
" said Company, and actually paid as aforesaid, or
" upon their Capital or Joint Stock, and in pay-
" ing such yearly or other sums of Money as are
" hereinbefore directed to be paid by the said
" West India Dock Company, as and for com-
" pensations for losses and deficiencies of Tithes,
" Taxes, Sewer Rates, and other Rates and As-
" sessments; and subject thereto, then in defray-
" ing the necessary charges and expenses of
" making, completing, maintaining, and sup-
" porting, and attending, managing, and regulat-
" ing the said Docks, Basons, Cuts, Quays,
" Wharfs, Warehouses and other Works, which
" are to be made and done by the said Directors
" in pursuance of this Act; and of any such
" extensions and improvements of the same re-
" spectively, as the said Directors may, from time
" to time, think necessary; and that the residue
" or surplus of such Monies shall from time to
" time be applied in or towards the repayment
" of the Principal Monies, which shall be bor-
" rowed by the said Company upon the credit
" of the Rates and Duties hereby granted to
" them, until all the same Principal Monies shall
" be repaid, and in or towards executing such of
" the other purposes of this Act, as are to
" be executed by the said Directors, or by and

"at the charges of the West India Dock Com-
"pany; and when by the means last mentioned
"or otherwise, the Principal Monies so to be
"borrowed by the said Company shall be all
"repaid as aforesaid, then and in such case, the
"Rates and Duties by this Act granted to the
"said Company, shall be lowered in the manner
"hereinbefore directed, as far as the same can,
"under the then existing circumstances, be done
"with prudence and safety."

No exception is made in respect to the manner in which any residue or surplus shall have arisen. A surplus (from whatever source derived) is alone contemplated, and its application peremptorily prescribed, after the demands upon the Company are satisfied. The demands on the Company, which were an obstruction to their acting on this clause, as it appears, have been at length discharged, (and why they were not discharged at as early a period as the state of the affairs permitted, has not been satisfactorily explained); they are, therefore, in the condition contemplated by the Act, and may be called upon to relieve the trade by a reduction of the Rates.

In the justice of this call Your Committee are happy to observe the Dock Company readily acquiesce; they have indeed already reduced their Rates considerably; first, in the year 1817, and still further in the last year; and it has been signified to Your Committee that they are prepared to carry the additional reduction of Rates prescribed by the law into effect, in such manner as may appear most conducive to the public interests, and most in conformity to the presumed intentions of the Legislature in framing the provisions of the Act relative to any surplus that might accrue to them. With a view to this, they have themselves submitted to Your Committee a proposition for the reduction of the sum of £393,910 now in their hands, to the sum of £100,000, deemed necessary as a reserve to meet contingencies, after the completion of certain necessary repairs, in the course of rather less than three years, being the period at which the exclusive privilege of the London Dock Company will expire.

The detailed proposition submitted by the West India Dock Directors will be found in the Appendix to this Report. It is one which Your Committee, after much consideration, has resolved to recommend to the approbation of the House, as, under all circumstances, appearing to them best calculated to meet the public interest, to remedy the error into which the Dock

Company had fallen in the accumulation of such a surplus, and to provide against the inconveniences any other application might occasion.

The Act of Parliament has it clearly in contemplation, that no large surplus should be accumulated, by the provision that any which should be found to exist, after some specific appropriations of the monies received by the Dock Company, should be applied to the reduction of rates. This reduction of rates, had the Act been literally executed, would have been for the exclusive benefit of the importers of West India produce. The proposition, therefore, although not perhaps conveying the benefit to the same individuals, is so far in conformity to the spirit and intention of the law, as that the West India Trade will receive the benefit of it, unless voluntarily relinquished. That the reduction of the surplus should take place within the limited period assigned, and by a large diminution of the rates, Your Committee feel to be rendered necessary by the situation in which the other docks will be placed on the expiration of their respective charters. In their resolution not to recommend to the House a continuance of the exclusive privileges to the West India Dock Company, Your Committee had in view the establishment of a general competition among the dock establishments at that period. In such a competition the power of applying of such a large sum to the reduction of rates below the amount for which the business of the dock could be probably conducted, must have a most injurious operation; and would, in fact, enable the Dock Company which possessed it, to cast the balance of competition in its own favour. While the exclusive privileges of those Docks are in operation, while competition is yet fettered by legal restraint, such a power is of comparatively little moment, and can have no ultimate influence on the competition which it appears to Your Committee so desirable to establish. Another reason has also had its effect on Your Committee in approving the proposed arrangement, which appears to possess an advantage in tending to preclude an inconvenience resulting from the adoption of the recommendation offered by them, which they could not but feel. It is true, that if the continuance of the exclusive privilege was withheld, there could be, in point of justice, no claim on the part of the West India Dock Proprietors. The pledge of the public has been redeemed, and the Company have received all they contracted for, in the maintenance of their exclusive privileges during the term specified. But it will not escape the observation of the House, that they must be exposed to considerable inconvenience if they should be compelled to meet a competition with those who, for a limited period, are in possession of exclusive privileges; which privileges secure to the Docks possessing them the whole of particular trades, a proportion of which might come to the West India Dock, while they will at the same time have a chance of receiving a part of that, of which those Docks have by law now the exclusive possession. To avoid this evident disadvantage, Your Committee considered how far it might be expedient either to continue the exclusive privilege to the West India Docks to the period of the expiration of that of the London Dock Company, unless that Company should be disposed to relinquish, during the remainder of their term, the exclusive privileges now possessed by them. Your Committee have found that such relinquishment is not practicable, either on their part, or on that of any other Company similarly circumstanced. It appears to them, however, that under the proposed application of the Surplus Fund, any extension of the operation of the compulsory clauses in the Act of the 39 George 3, is not necessary, as that application must so operate upon the rates in respect to West India produce, during the term of the exclusive privilege possessed by the London Dock Company, as to leave a great proportion of the West India Trade to the West India Docks nearly as effectually as could be done by a continuance of the clauses referred to, and fully to counterbalance the advantage derived to the London Dock from receiving and warehousing the several articles now strictly by law appropriated to it.

Although the effect of this arrangement is, in fact, partially to continue the system of exclusive privileges among the Docks for two or three years to come, Your Committee, under the conviction of the advantages that would be derived from an open competition, are anxious that the operation of this system should be as limited as consistent with existing laws it can be rendered. On reference to the laws, under which the other Docks are established, it appears that the exclusive privilege of the London Dock Company, granted by the 39 and 40 George 3, is confined to the warehousing of the articles of Rice, Wine, Tobacco, and Foreign Spirits; and that, with certain exceptions, all other articles are confined to it by Orders or Warrants of the Treasury, issued in the exercise of the authority conveyed by the 43 Geo. 3.

That to the East India Docks is confined, by the 43 and 46 of George 3, to the landing of goods and merchandize, the produce of the East Indies or China, which shall arrive in the river Thames; but by the 54 George 3, c. 36, all goods imported from countries within the limits of the Company's Charter, by any person trading under the 53 George 3, may be lodged in warehouses belonging to the East India Company, or in any other warehouses approved by the Commissioners of the Customs; nothing in the Acts referred to compels the warehousing within the East India Docks; the restriction is confined to landing only. The warehousing depending on the approbation of the Commissioners of the Customs, they appear to have exercised the discretion vested in them, by limiting their approval to the warehouses of the East India Company, which, not being situated within the Dock, offer no greater security than others that might have been selected, or seem to afford any reason for such a preference.

It is, therefore, the opinion of Your Committee, that great advantage would arise to the Public, and the benefit of a free competition amongst Docks in the port of London be in a great degree established, if the Treasury should consent to recall the various orders and warrants, issued under the authority vested in them by any Acts of Parliament, confining the landing or bonding of particular articles to particular docks or places, and allow them to be landed and bonded wherever a sufficient security could be afforded to the Revenue, and to the property of the Merchant; and that orders should be given to the Commissioners of Customs to inspect other warehouses, for the purpose of ascertaining if, with adequate security to the Revenue, the privilege of warehousing East India Goods may be extended to them; and, if such be the result of the examination, that it should be so extended.

By this means, the object of setting free many articles of Trade, and establishing competition, may be in a great degree obtained at an early period, and provision effectually be made for its complete and undisturbed operation in the year 1827, when all the Acts conveying exclusive privileges will have expired.

Your Committee have abstained from entering in their Report into many details to which a more minute consideration of the evidence might have led, and which they should have thought it a duty to enter into, had such a case been made out in behalf of the West India Dock Company in respect to security to the Revenue, or protection to the Merchant, as might have raised any considerable doubt in their minds as to the recommendation they should offer touching a renewal of the compulsory clause of the 39 George 3. The expiration of this opens the way to free competition among the Docks; and they feel assured that, by free competition, the accommodation of the Commerce, in every particular, will be best provided for. In deliver-ing an opinion in favour of this competition, they entertain none of the fears that have been sug-gested of combination among the Docks, op-pressive to Trade and hostile to the Public In-terests: if they did not entertain the confidence already expressed in the situations and charac-ters of those to whom the direction of the re-spective establishments is committed, they can-not believe in the accomplishment of any such combination that would be effectual: they feel that Parliament will always have the ready means of defeating an attempt so injurious to the Pub-lic Interest, and, in case of necessity, will not be backward to employ them.

They have also less reluctance in offering the opinion contained in this Report, because, although the system of the West India Docks, applicable now exclusively to the Trade received into them, must, if it should be adopted, undergo some alteration, yet there is reason to believe the interests of the Proprietors will not incur any hazard; and from the character, regulations, si-tuation, and other advantages possessed by these Docks, they are at all times sure of commanding that proportion of the commerce of the country to which they are justly entitled.

Consistently with the opinions entertained by Your Committee, of the important advantages already derived by the Commerce of the country, the establishment of Docks, and the encouragement they are desirous of giving to their construction, wherever the means for it can be found, they cannot conclude this Report without bearing testimony to the wisdom evinced in the original design of this, the first establishment that was completed, and the public spirit and perseverance with which it was carried into execution; and in doing this, they feel it a debt of justice to mention the names of Mr. George Hibbert and the late Mr. Milligan, who, by devoting their time and talents to its accomplishment, have rendered an inestimable service to the Trade of the Metropolis.

3 *June*, 1823.

Hughes, Printer, Maiden Lane, Covent Garden.

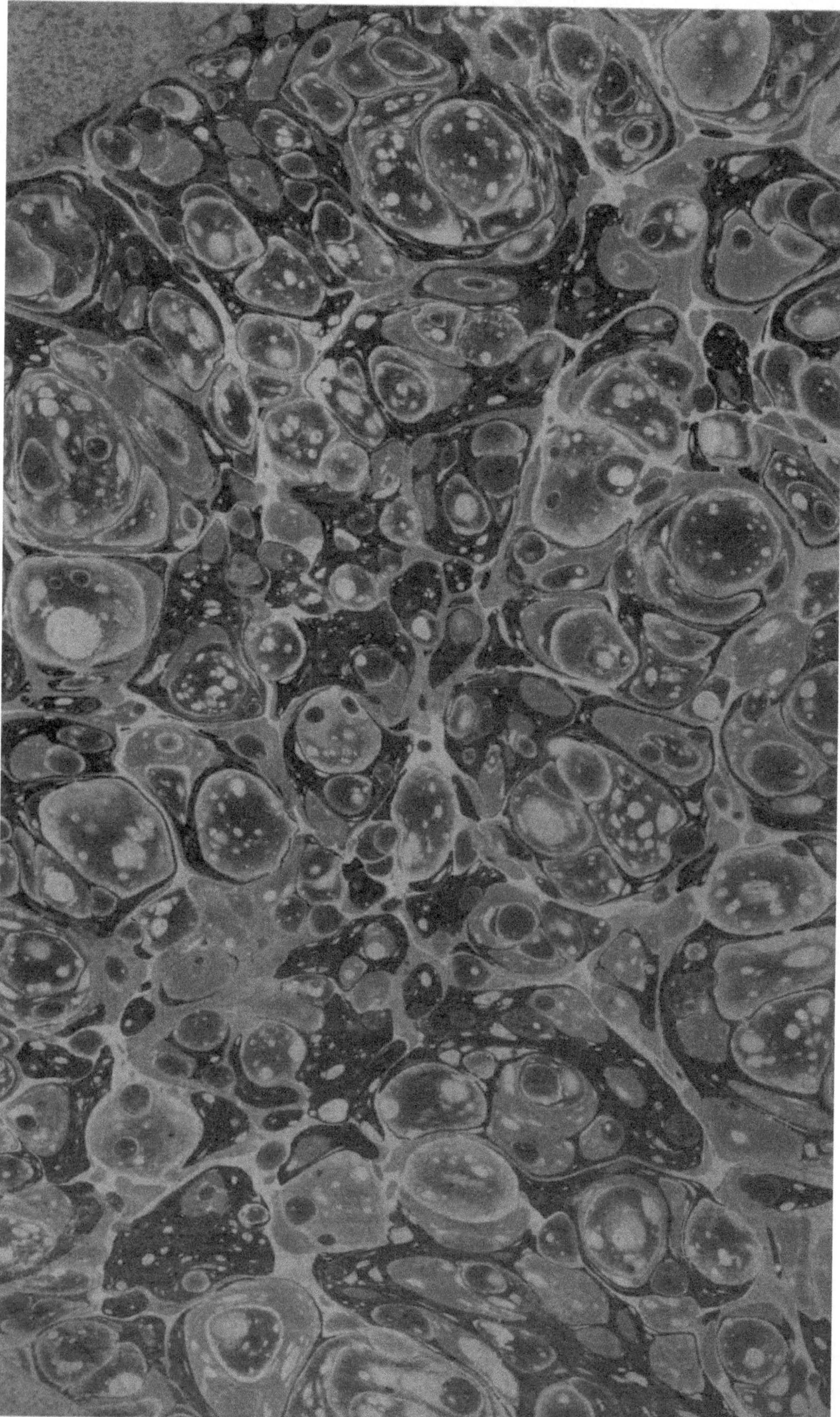